IMAGES
of America

SPOKANE HOT RODDING

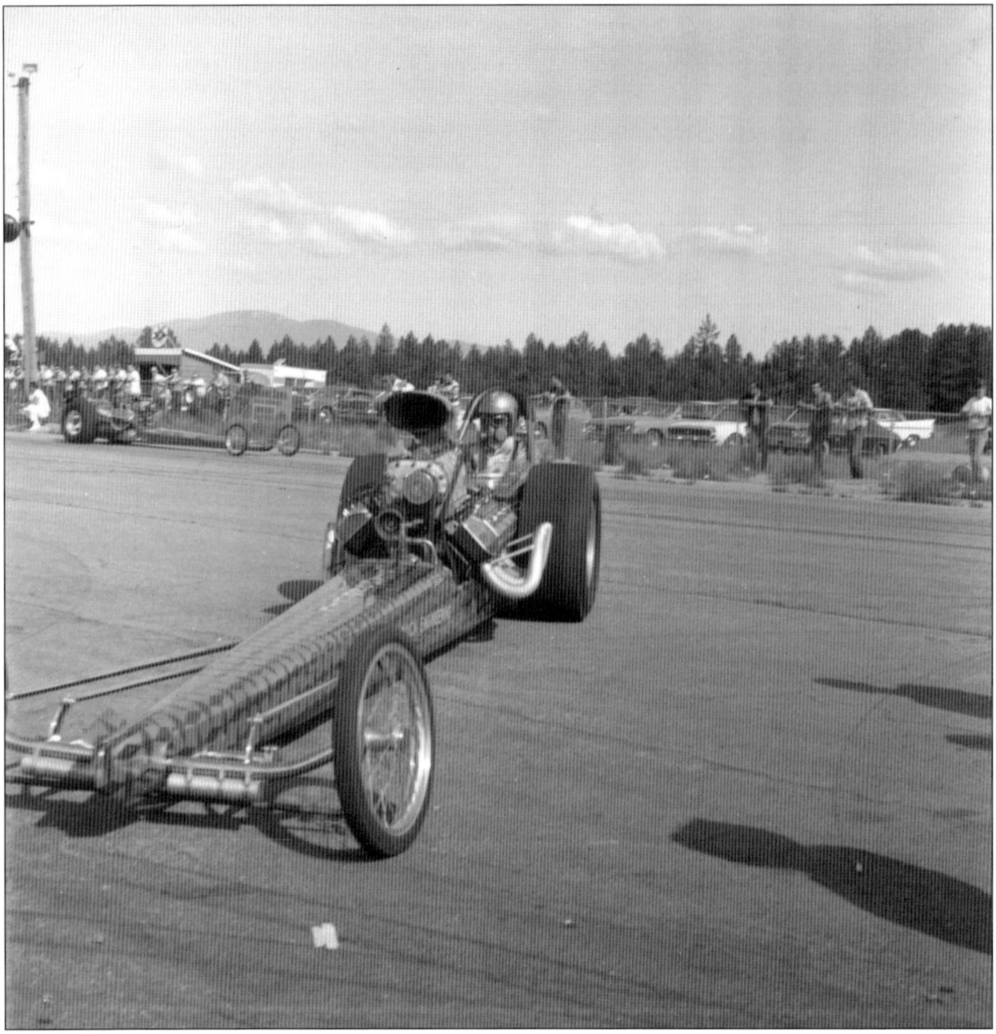

"Diamond Lil," sponsored by Dixon Engineering, became a major competitor in the Northwest drag-racing circuit and was led by John Dixon, one of the most talented automotive fabricators to come out of Spokane. The Dixon, Niederiger, and Bennett dragster was powered by a 392 hemi. John and Walt Johnson took turns driving the rail while Ron Niederiger and Clarence Bennett took care of the mechanical components. Clarence Bennett owned the Hillborn setup and loaned it out to many Spokane teams in the late 1960s. (Courtesy of Greg Fury.)

On the Cover: Anyone who has ever worked on a hot rod can appreciate this photograph. It captures the feeling one gets after stepping back and realizing the work that has been done. The hot-rodder can finally see the car, not as a half-finished mess, but as a completed project ready to hit the streets. Brothers Bill (left) and Butch Miller, leaning on the swing set, are with Stu Young in Joe Kostelecky's backyard. They are taking in this 1934 Ford coupe project and imagining what it will become. (Courtesy of Ludy Kostelecky.)

IMAGES
of America

SPOKANE HOT RODDING

John Gunsaulis

ARCADIA
PUBLISHING

ISBN 978-1-4671-3300-5

Published by Arcadia Publishing
Charleston, South Carolina

Printed in the United States of America

Library of Congress Control Number: 2014948185

For all general information, please contact Arcadia Publishing:
Telephone 843-853-2070
Fax 843-853-0044
E-mail sales@arcadiapublishing.com
For customer service and orders:
Toll-Free 1-888-313-2665

Visit us on the Internet at www.arcadiapublishing.com

This book is dedicated to Richard "Speedy" Gunsaulis and Clarence Bennett.

Contents

ACKNOWLEDGMENTS

I would like to thank the following people for their photographs, support, and hours of interview time: Barbara Bennett, Harry Prouty, Tim Hein, Ludy Kostelecky, Don and Nancy Wilbur, Art Santa Rosa, Gary Harms, Toni Reidburn, Gary Hordemann, Jack Hordemann, Dick Flynn, Bob Coutts, Scott Parrot, Bob "Butch" Miller, Greg Fury, Bob and Shirley Adams, Bob Frankovic, Dusty and Gael Rhodes, Larry Taylor, Bob Knowles, Jim Tipke, Dan Martin, Pat Riggings, Tamatha Shockley, Frank Moyer, Dan Weaver, John Mehl, Brian Kelly, Buzz Storch, Art True, Roger Domini, Jeff Allison, Connie Sullivan, Don Audel, Claude Cuzzetto, Tom Ryan, Ronnie Corcum, Larry Skidmore, Chuck Schwartzenberger, Mike Robinson, Josh Scott, Gary Hustad, Chris Shelton, Sue Fruend, Glen Harbison, Lloyd Johnson, Darrell Larson, Bob Morrill, Jack Henderson, Jim Kelly, Don Gorman, Korey Heunick, Chris and Duke Cornell, Billy Payne, Frank Rupert, and Molly Gunsaulis.

This book is meant to showcase a small slice of the hot rodding that was going on in Spokane from the 1940s through the 1960s. I have done my best to tell the story of Spokane hot rodding by interviewing many of the local hot-rodders. I know that some cars traded hands multiple times, and I apologize in advance for any incorrect information or omissions. I hope you enjoy the book.

Unless otherwise noted, all images appear courtesy of the author.

INTRODUCTION

Spokane, located just 20 miles from the Idaho border, is the largest city in Eastern Washington. During the 1940s, it became a center of an evolving postwar hot-rod community. Automotive sports were expanding at this time, from stock-car and midget racing to street cars and drag racing. Local car enthusiasts joined with an influx of military personnel and college students who were just as passionate for hot rodding, and it was during this time that the Spokane hot rodding culture began to flourish. Together, they pushed the boundaries of hot rodding, creating lifelong bonds in the process. This book explores that evolution of Inland Northwest hot rodding from the mid-1940s to the mid-1960s, starting with jalopy-style hot rods that began popping up on local streets, to the formation of new clubs and organized racing.

One

Street

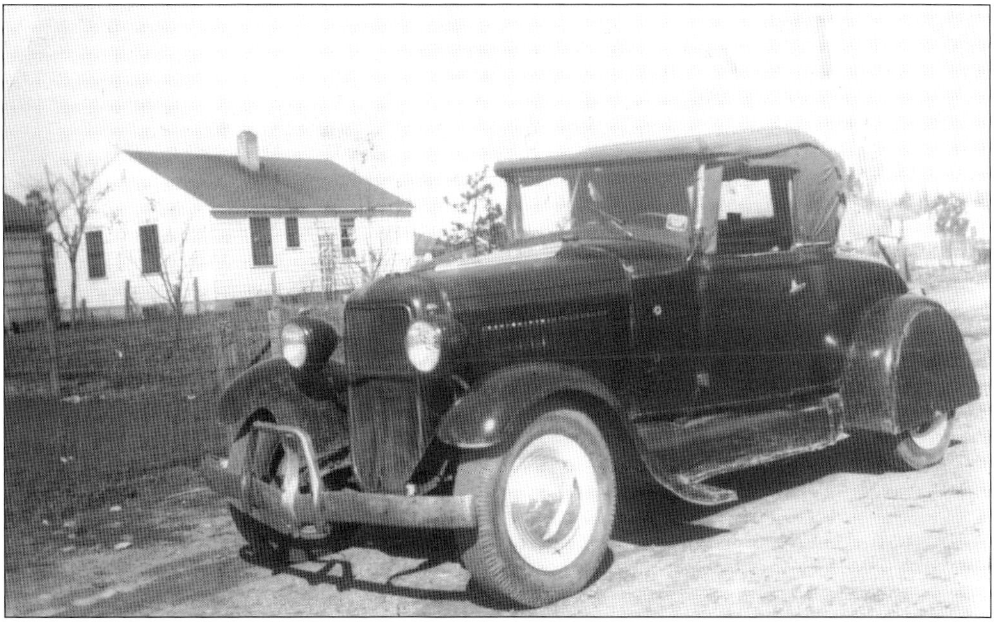

In 1946, Harry Prouty was 15 years old and the proud owner of this 1931 Model A, which he built out of parts from wrecking yards. This was just the beginning of his fascination with hot rods. The A is still banger-powered, but it now features a '33-'34 Ford truck grille, '28-'29 front fenders, Hollywood hubcaps, and custom fender skirts. The fins added to the top of the hood and markers on later 1930s headlights are visible. The running boards were removed to give it a more modern look. This photograph was taken in front of Harry's parents' house. (Harry Prouty.)

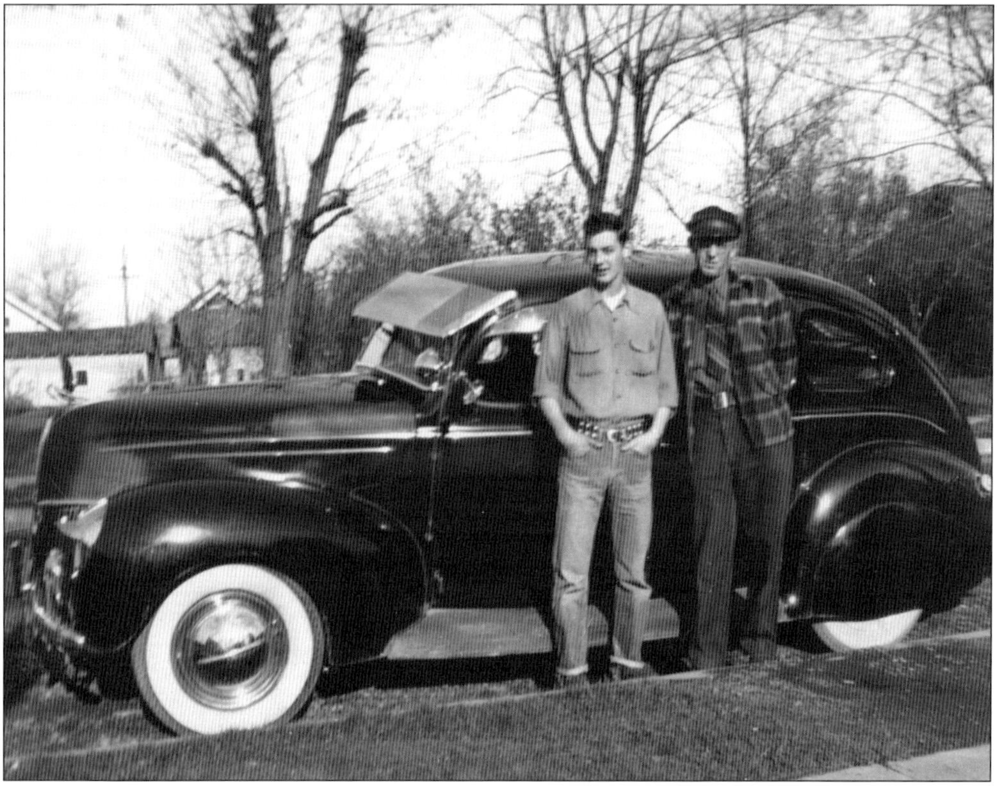

Bob "Butch" Miller and his father, Everett Miller, stand in front of Butch's 1939 Ford four-door; "with a lot of junk hung on them, that was the thing to do at the time." This photograph was taken in front of the Miller house at 1900 North Napa Street around 1949. Butch later traded the four-door for a 1947 Harley 84 Springer. (Butch Miller.)

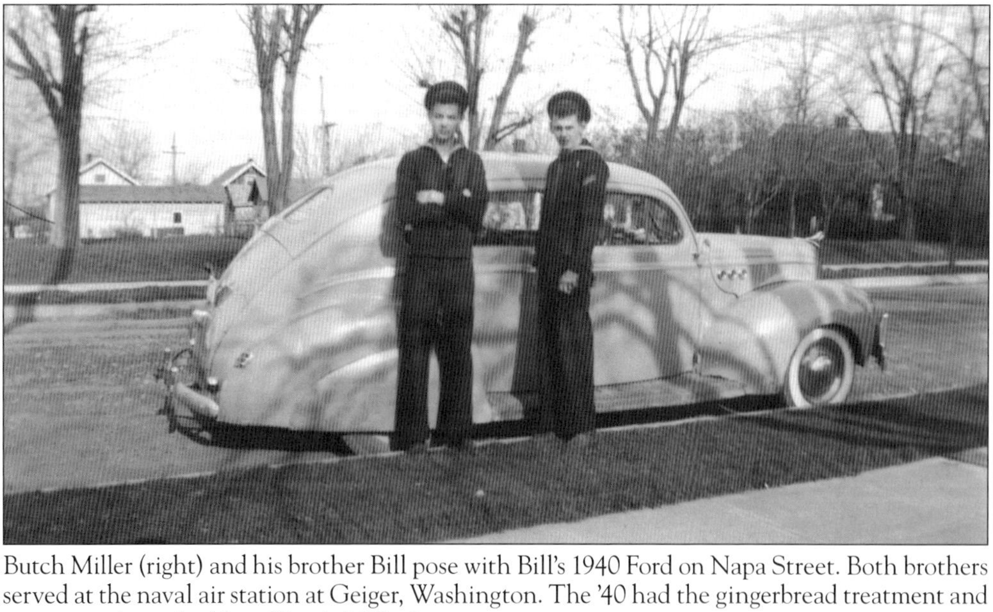

Butch Miller (right) and his brother Bill pose with Bill's 1940 Ford on Napa Street. Both brothers served at the naval air station at Geiger, Washington. The '40 had the gingerbread treatment and was painted powder blue. (Butch Miller.)

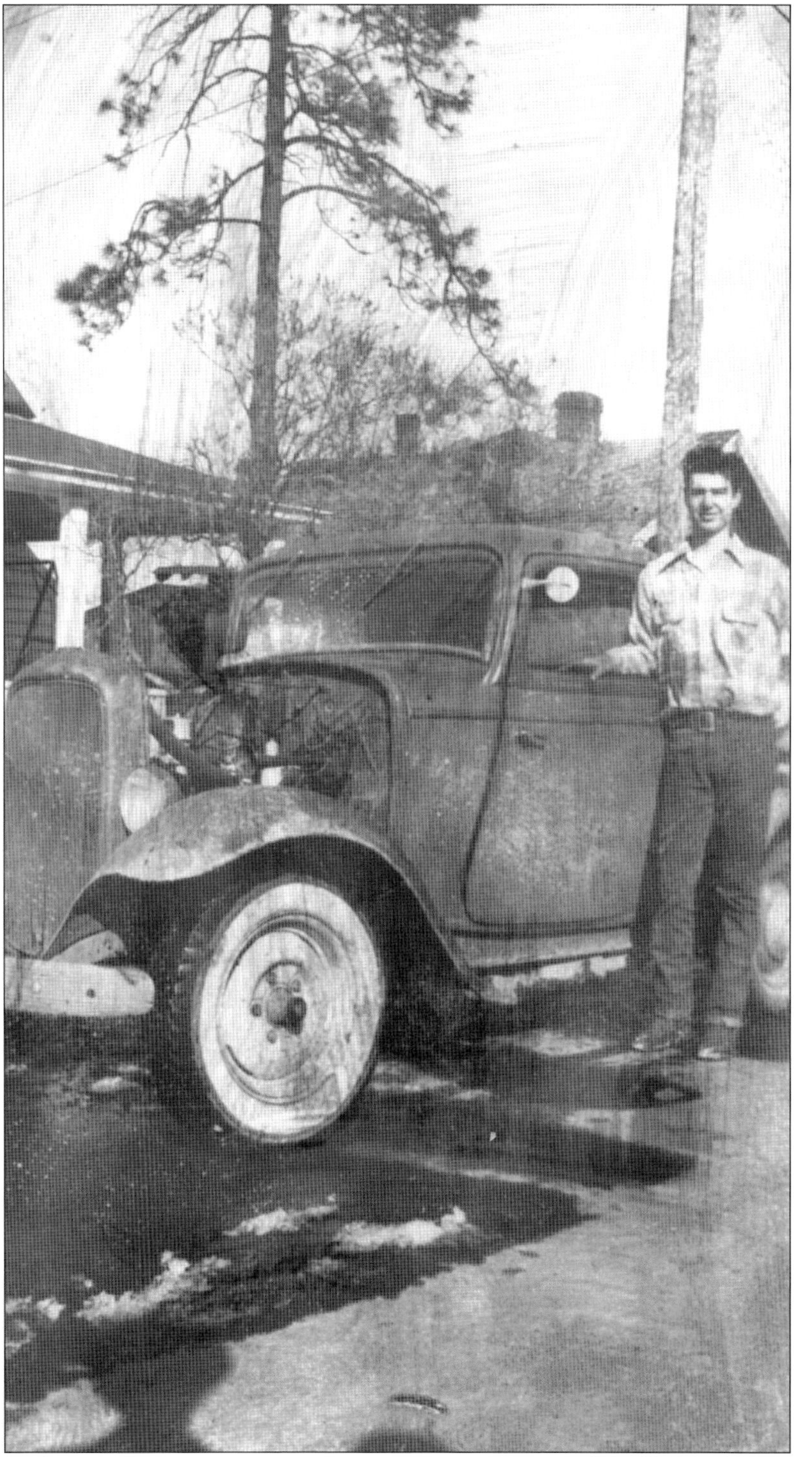

Steve Pick poses with his 1932 Ford three-window coupe, which he bought from an older couple in the Corbin Park area in 1950. He removed the hood and running boards and shaved the grille shell. (Gary Hustad.)

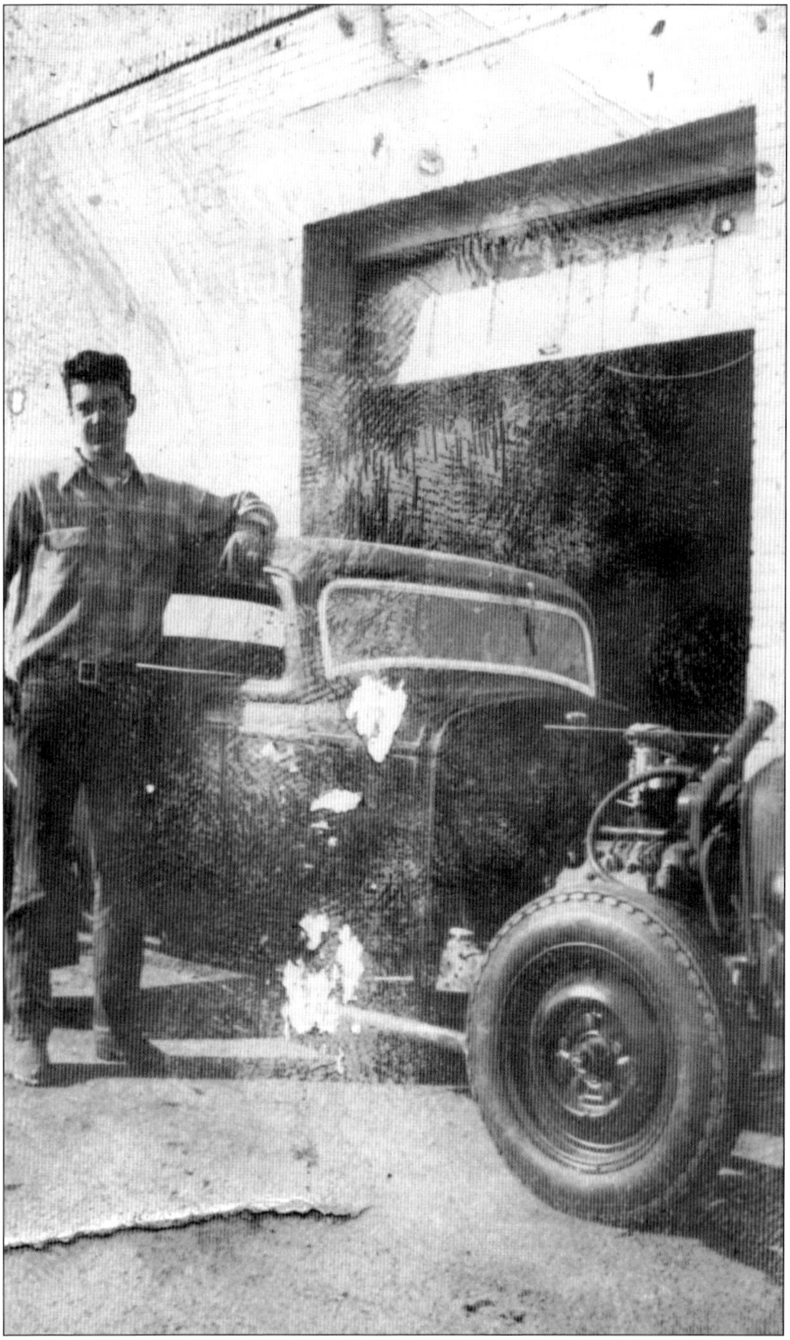

Steve Pick poses with the same '32 coupe in front of Custom Auto Body, where he worked at the time. The car has been heavily modified, chopped, and channeled over the frame. The front suspension has also been modified, and the windshield has been plated. When Steve and his wife, Connie, left Spokane, he was stationed at Fort Ord near San Luis Obispo, California. Some friends drove the car down in the middle of winter so he could have it in California. When the base was decommissioned, Pick was moved to the Midwest, and the '32 came back to Spokane. (Gary Hustad.)

Butch Miller's 1932 Ford five-window is parked in front of his parents' house in the winter of 1950–1951. The top was chopped by Joe Kostelecky on Nora Avenue, just past Division Street in the Gonzaga area. Joe would chop cars for $50 at his place, and performed other body modifications. In the background is Miller's Ford convertible covered in snow. The front of the '32 featured an undropped headlight bar with small aftermarket lights and a filled grille shell. The back of Miller's deuce coupe was basically stock, with late-model bumper guards and an early clear-plastic Dukes Auto Club plaque. (Butch Miller.)

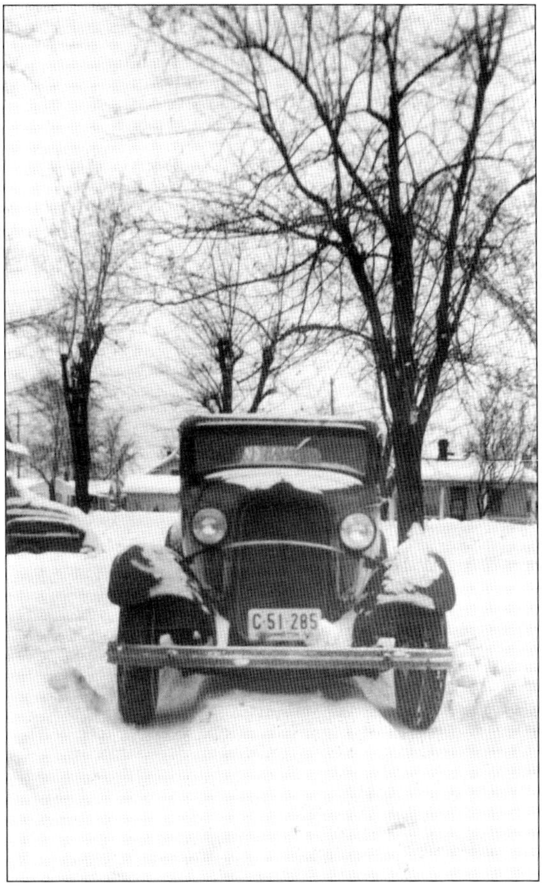

At this point, Butch Miller's coupe is running the 1932 21-stud flathead and bone stock running gear. The paint is factory black, mixed with primer spots from the chop and nose job. Later, the car was also channeled by Joe Kostelecky and received a built flathead to go along with the new look. (Butch Miller.)

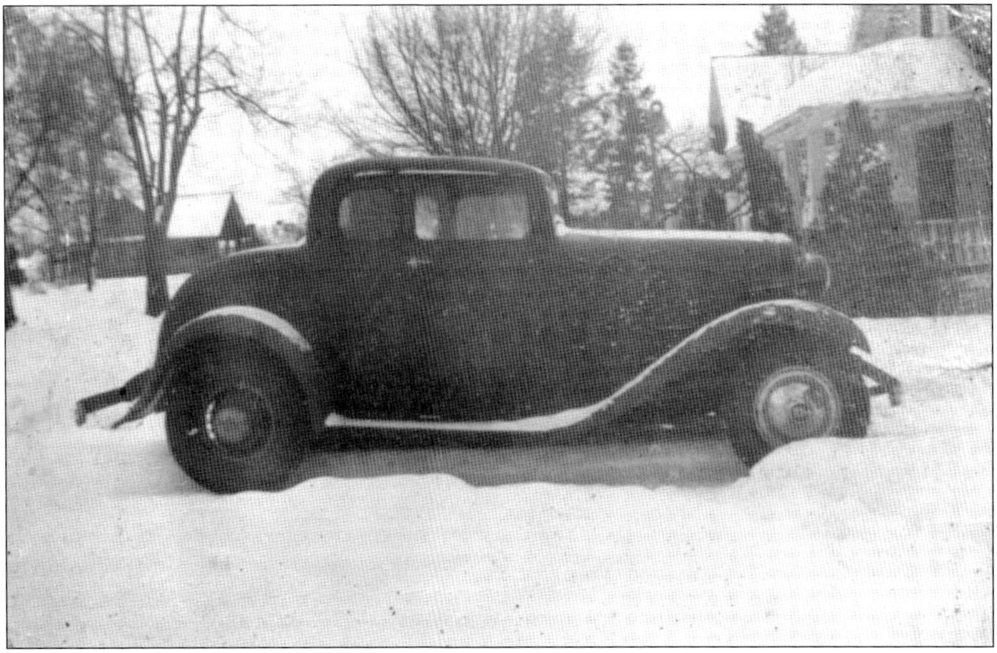

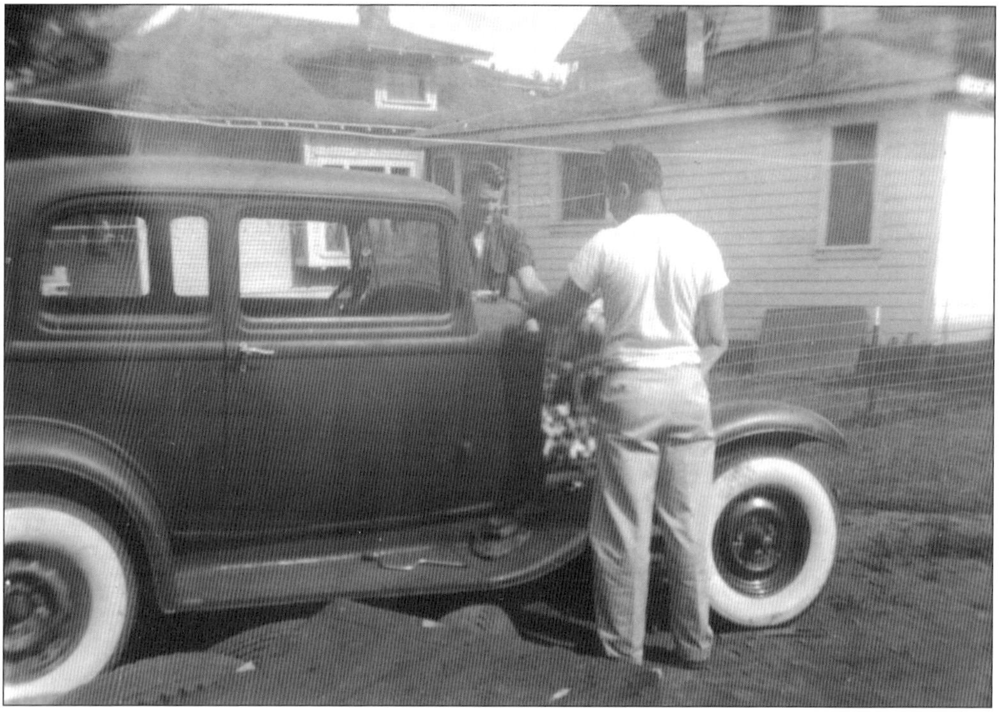

John Mehl bought this 1932 Ford Victoria from its original owners for $150 around 1952. The Vic was a bone stock V-8 car, except for the headlight conversion, and was painted Washington blue with black fenders. Mehl (back to camera) and some friends are looking at the newly installed 59A motor, which included an Offy tri-power and Edelbrock heads. Mehl did not convert it over to juice brakes at this time; he said he left the old "push and pray" rod brakes in the deuce. The wheels on the back of the car are from a Chrysler Airflow. The front wheels are 1940-Ford style. Mehl sold the Vic to Len Sutton, and then it went to Bill Bongers, Don Wilbur, and Richard "Speedy" Gunsaulis before it headed to Oregon in 1970. The deuce would end up being pictured in *Hot Rod* magazine when Wilbur owned it, and in *Rod & Custom* when it belonged to Gunsaulis. By the 1960s, the Vic was a full show car, appearing all over the Northwest, including as far north as Calgary, Alberta. (Both, John Mehl.)

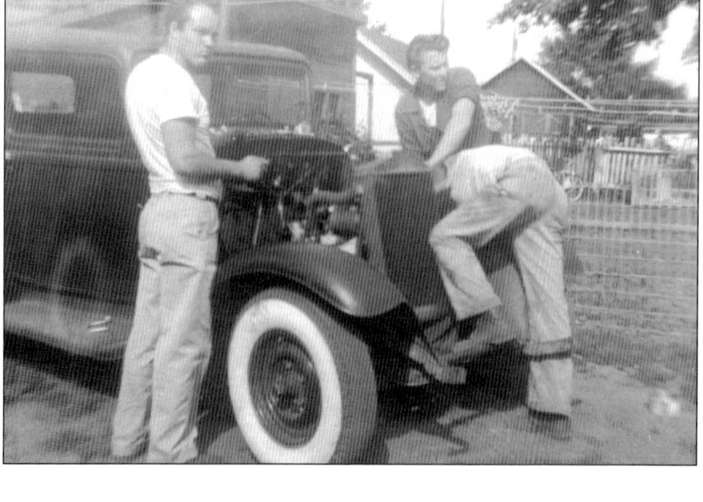

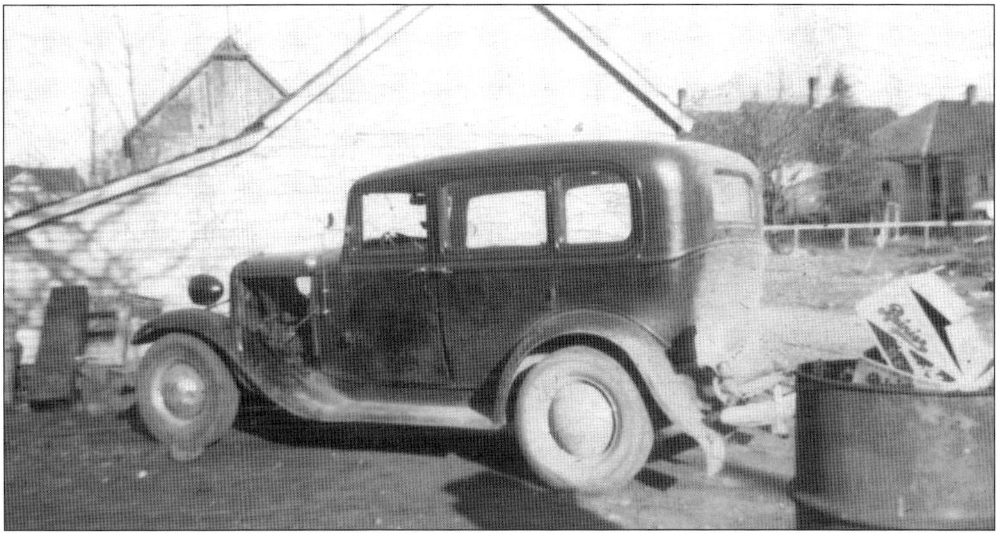

This is the first car of Jack Hordemann, 17, shown behind his parents' store at 1624 North Ash Street. This nearly stock 1932 Ford four-door is running a rebuilt 21-stud flathead out of a '36 Ford and is starting to get the gingerbread treatment with full wheel hubcaps, smaller headlights, and a later bumper. Hordemann found the car at the Silverloaf Bakery, where an industrial fan had fallen out of a window and went through the car's top. He covered the seats in Army surplus blankets before the deuce met an untimely fate. A Packard ran a stop sign on Normandie Street and punched the deuce in the drivers' door. It was wrecked, but the chassis was fine, and Hordemann located a '32 roadster body to put on the frame. (Gary Hordemann.)

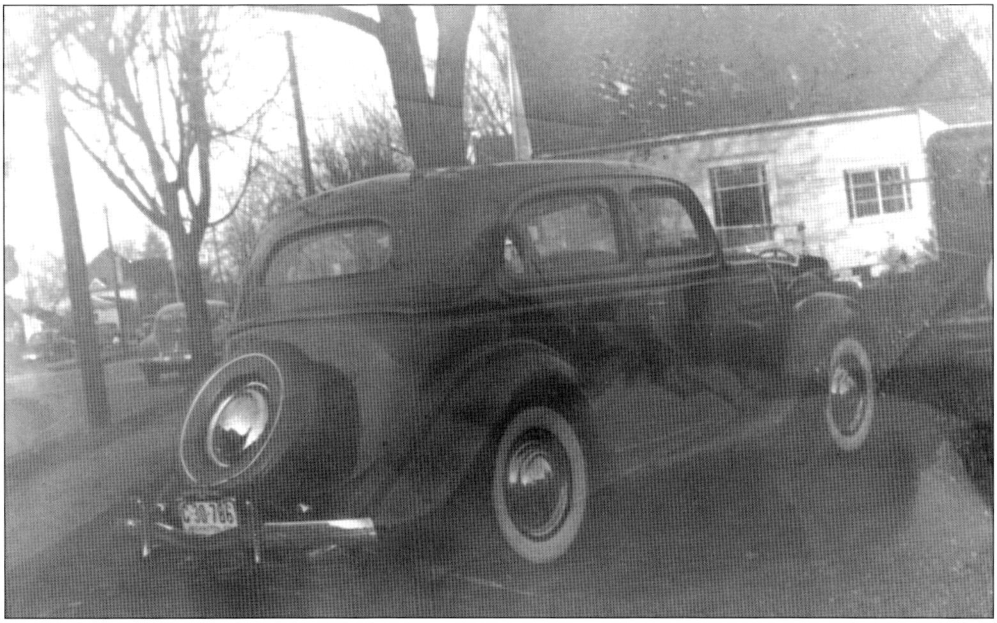

Jim Hordemann's 1935 Ford two-door sits behind brother Jack's new '32 roadster. Above the license plate is a topper for the newly formed Spokane Roadsters Racing Association (SRRA). The roadster was towed behind the '35 to SRRA races in Deer Park. The sedan was no dog itself, powered by a built flathead; it later raced at Bonneville. The taillight treatment, coming off Harley Davidson motorcycles, was common in Spokane and called "buddy lights." (Gary Hordemann.)

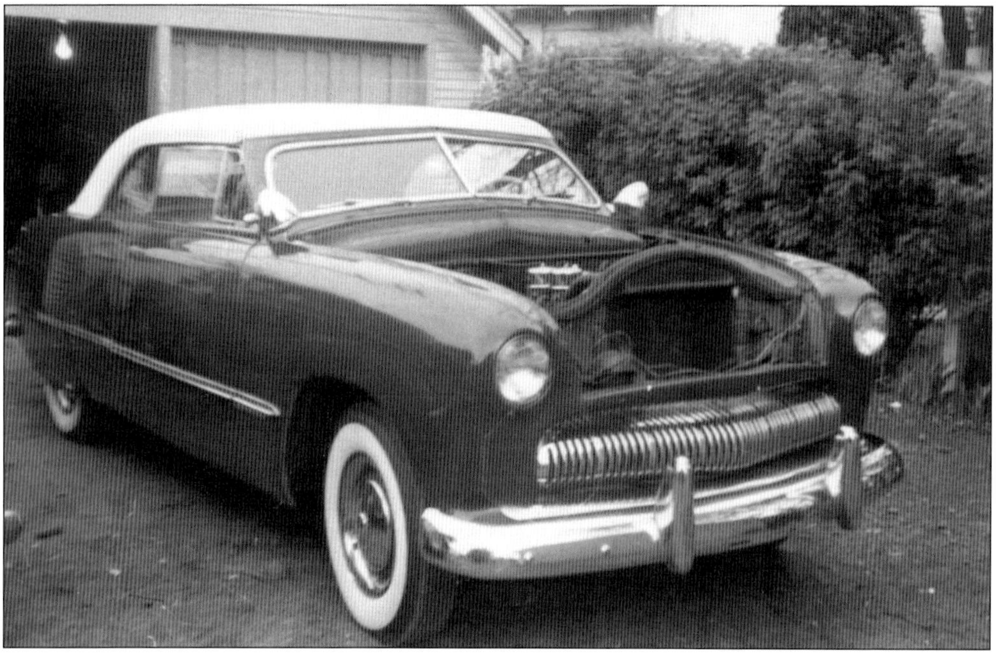

Tim Rochlitzer brought his 1949 Ford custom convertible with him when he came to Spokane to study mechanical engineering and ROTC at Gonzaga in 1950. Rochlitzer, from Santa Barbara, California, brought his hot-rod connections with him. The car was customized by Gil Ayalis and had a full race Evans flathead in it. (Bob Coutts.)

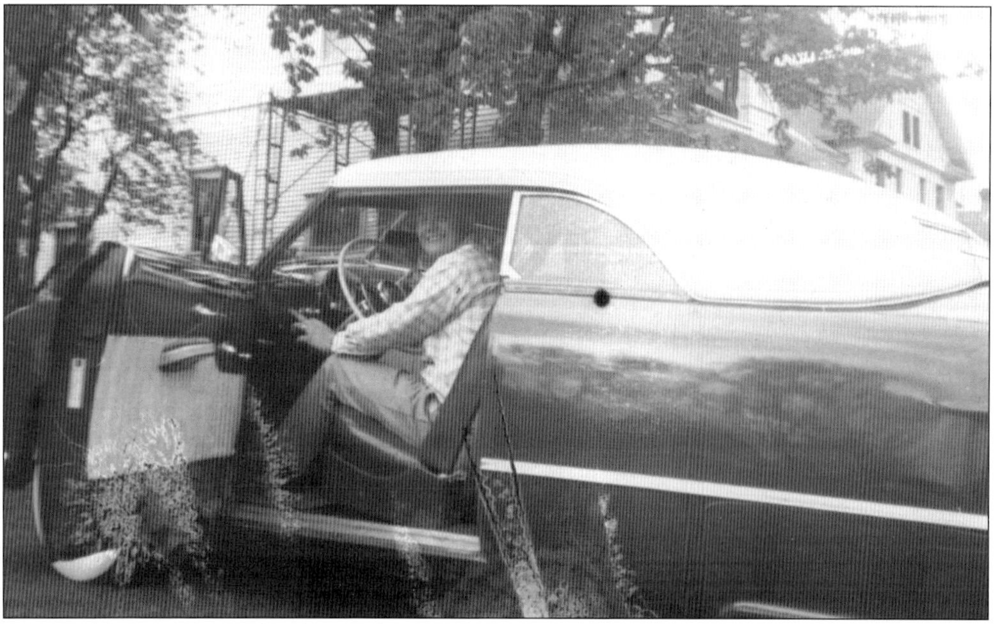

Tim Rochlitzer sits in his bright red shoebox. The door handles where shaved, and a microswitch was hidden behind the side trim behind the B pillar. He used his knee to push the trim back slightly, which actuated the door solenoid. The flawless interior was done by Gaylord Kustom Tops & Interiors in dark red and cream with red carpet, accented with cream trim and custom floor mats sewn in. The top was a real Carson top, a rare sight in Spokane. (Bob Coutts.)

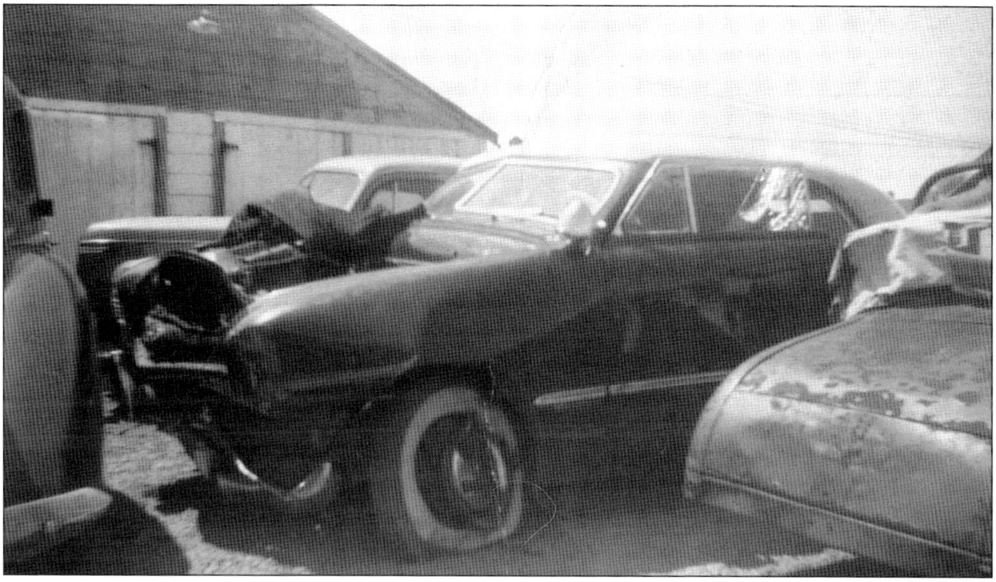

Tim Rochlitzer's car sits behind Duke Rogers's shop on North Elgin Street after the shoebox was wrecked. Luckily, Rogers bought the car from the insurance company after the wreck and took it to Pat's Frame Shop in Spokane. The impact of the collision was so intense that the motor cracked. The Evans motor was replaced with a stock flathead. After the car was fixed, Rogers drove it back to Los Angeles to show Gil Ayalis. Note the Model T at right; it will end up being a major part of Spokane hot rodding. (Bob Coutts.)

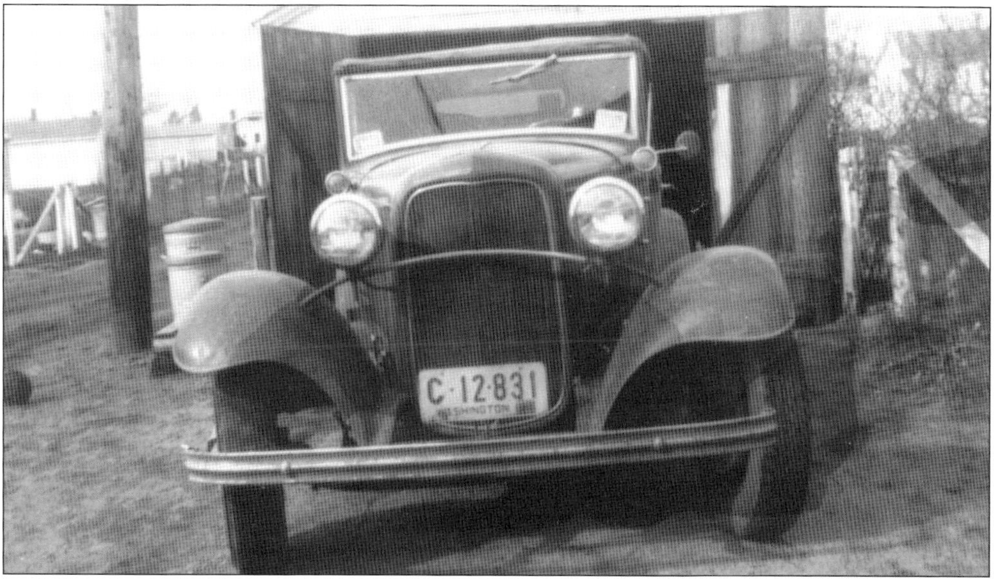

When Art Santa Rosa was in his early teens, he discovered freedom by exploring the north side of Spokane, searching for cars on his motorbike. One day, he found a 1932 Ford Cabriolet just off Wellsley Avenue and Division Street, in a backyard behind Kirk's Drive Inn. It was a bone stock V-8 car, and the owners were asking $250 for it. Art tried to talk his dad into letting him get it, with no success. So, he told his friend Buzz Storch about the deuce. Storch talked the owners down to $125 and hauled it to his parents' place in Morgan Acres. He then started to build it into a hot rod. (Buzz Storch.)

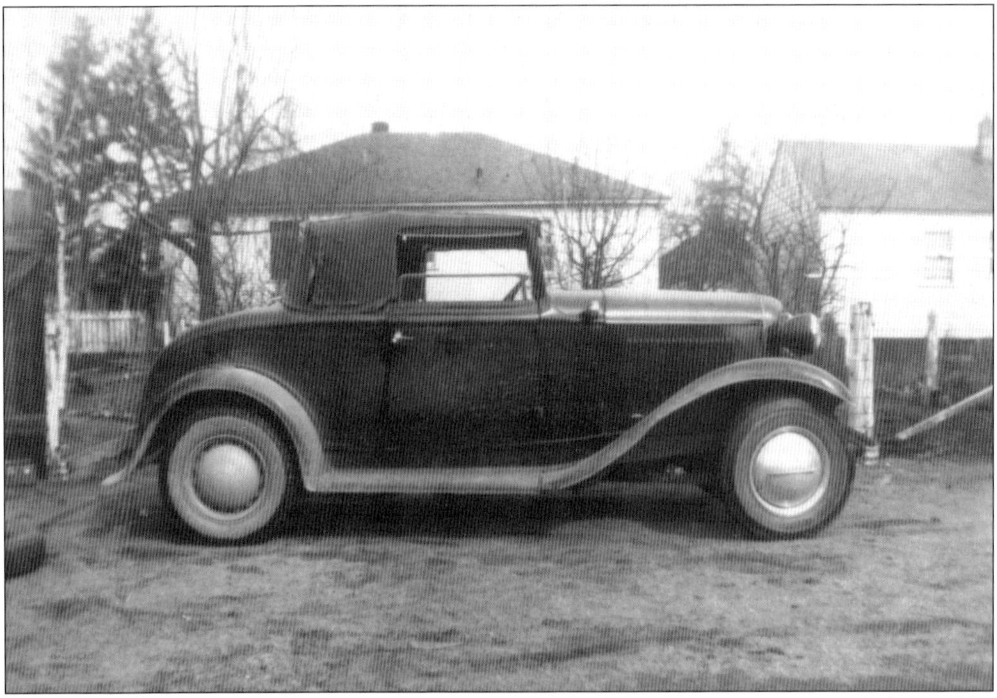

The grille shell of Buzz Storch's car was filled and peaked by West End Auto Body, located at the bottom of Sunset Hill in Spokane. Storch found a set of '39 Ford juice brakes and wheels at a wrecking yard, and changed out the stock headlights with a more streamlined set. His car became one of four 1932 Cabriolet hot rods that roamed the streets of Spokane in the early to mid-1950s. (Buzz Storch.)

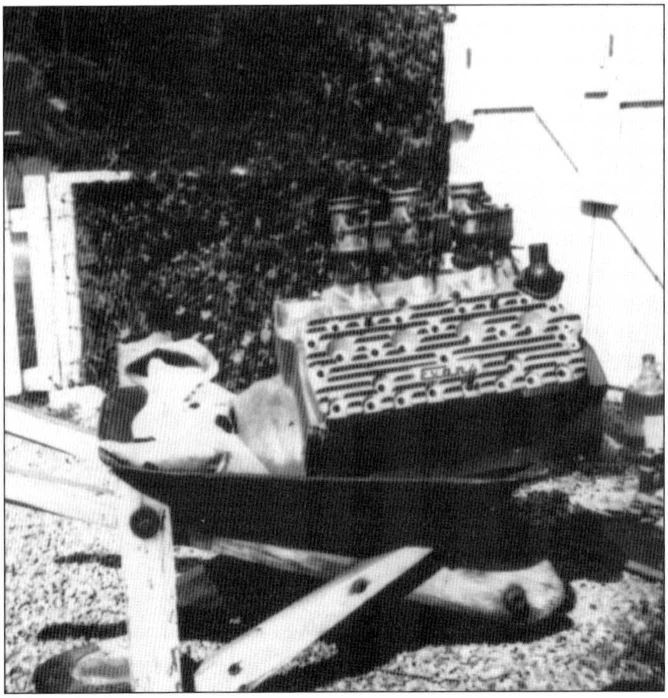

Buzz Storch's new mill for the Cabriolet was a 59A, equipped with Evans 8BA heads and intake with three 97s. The speed equipment came from Thrifty Auto on Division Street, as did the dropped axle, but the machine work on the motor was done down the street from Storch's house. The new motor was transferred around in a wheelbarrow before coming to rest in the '32. (Buzz Storch.)

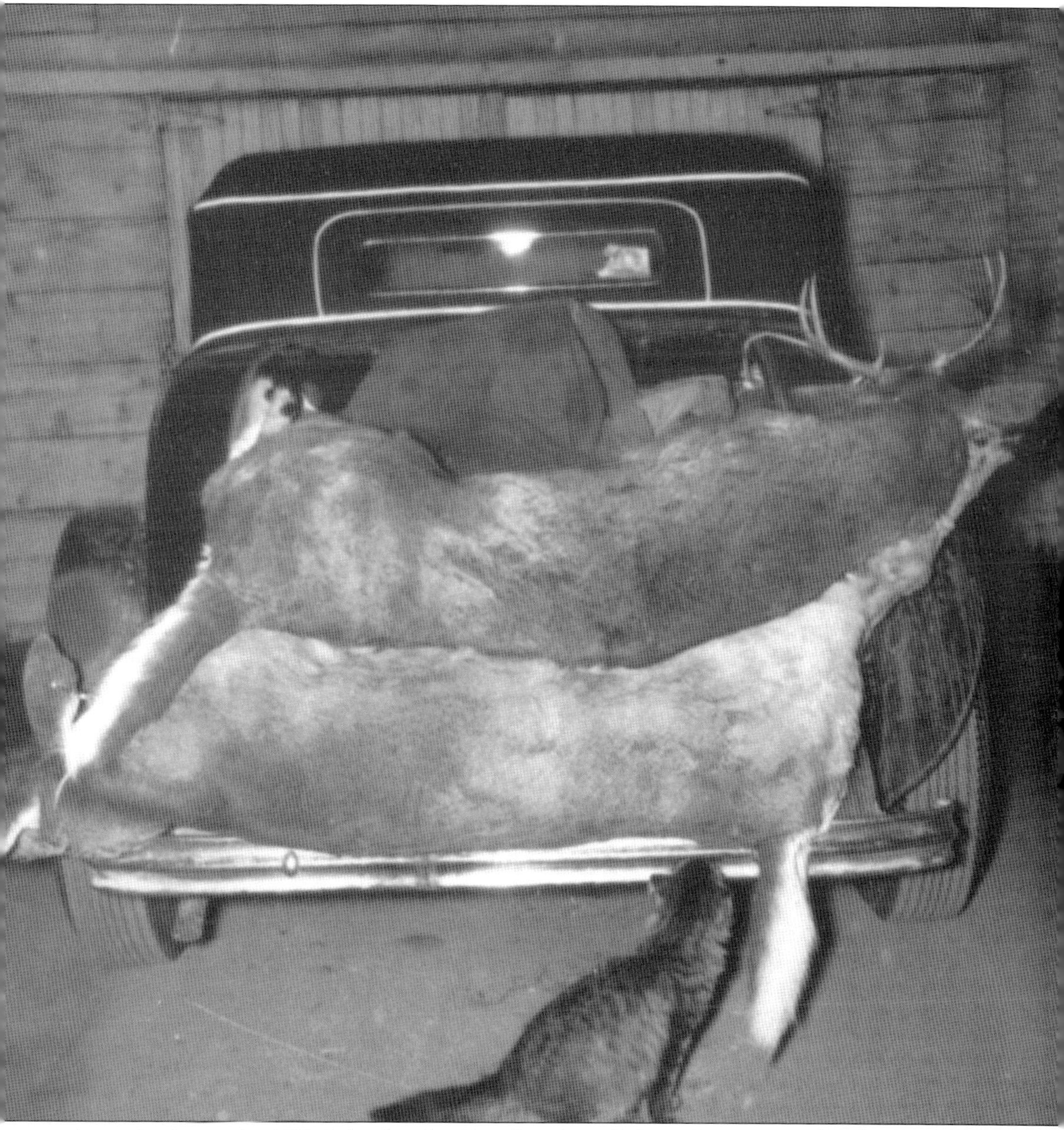

A cat checks out the 1932 Cabriolet after Buzz Storch and Monty Bonnet completed a successful day of deer hunting. The pair took the deuce up to the Colvile, Washington, area. It is hard to see in this photograph, but the car has come a long way: bobbed back fenders with cycle fenders are in the front, and the back bumper has been narrowed and Pontiac taillights added. Del George at West End Auto Body chopped and channeled the car and leaded in the cowl vent and tops of the doors in this version. The car was used as an everyday family car; when Storch was working in Moses Lake, his daughter rode on the package tray. Later, the car was sold to a Spokane police officer, and then to local hot-rodder Bill Payne, before it ended up in the hands of Stan Canter. He sold the deuce to Ronnie Corcum with the stipulation that if he ever parted with it, Canter would have the first chance to buy it back. Decades later, Corcum decided to sell the car back to Canter, who is still driving it on the streets of Spokane. (Buzz Storch.)

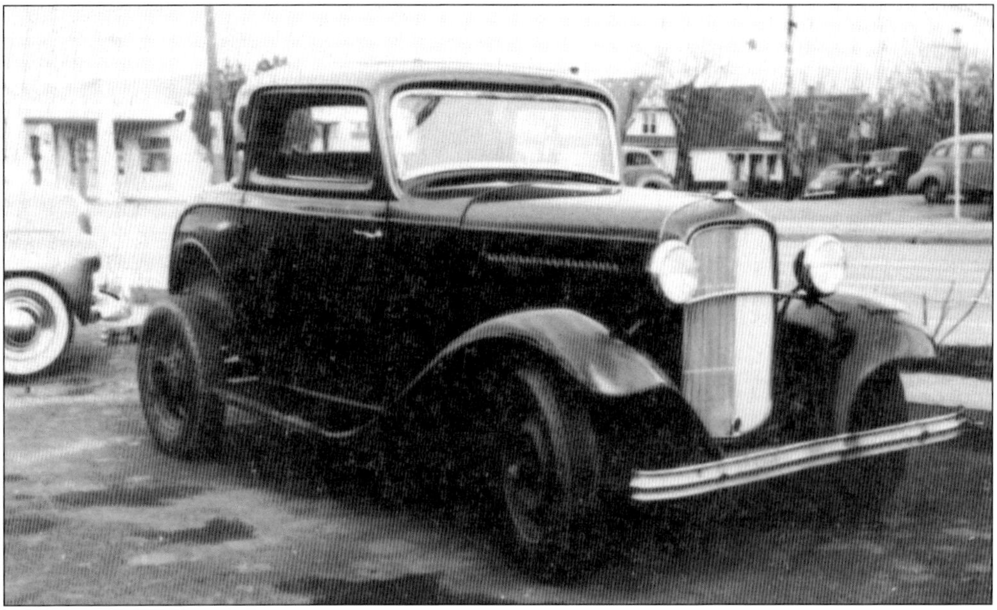

Jack Hordemann's coupe is seen here in 1951; very little is done to the car at this point, with the exception of later headlights, shaved cowl lights, and part of the nose trim having been removed. The coupe had just 38,000 miles on it when Hordemann bought it from the original owner. He owned the car until 1954, when he sold it to Dick Flynn. (Gary Harms.)

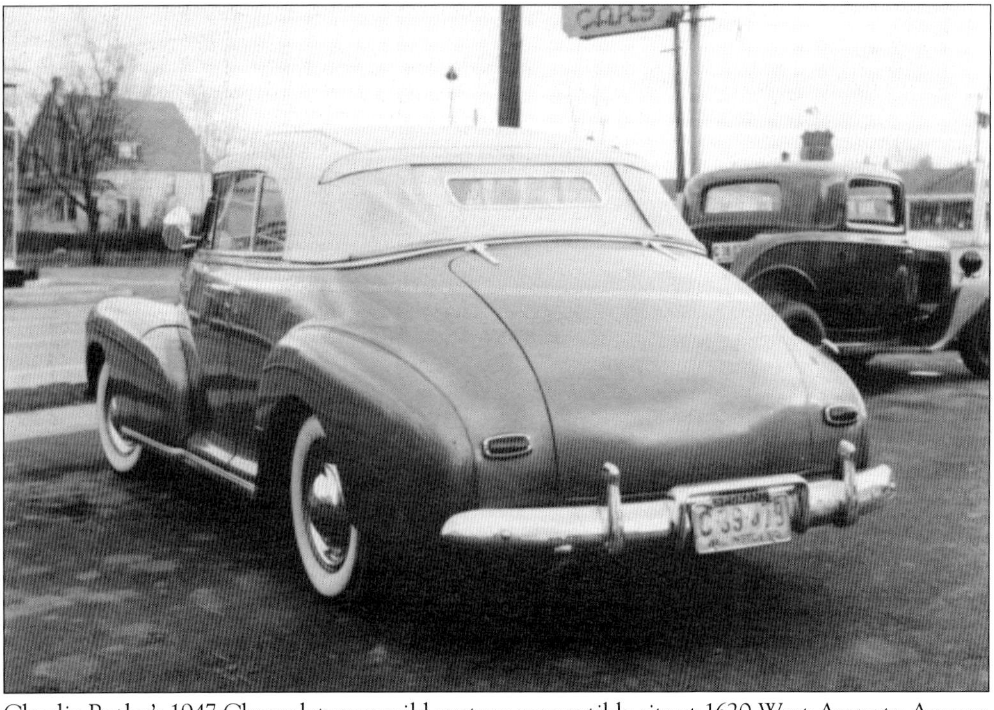

Charlie Butler's 1947 Chevrolet very mild custom convertible sits at 1620 West Augusta Avenue on Spokane's north side. In the background is Jack Hordemann's '32 three-window; its deck lid and rear fender have been removed, and the license plate is tied up between the rain channels. (Brian Kelly.)

Jack Hordemann works on his '32 Ford three-window in front of his parents' garage on North Ash Street in 1951. Jack's brother, Jim, was an Edelbrock and Howard Cams dealer, and the coupe was running a built flathead featuring those speed parts. This is the beginning of a hot rod that became a major piece of Spokane history. By the end of the decade, the coupe would have four different owners, drag race at Deer Park, compete at the Bonneville Salt Flats, make it into *Hot Rod* magazine (in 1956), and participate in numerous indoor shows in Spokane. (Gary Hordemann.)

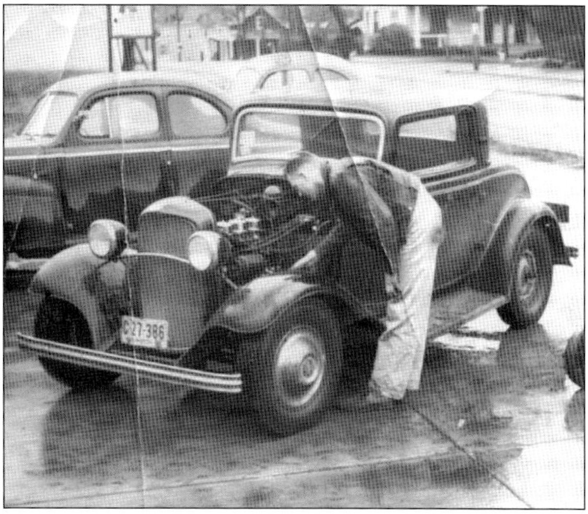

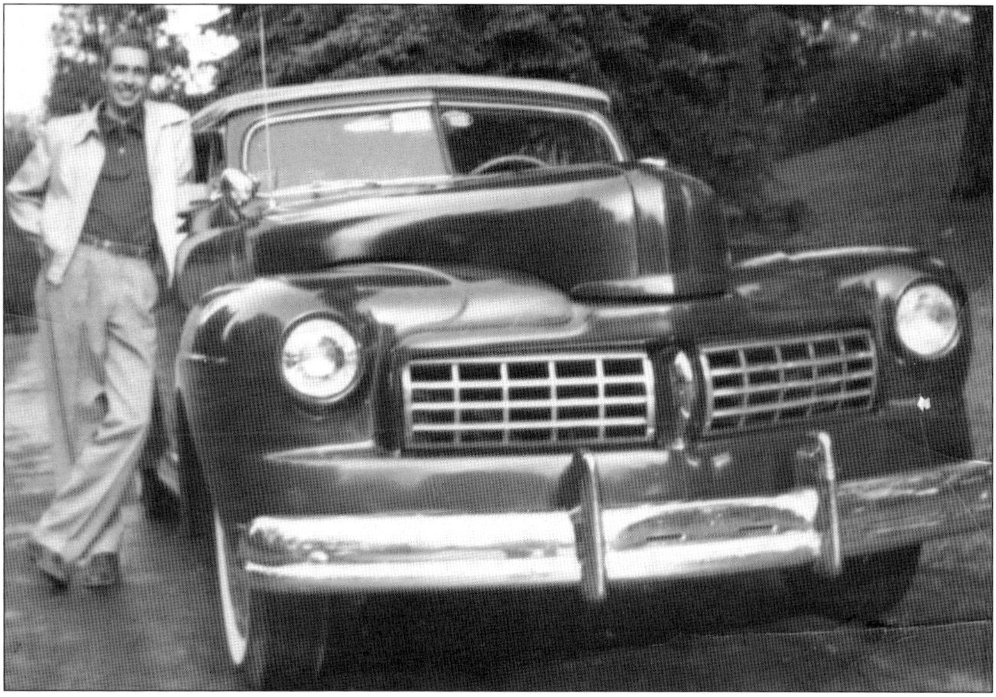

Dusty Rhodes drove his 1947 Mercury convertible all the way from Spokane to East Los Angeles so he could have Gil Ayala chop it. A real Carson top was added to the Merc on that trip. Here, Rhodes stands next to his Merc convertible, with its new custom front end done by Taylor Baker at West End Auto Body, located at the base of Sunset Hill in Spokane. The grille is made out of pieces of late 1940s Lincoln grilles. The hood was louvered and the headlights frenched before the car was sprayed organic purple. (Dusty Rhodes.)

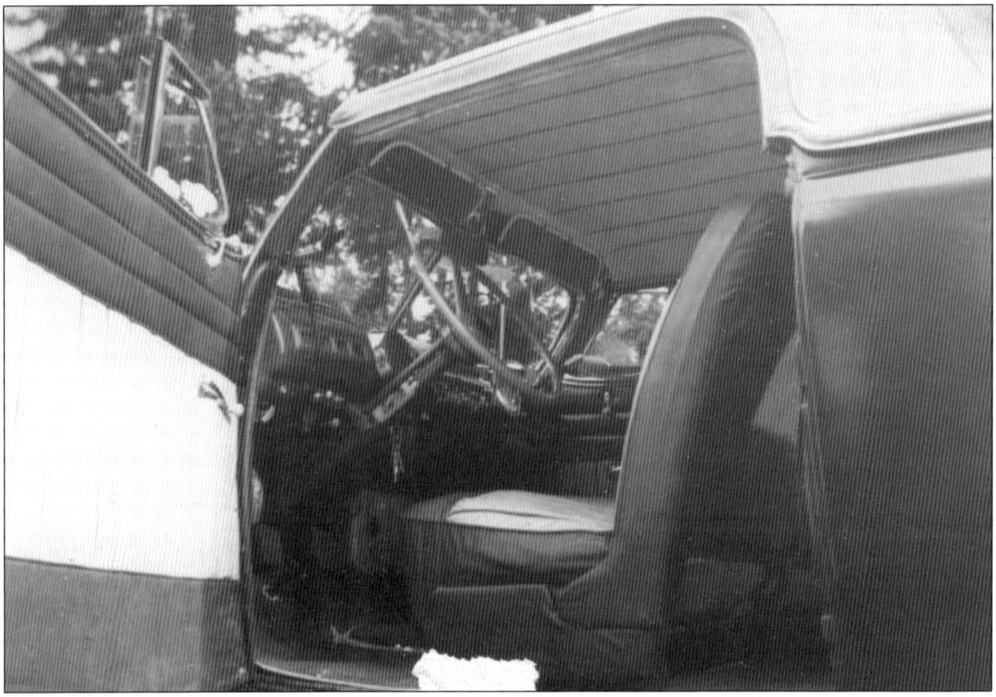

The Mercury's upholstery was finished in maroon and cream by Slow Annie, on Spokane's north side, where many early Spokane rods and customs were done. By this time, the car received Pontiac taillights, a sunken license plate, and shaved door handles. Dusty Rhodes remembers that he sold the Merc in the mid-1950s for $1,145. (Dusty Rhodes.)

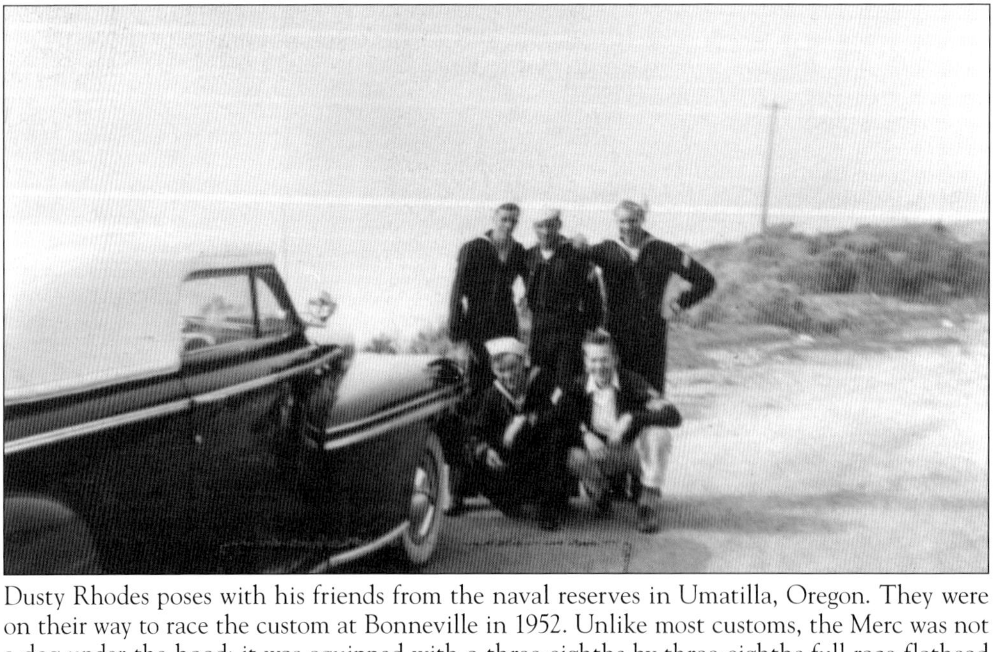

Dusty Rhodes poses with his friends from the naval reserves in Umatilla, Oregon. They were on their way to race the custom at Bonneville in 1952. Unlike most customs, the Merc was not a dog under the hood; it was equipped with a three-eighths-by-three-eighths full race flathead with Edelbrock heads and intake. The rear end was a Columbia two-speed, and the transmission had Zephyr gears in it. (Dusty Rhodes.)

Early Dukes Auto Club member Don Noack (right) and a friend stand next to his 1936 Ford Cabriolet in 1951. The car featured a sectioned body with Cord-like custom pipes coming out of the stock hood sides. Spotlights and Hollywood flipper hubcaps finish off the early custom look. (Connie Sullivan.)

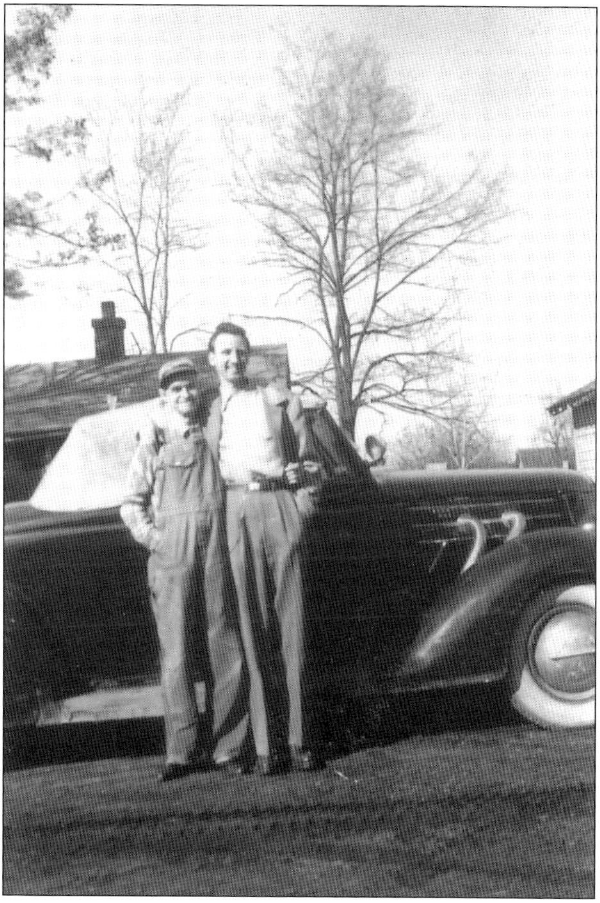

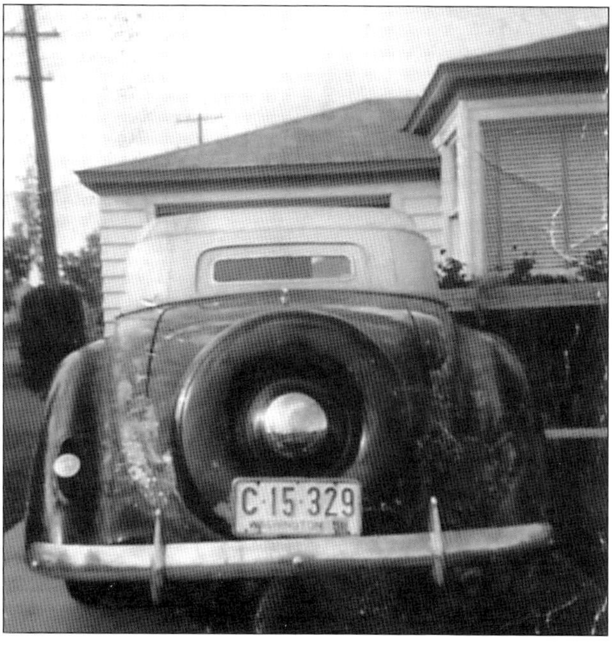

This photograph of the rear of Don Noack's Cabriolet illustrates how the proportions were spot on and the stance perfect. The fenders are molded into the body, and the stock bumper is replaced with a later one. The stock taillights are removed, but replacements are not yet added to the car. (Connie Sullivan.)

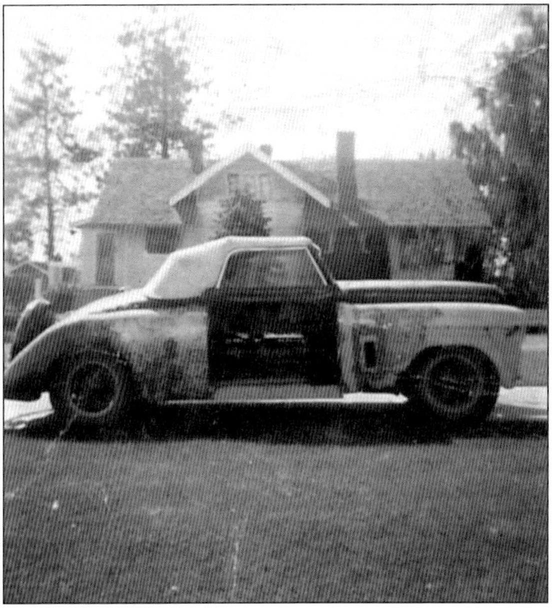

Like many customs, Don Noack's Cabriolet did not make it through to the second stage of its life. Parts of early 1950s GM cars were used to modernize the Ford, partially replacing the original 1936 sheet metal and used over the top of factory components. In the quarter panel, that blend is easy to see, and the GM B pillar blends into the Ford rear fender, deleting the running board in the process. (Connie Sullivan.)

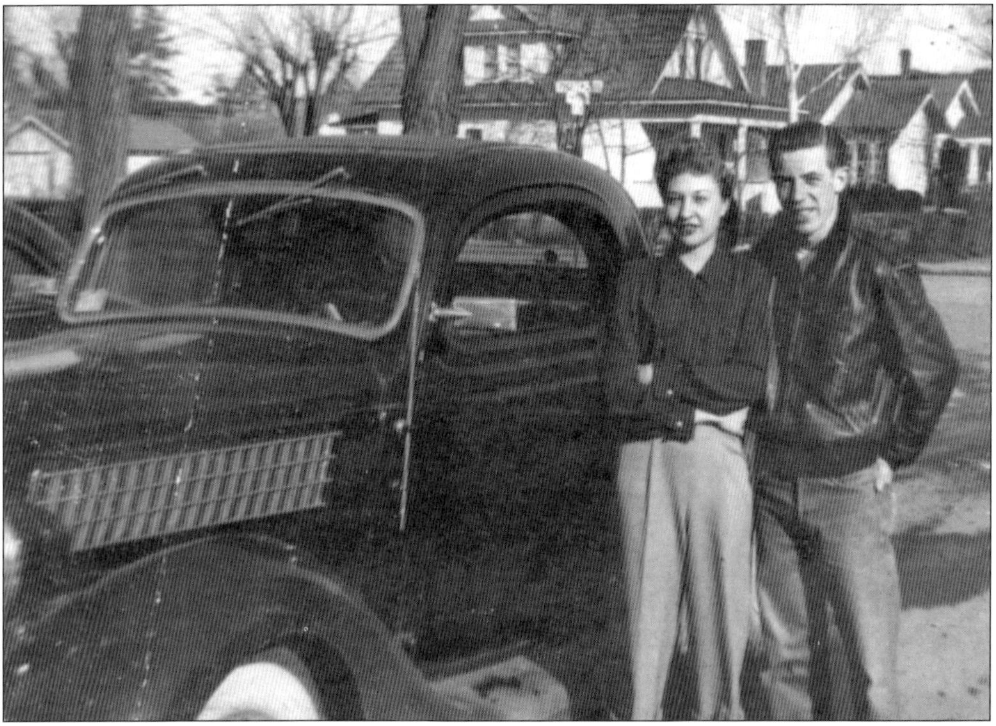

Original Dukes member Floyd "Kayo" Reidburn, 18, poses with Toni Reidburn, 17, and the 1935 Ford in front of her parents' house at 808 West Providence Avenue. The '35 Ford three-window was painted a dark royal blue with matching rolled and pleated interior. Kayo's contribution to the history of the Dukes is long lasting and sometimes overlooked. He was the designer of the Dukes top-hat-and-cane logo, still used on the club plaques. Kayo sold his 1935 to a kid who lived on the South Hill, who then painted it green. Rectangular rearview mirrors were common at this time. (Toni Reidburn.)

Kayo Riedburn poses in his '26-'27 T modified in his backyard in 1952. The car still has the stock firewall and is fitted with a 24-stud Ford flathead. The building in the background with the chimney was Sigmond's grocery store on Post Street and Garland Avenue. Several local hot-rodders worked at the store when they were younger. (Toni Reidburn.)

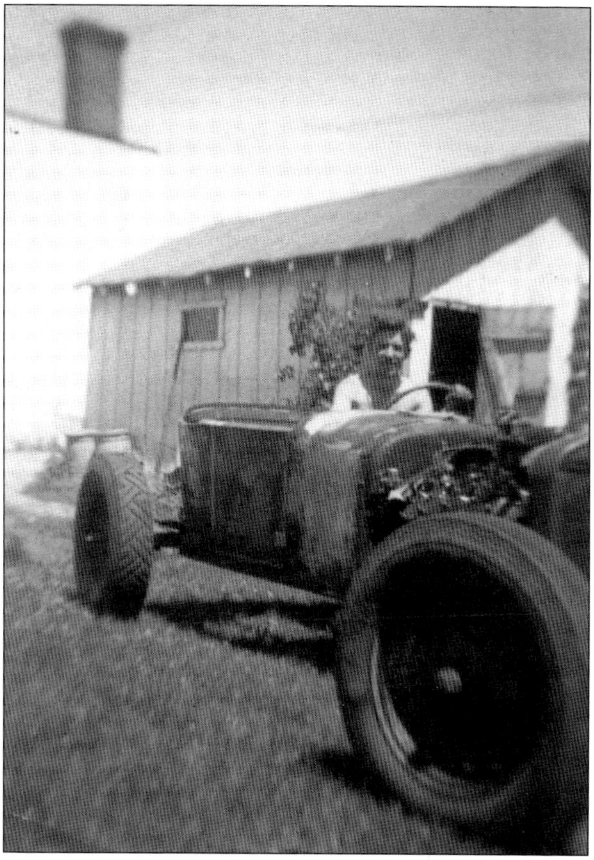

The same '26-'27 T of Kayo Riedburn is seen here just a little further along in its remodeling. The stock firewall has been replaced with a flat sheet of metal, a banjo steering wheel was installed, and the modified was painted white. From left to right are Toni's niece Connie Clark, Jerry Riedburn, and Jeff Clark (at the wheel). (Toni Reidburn.)

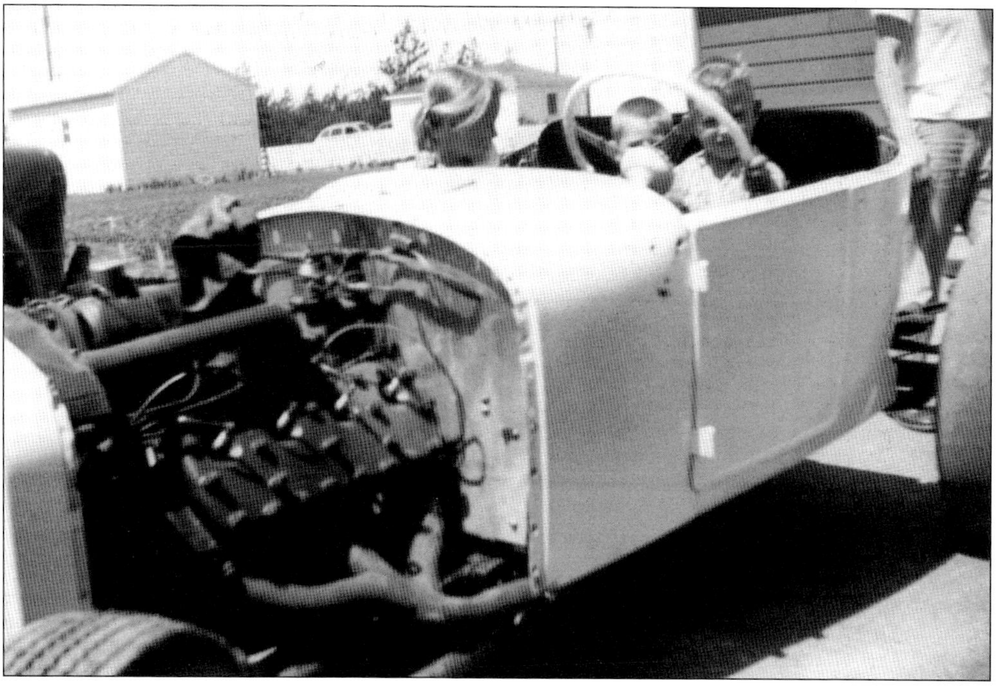

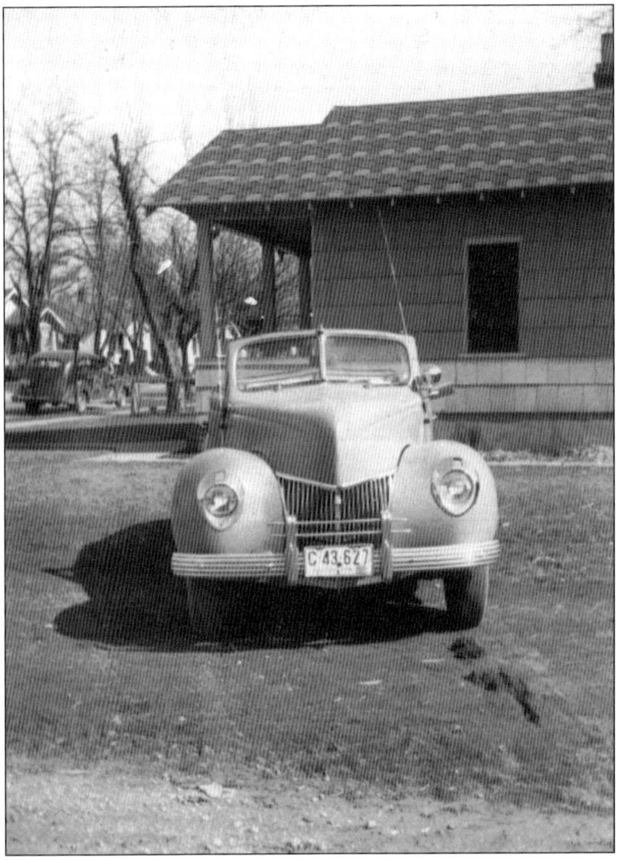

Dukes member Harry Prouty's 1939 Ford convertible custom is seen here in gray primer. The car was a very mild custom, with all-stock running gear and interior. The hood trim has been shaved, and 1937 Desoto bumpers and '40 headlight rings replaced the stock components. Prouty was working at Buchanan Chevrolet at Third Avenue and Wall Street when someone saw his '39 parked on the street and tracked him down to purchase it. (Harry Prouty.)

Harry Prouty already owned this green '41 Ford convertible when he sold his 1939 Ford. It is seen here in front of his house on the north side, still sporting Idaho plates from the previous owner. Prouty was starting to give it a mild custom look. The rectangle side mirror was a common addition to early Spokane customs. (Harry Prouty.)

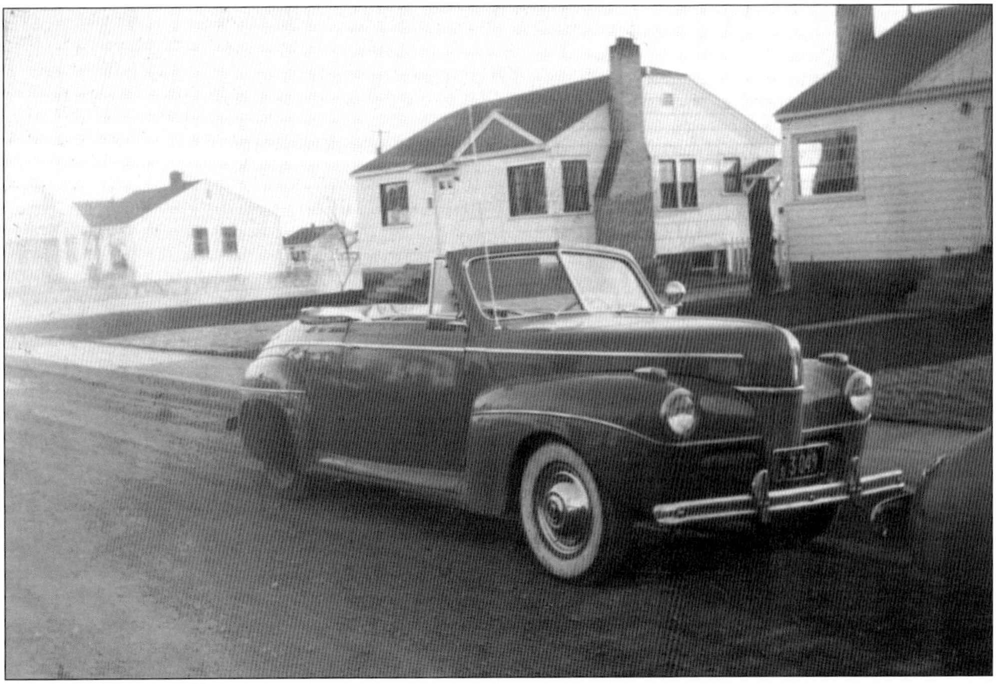

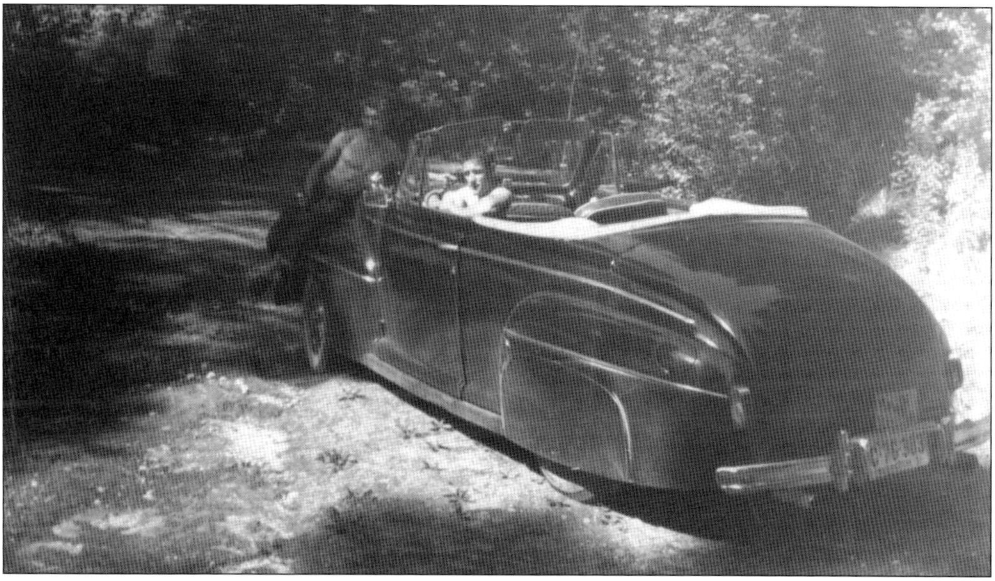

Harry Prouty (left) and a friend pose with the 1941 convertible after it was painted black in Buchanan's paint department. The interior was stock with seat covers, but the motor has been changed out at this point to an 8CM flathead out of a 1951 Mercury. Above the license plate surround that was added to the stock bumper is an early clear Dukes plaque. (Harry Prouty.)

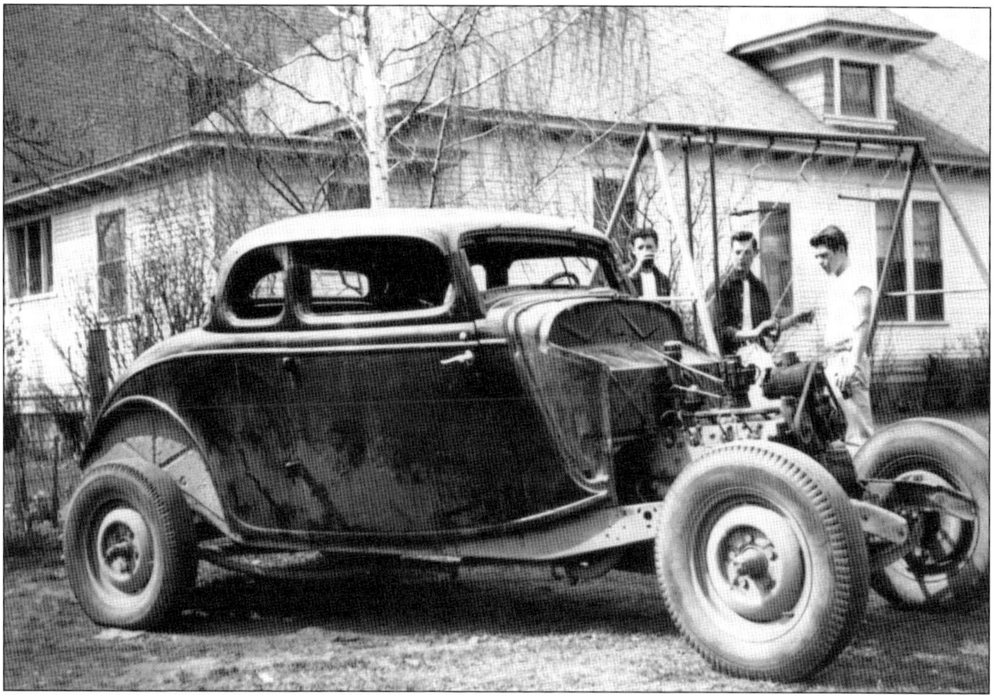

Anyone who has ever worked on a hot rod can appreciate this photograph. The hot-rodders can step back and appreciate the work they put into a car, which is now not a half-finished mess, but a completed project ready to hit the streets. In this case, the car is a 1934 Ford coupe. Brothers Bill (left) and Butch Miller, leaning on the swing set, are with Stu Young in Joe Kostelecky's backyard. (Ludy Kostelecky.)

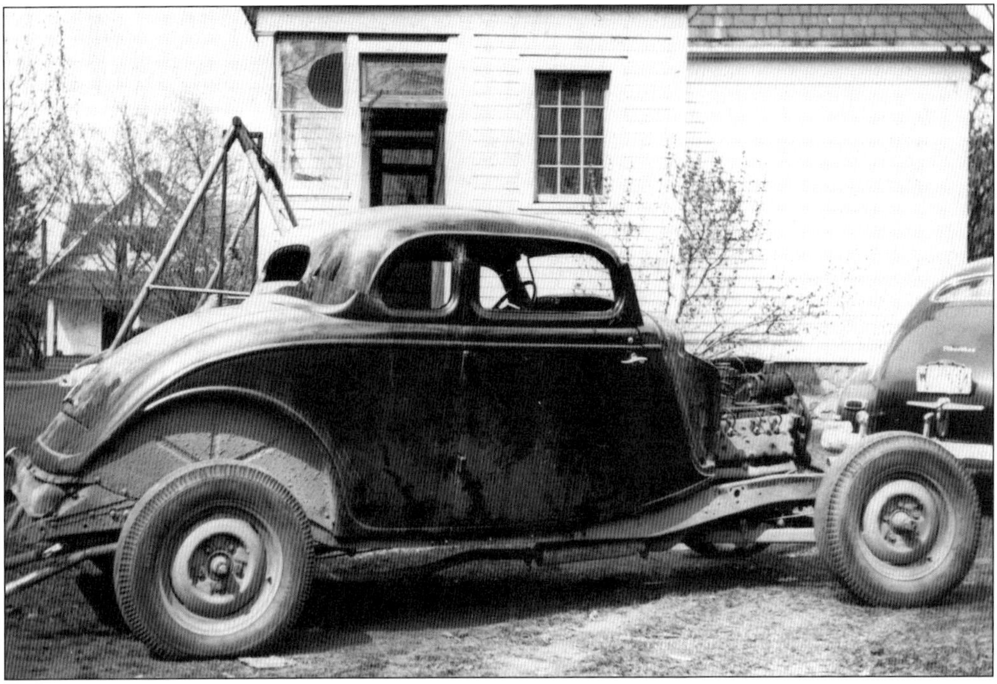

Joe Kostelecky's backyard, on Sinto Avenue between Division and Ruby Streets, is where many early projects like this were done. Joe and his wife, Ludy, moved to Spokane in 1950 from Dickerson, North Dakota. The 1934 five-window is still running the stock motor. Visible is the raised oil fill tube and breather that Ford added in '34s to clear the firewall. (Ludy Kostelecky.)

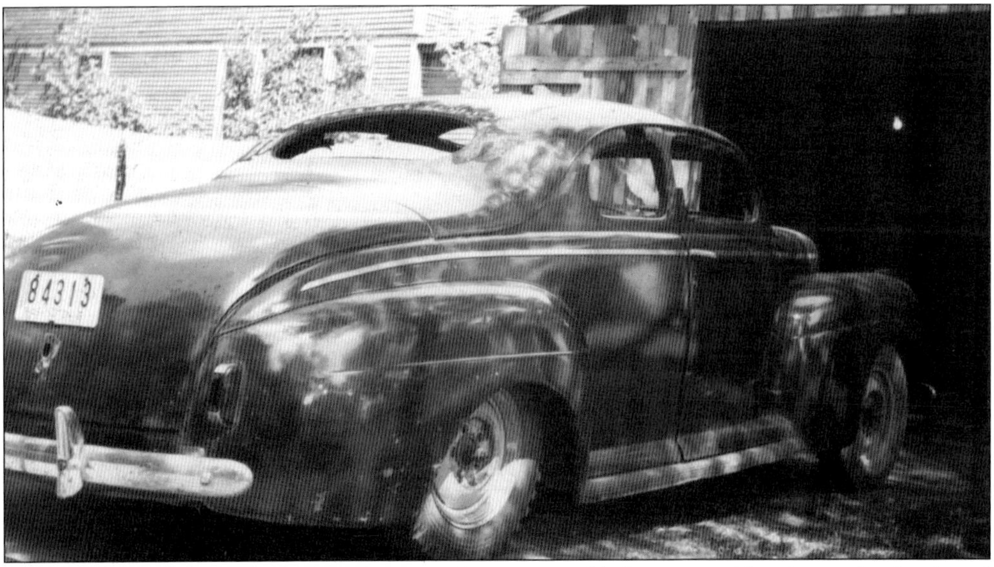

Joe Kostelecky, known in Spokane as a craftsman, would chop a car like this in his backyard for $50. It is said he traded work on this 1941 Ford coupe for a new refrigerator. His day job was working with his uncle at a body shop on Washington Street. The house in the background is where Ludy and Joe raised six children. In the yard and small garage, Joe created some of the best rods that have ever hit the streets of Spokane. It became a hangout where local hot-rodders dreamed of their next custom project. (Ludy Kostelecky.)

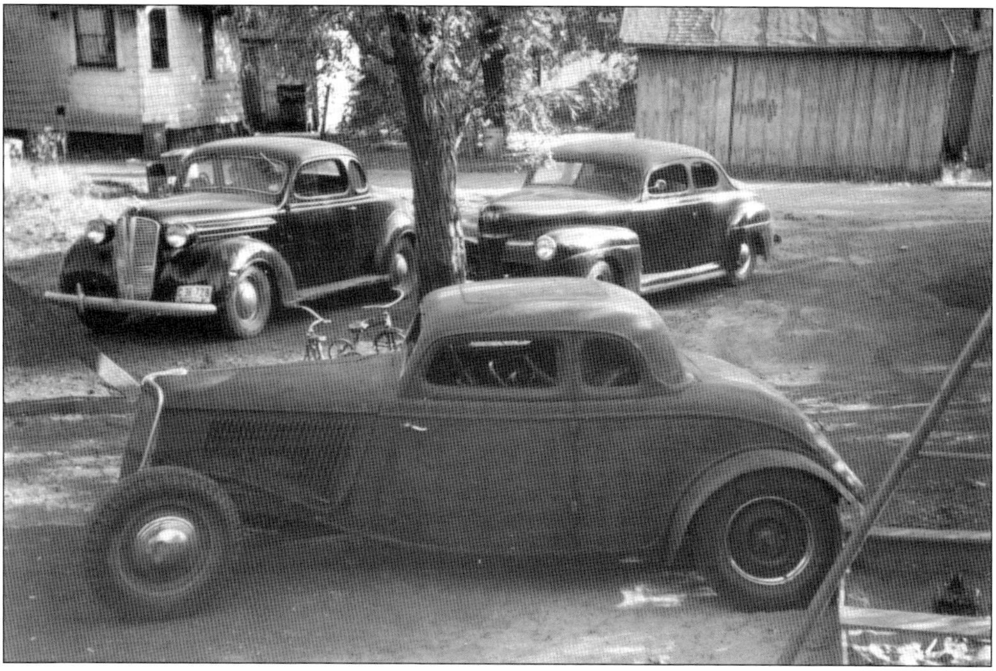

Both the 1934 and the 1941 coupes are now back together in the Kosteleckys' yard. The '34 five-window (center) is now channeled, too, with bobbed back fenders and a coat of primer. The interior is filled with the garnish moldings. The '41 (top right), partially primed, looks like it could hit the road at any point. (Ludy Kostelecky.)

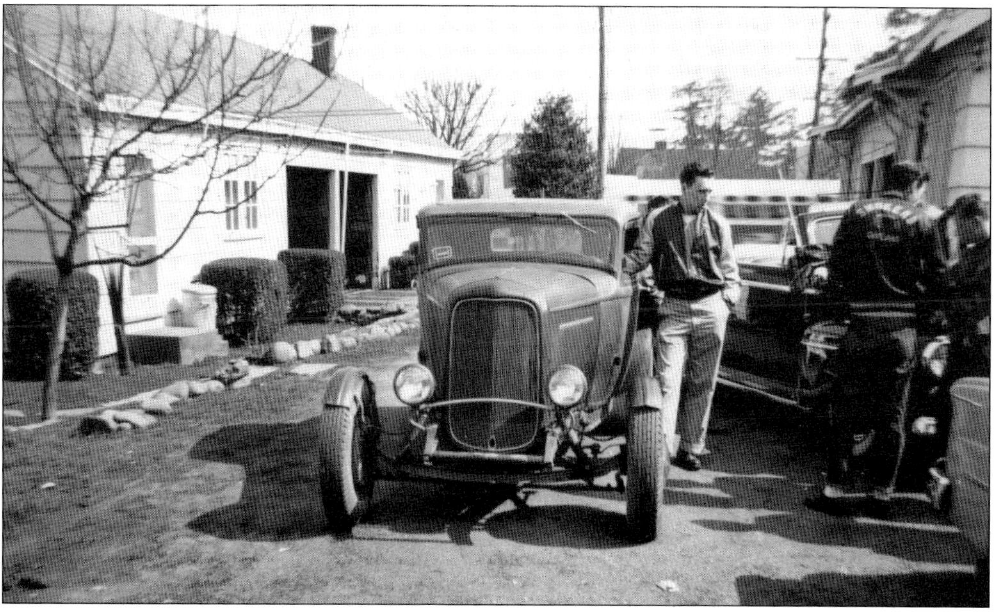

The Dukes hang out in their hotel parking lot in Portland, Oregon, after driving down to participate in the 1953 Portland indoor show. Duane Wolf (center) stands next to his chopped 1932 five-window coupe with filled grille shell, bobbed fenders in the back, and fronts made out of Ford spare-tire covers. George Chilimidos (back to the camera) wears a Smokers Car Club jacket. Larry Hovick is next to him. The convertible in the background is Jack Currie's 1948 Ford. (Butch Miller.)

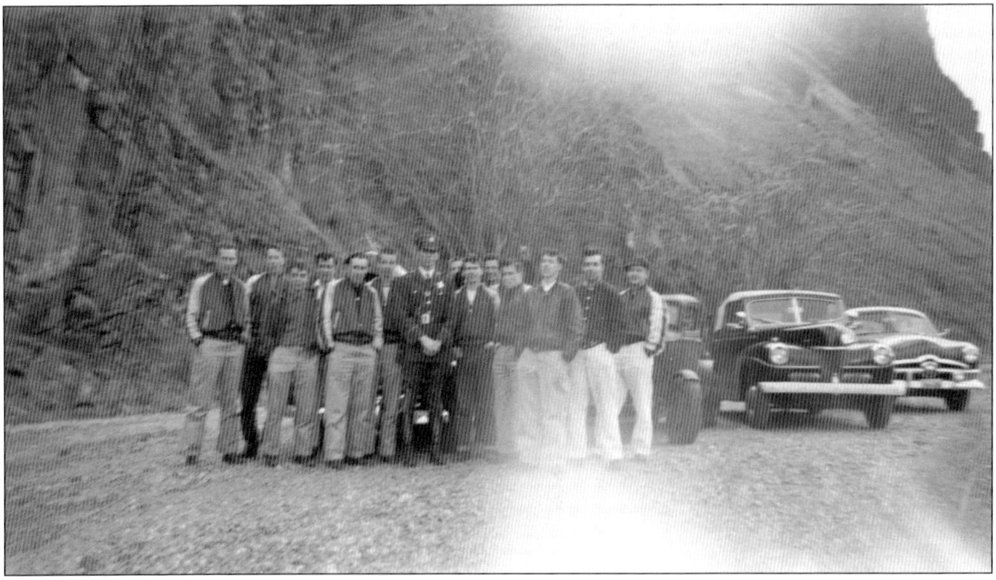

Members of the Dukes Auto Club pose with the police officer who just pulled them over for street racing in the Columbia Gorge on their way back home to Spokane. The highway patrolman caught Duane Wolf in his '32 coupe and made him chase down the others so he could talk to them. Among those shown here are Don Miner, Bill Wyman, Stu Young, Duane Wolf, Bob Brown, Harry Prouty, Jerry Hoover, Kayo Reidburn, and Durwood Johnson, with the police officer in the center. (Harry Prouty.)

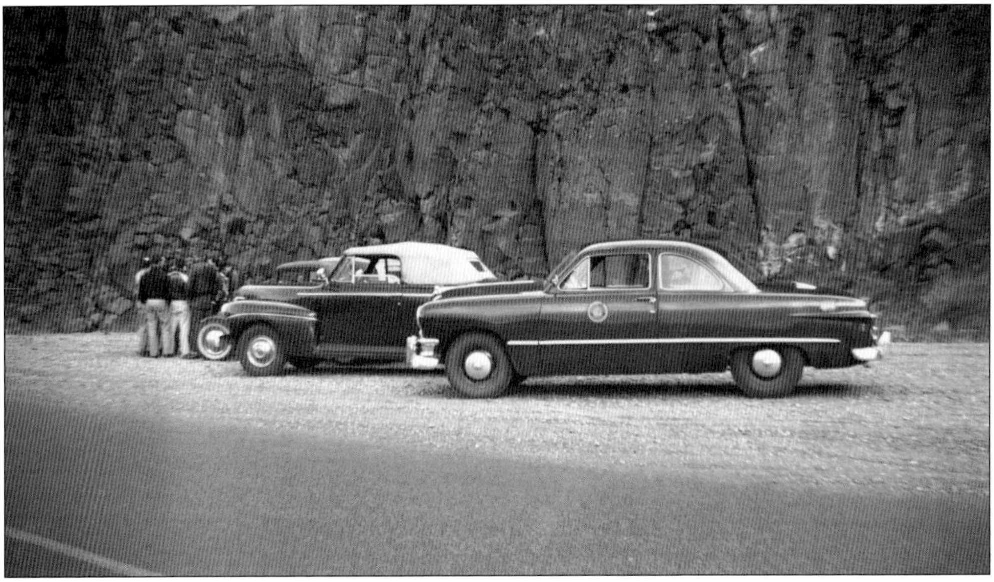

The highway patrol's 1950 Ford coupe (right) is parked alongside Harry Prouty's '41 (center) and Duane Wolf's five-window (rear). The group is in a huddle in front of the cars. The rock walls of the Columbia Gorge provide a great backdrop. (Harry Prouty.)

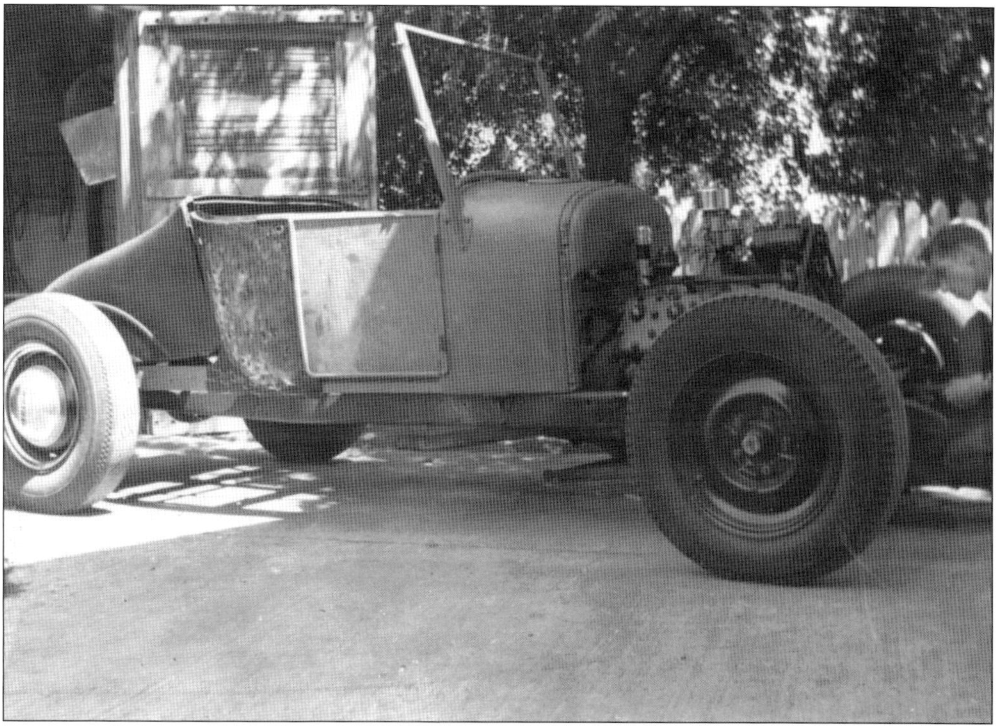

Gary Harms, 15, works on his 1926 Model T in his parents' driveway. Gary and Art Santa Rosa found the roadster in a wrecking yard on North Division Street, and talked Gary's dad into borrowing the neighbor's utility trailer and hauling it home. The frame belonged to Dick Chastek and was stepped in the rear. Chastek, a Spokane hot-rodder, met Rochlitzer when they both attended Gonzaga University. (Gary Harms.)

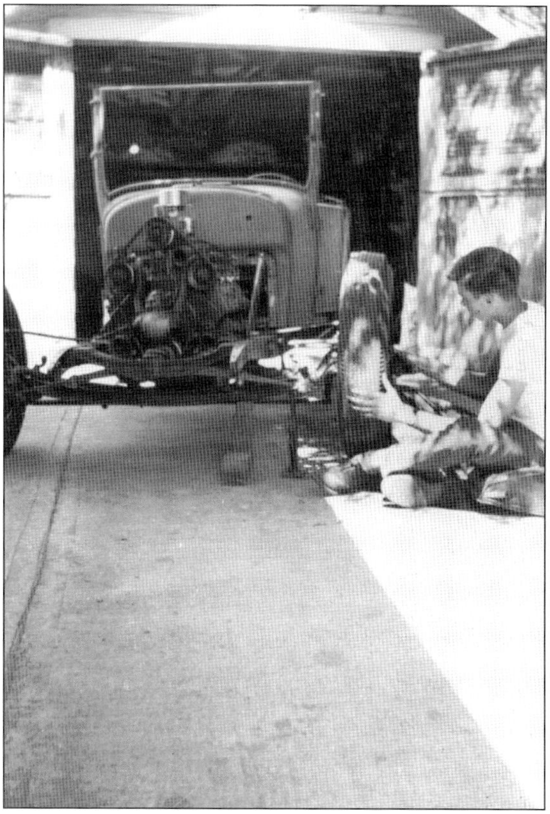

The axle and spindles were dropped in Spokane by the Muir brothers at their shop on Francis Avenue, later the site of Bennett's Auto Wrecking. The Muirs' shop catered more to midget racing than to hot rodding, but they unknowingly helped give Spokane hot rods a unique look. After the brothers closed their shop, they sold Gary Harms their homemade louver dies; Harms has been punching the louvers in this area since then. Harms and Santa Rosa parted out a 1936 Ford for the running gear, but Harms sold the Model T before it saw the road. (Gary Harms.)

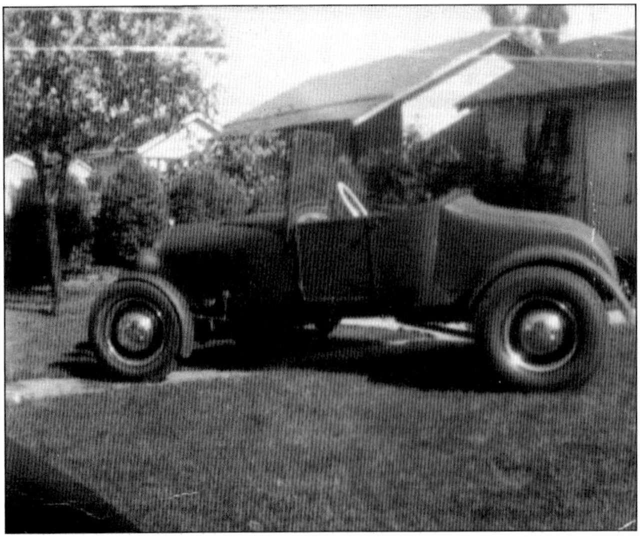

Originally built by Tim Rochlitzer and Duke Rogers to race at Bonneville in 1952, this little roadster would see street and racing time by numerous owners in Spokane. When Rochlitzer moved up to Spokane, he brought with him a full race Ford V-8 60 motor that was built by Taylor and Ryan in Los Angeles. The turtle deck was a NOS part that Duke was able to locate at a Ford parts warehouse. This photograph was taken in Steve Pick's back yard when he and Rochlitzer were partners in the car. (Gary Harms.)

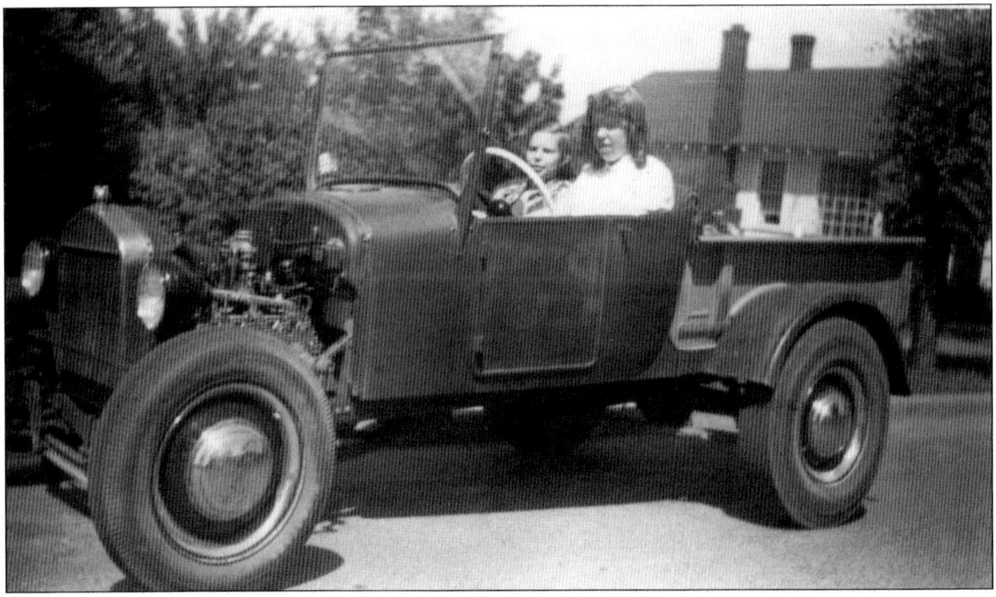

This is the same Harms and Rochlitzer T roadster, with a pickup box on it and the hood removed. This is the street motor that they had for the car with the Evans race heads on it. The remnant of a racing number is visible on the side of the body. The motor was equipped with Evans speed parts. On trips to California, Rochlitzer would load up Evans parts and bring them back to sell in Spokane. Sitting in the car on East Providence Avenue is Gary's sister Julie Harms (left) and his cousin Caroline Crothers. After using it as a street car, Harms sold it to Gary Hordemann and Bob Frankovic, who turned it back into a race car. (Gary Harms.)

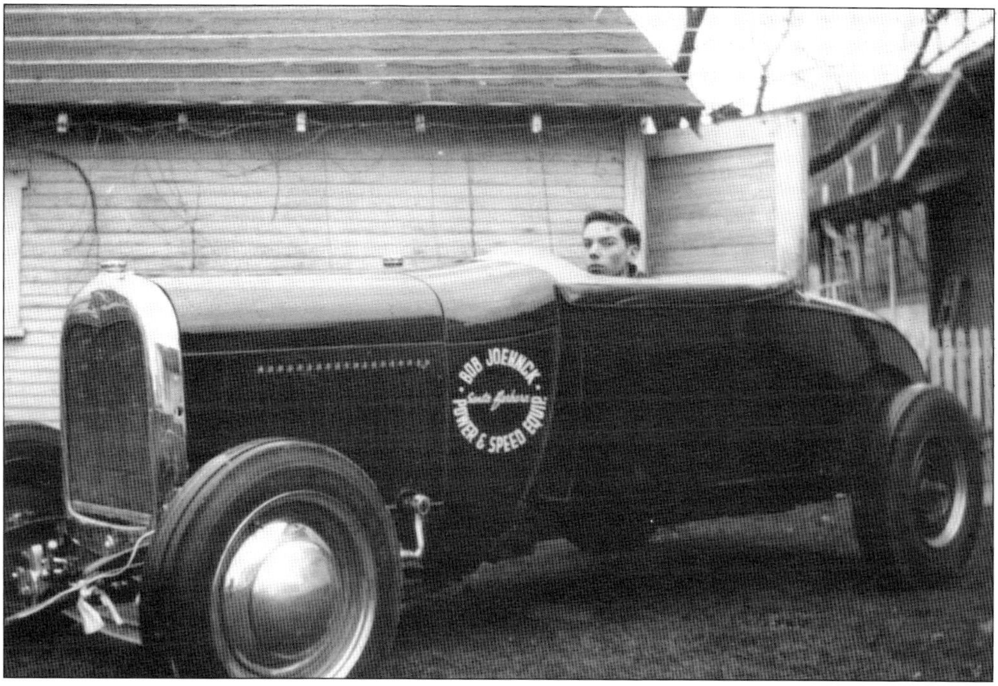

Gary Harms sits in Bob Joehnck's roadster, which he and Tim Rochlitzer bought. Harms and Rochlitzer went in as partners on this car, too. Rochlitzer was going to get the quick-change rear end, and Harms was going to keep the rest of the car. The A roadster came to Spokane in 1953, when Rochlitzer drove down and picked it up in Santa Barbara. This photograph was taken on the day it was dropped off at Harms's house, with the California lettering still on it. The car was covered with great details, including the body-line that was added to the hood around the steering box. (Gary Harms.)

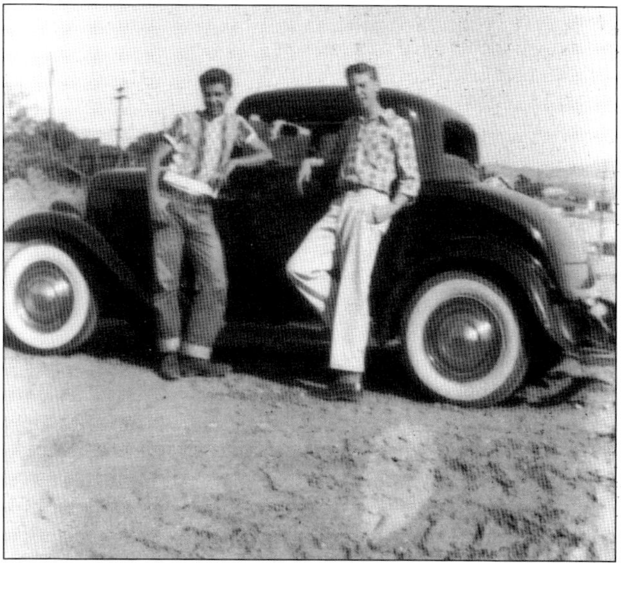

Art Santa Rosa (left) and Gary Harms lean on Tom Bellmore's '32 Ford three-window. Both guys are no more than 15 years old in this photograph. Bellmore's parents owned an auto-repair shop on the southwest corner of Division Street and Gray Court. The car is basically rock stock at this point, running the 1932 Ford 21 stud motor and sporting the factory interior. The only real changes were the jumbo wheels with aftermarket hubcaps, a headlight bar and headlights of a different make, and a gloss black paint job applied with a brush. (Gary Harms.)

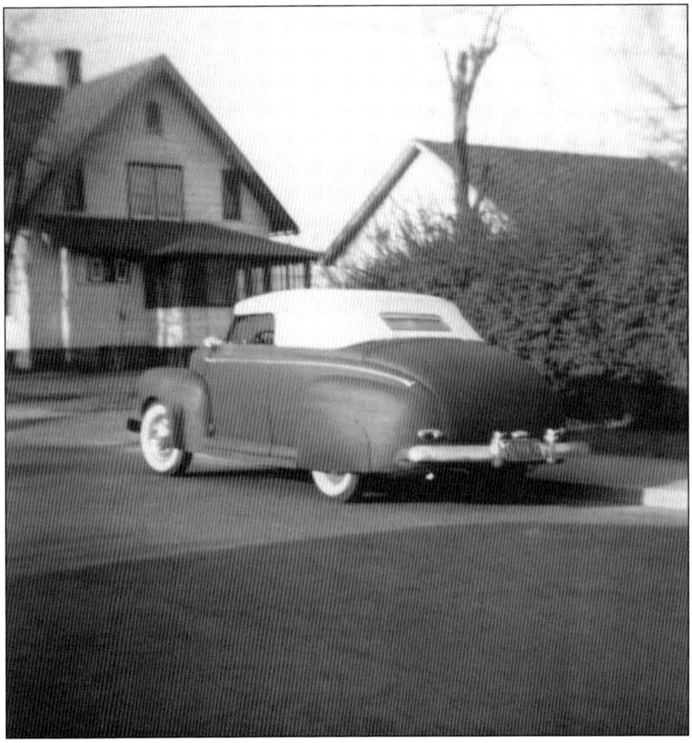

Bob Coutts bought his 1941 Ford convertible for $450 from the manager of the Early Birds Night Club, located in the basement of the Davenport Hotel. He added a fully built flathead with two 94 carburetors and finned heads. The top was chopped two-and-a-half inches by a body shop on Trent Avenue, and Bob Baker upholstered the top and interior in white, including the carpet. The car was painted with dark gray primer; other custom touches include 1950 Chevrolet taillights and a shaved deck lid. Coutts ended up trading the car for a new 1956 Chevy two-door sedan. (Bob Coutts.)

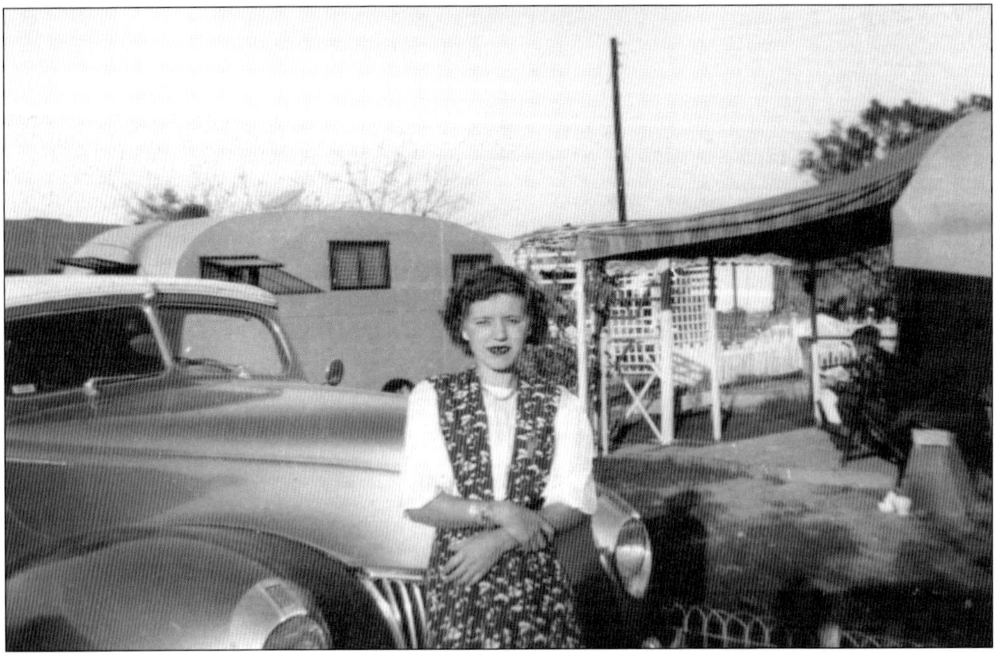

Shown here is Chuck Schwartzenberger's chopped custom '39 Ford deluxe convertible with '40 Ford headlights and shortened hood chrome. The car, of a silver color with a purple tint, was powered by a flathead with Edelbrock heads and a two-pot intake. Schwartzenberger bought the car in Missoula, Montana, for $150 and sold it to buy a 1941 Mercury convertible. Chuck was a member of the King Pins in Spokane. (Chuck Schwartzenberger.)

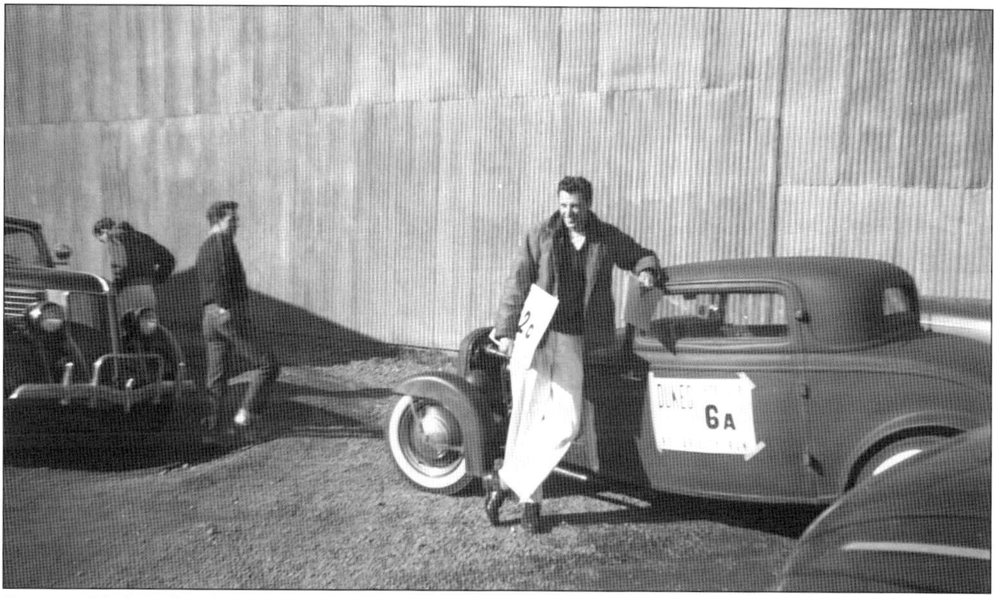

George Chilimidos, leaning on Steve Pick's '32 three-window, was a member of the Smokers Car Club from Oakland, California. The military brought Chilimidos to Spokane, and he brought with him a 1936 Ford two-door sedan that had the roof cut off. On this day, he is the chairman of a reliability run that the Dukes were having. On the front wheels of the coupe are a pair of motorcycle fenders, attached by drilling and tapping the end of the spindle, then drilling a hole though the hubcap to run a bolt through. (Harry Prouty.)

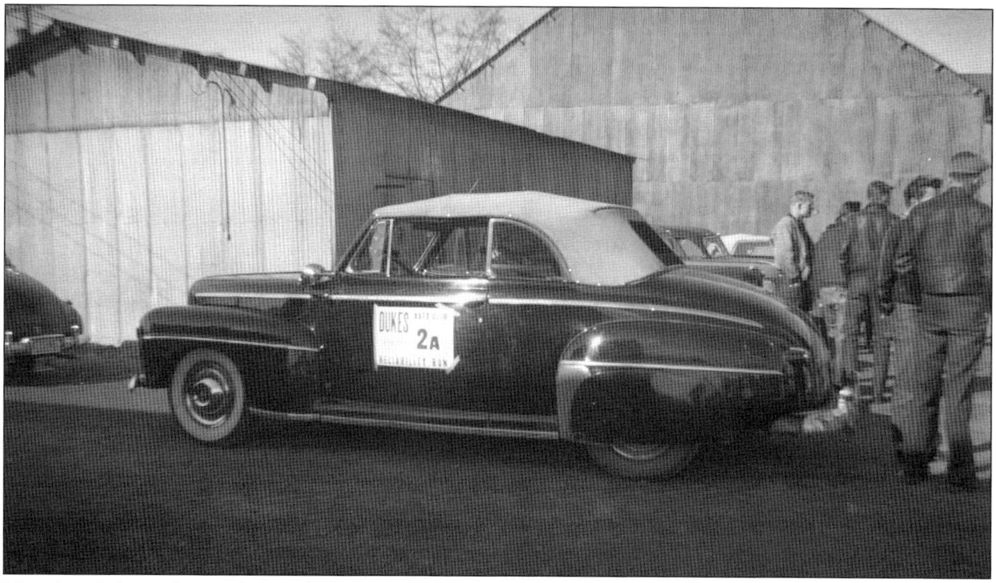

Number 2A in the Dukes' reliability run is club member Harry Prouty's 1941 Ford convertible. Prouty had been a Dukes member since it was formed in 1949, the same year he graduated from high school. He was well known in the Spokane area as a participant in many automotive sports, from hot rodding to motorcycle and stock-car racing. (Harry Prouty.)

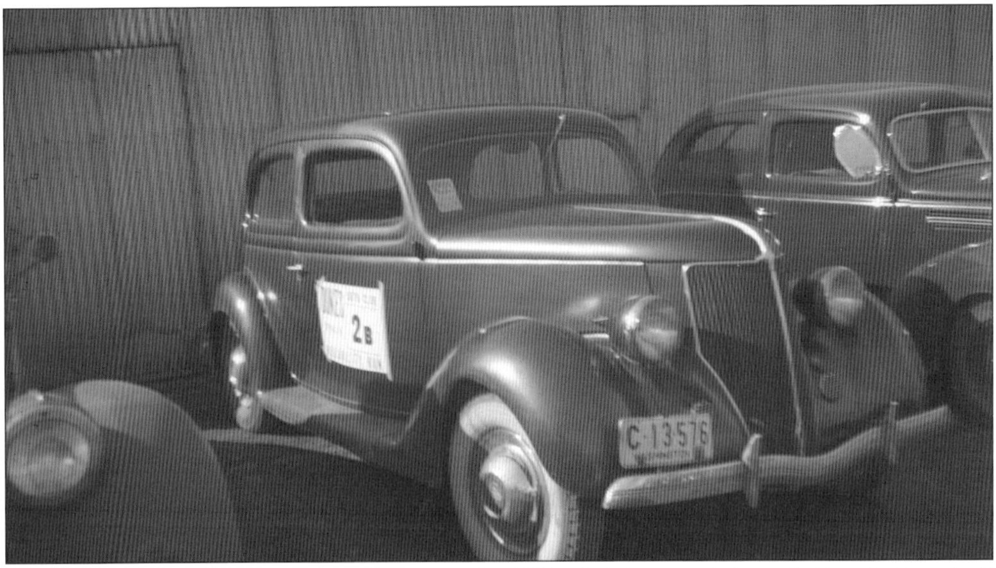

This unknown 1936 Ford two-door also ran in the 1952 reliability run. It has solid hood sides, a bull nose, and aftermarket hubcaps. The Dukes and the highway patrol laid out the 60-mile racecourse. The run was won by Butch Miller, another original member of the Dukes. (Harry Prouty.)

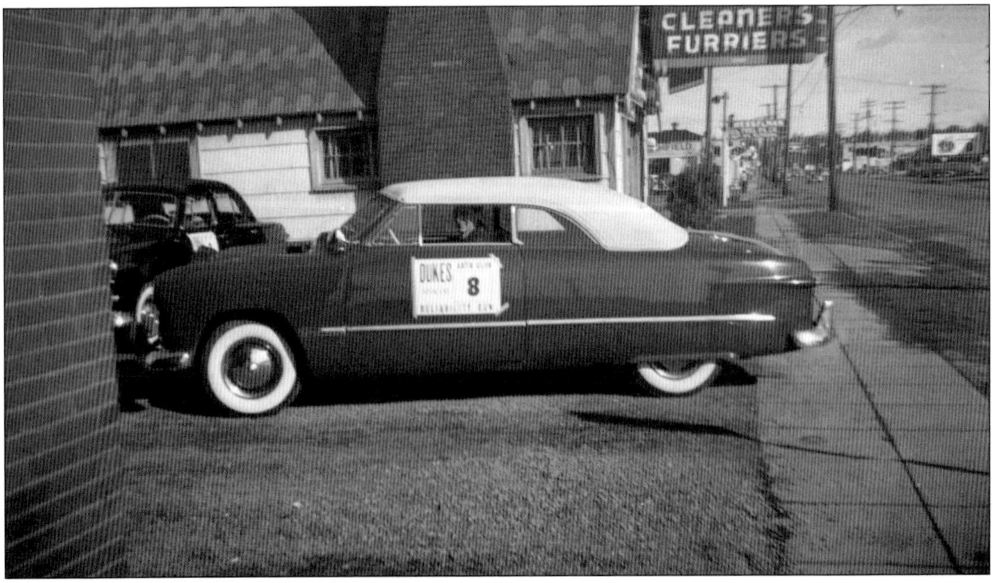

Tim Rochlitzer's 1949 Ford convertible ran as No. 8 in the event. The run was not based on time; the drivers were scored based on their driving skills and their ability to follow the rules of the road. It looks like the '49 Ford four-door at left also participated in the run. The man in the car is not Rochlitzer. This photograph was taken on Monroe Street, just north of Northwest Boulevard. (Harry Prouty.)

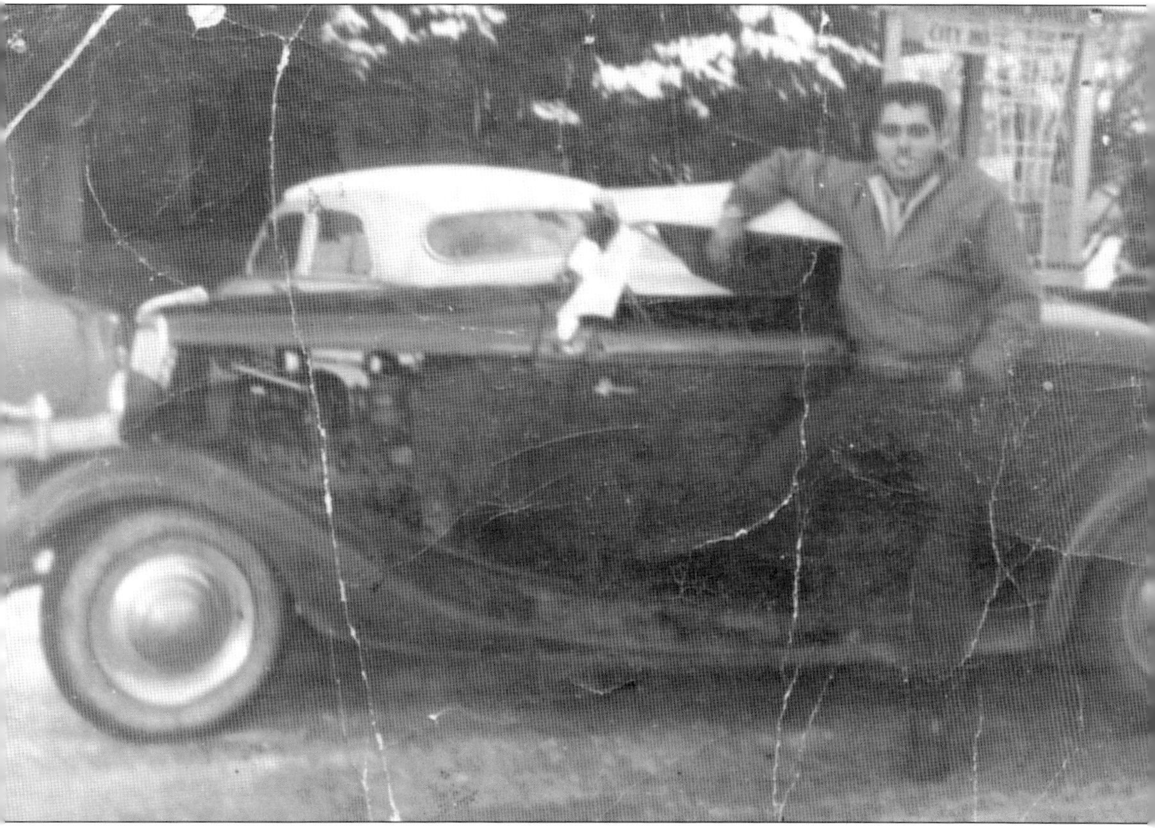

Standing in front of Larry Skidmore's chopped black 1933 Ford roadster is Skidmore's friend Nick, who bought the roadster first. It was already a hot rod in the Colville area. Nick was originally from Rock Island, Illinois, and was stationed at the Air Force radar base. Skidmore paid Nick $100 for the rod after he was transferred to another base. The roadster had a '59A flathead in it, with an Offenhouser dual-carb setup and aluminum heads. (Larry Skidmore.)

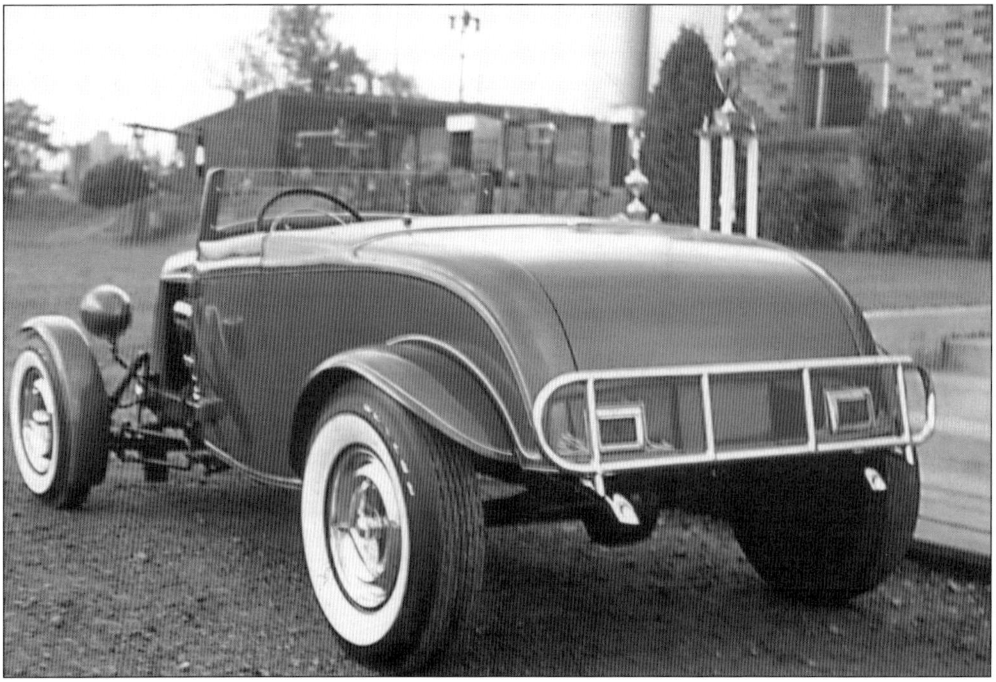

Art True's 1932 Ford Cabriolet sits in front of the True's Oil Company building on Hamilton, just south of the Gonzaga campus. Joe Kostelecky did some of the bodywork on the car for Jack Currie, then finished it up for True. For the section that covered where the original top was, Kostelecky used the tops of two Ford doors. He also bobbed the back fenders and added Olds taillights. The nerf bars were also hand-built by Kostelecky. Before the car was painted maroon, it was a bright blue, and in that version, the top of the Cabriolet windshield is still there. (Art True.)

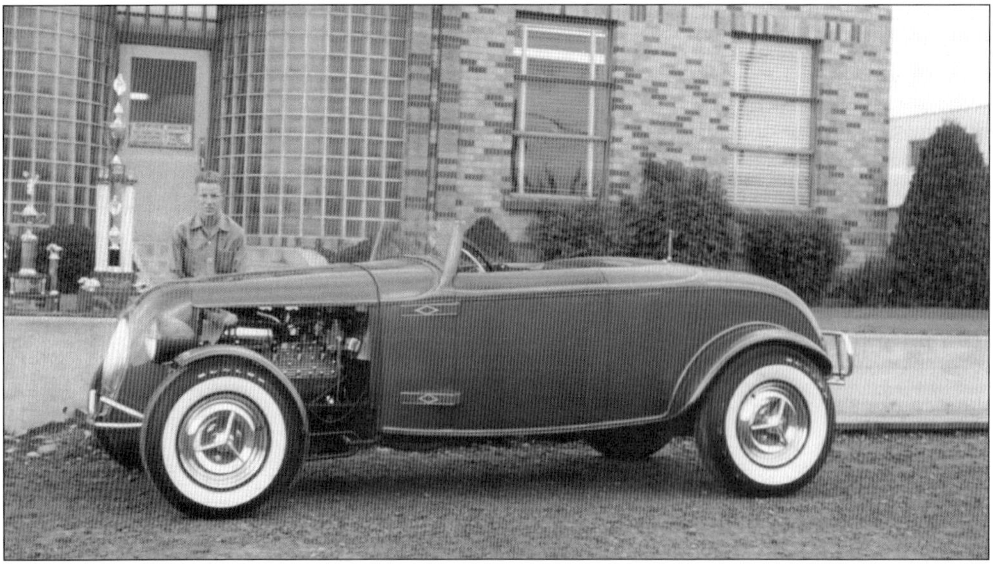

Art True sits next to the deuce and the trophies the car won in various Northwest shows, including the Seattle Seafair. It was at the Seattle show that Jack Currie applied the white lines. Visible in this side view is the track nose that Joe Kostelecky built in his backyard garage. A full-dressed flathead is under the hood, and the car sports Dunlop tires with Fiesta hubcaps. (Art True.)

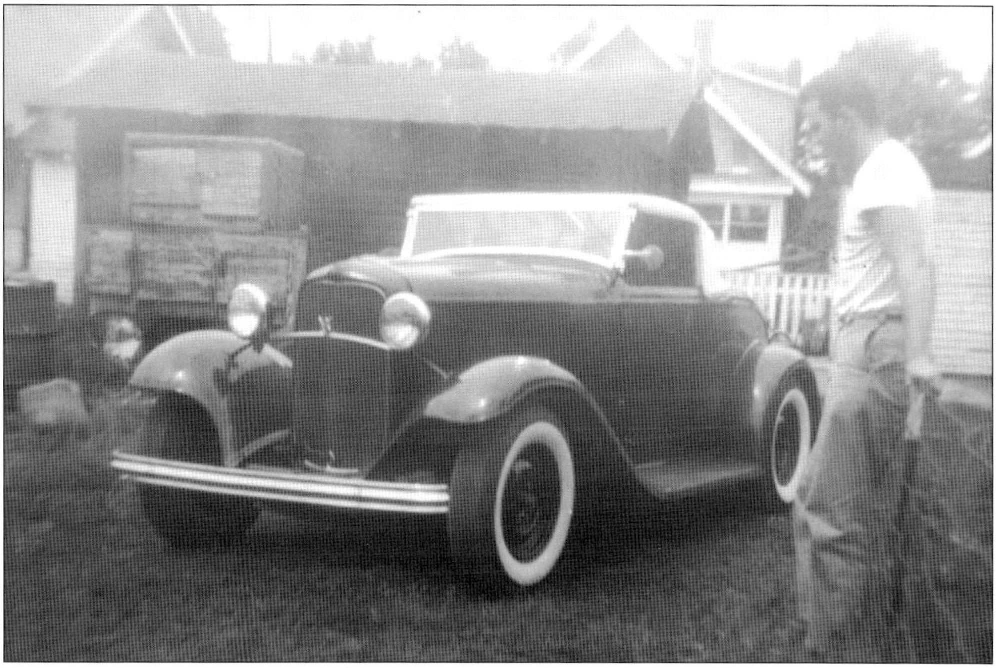

John Mehl's new roadster is seen in his backyard at 224 West Maxwell Avenue, on Spokane's north side. The 1932 Ford, previously owned by Jim Kennedy, was bright red with red-and-white tuck and roll. Kennedy was running a Desoto hemi with two 97s on it; the transmission and steering column were from a '40 Ford. (John Mehl.)

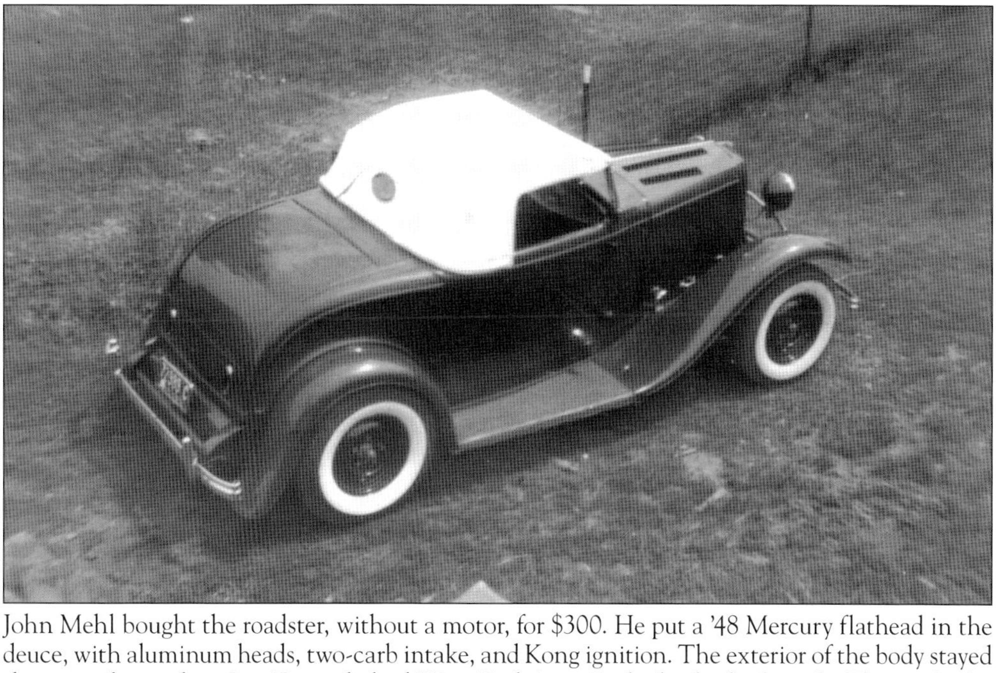

John Mehl bought the roadster, without a motor, for $300. He put a '48 Mercury flathead in the deuce, with aluminum heads, two-carb intake, and Kong ignition. The exterior of the body stayed the same from when Jim Kennedy had West End Auto Body do the bodywork. The car had a classic look, with 1938 Ford taillights, solid hood sides with a louvered hood top, and a white canvas top with an oval back window. (John Mehl.)

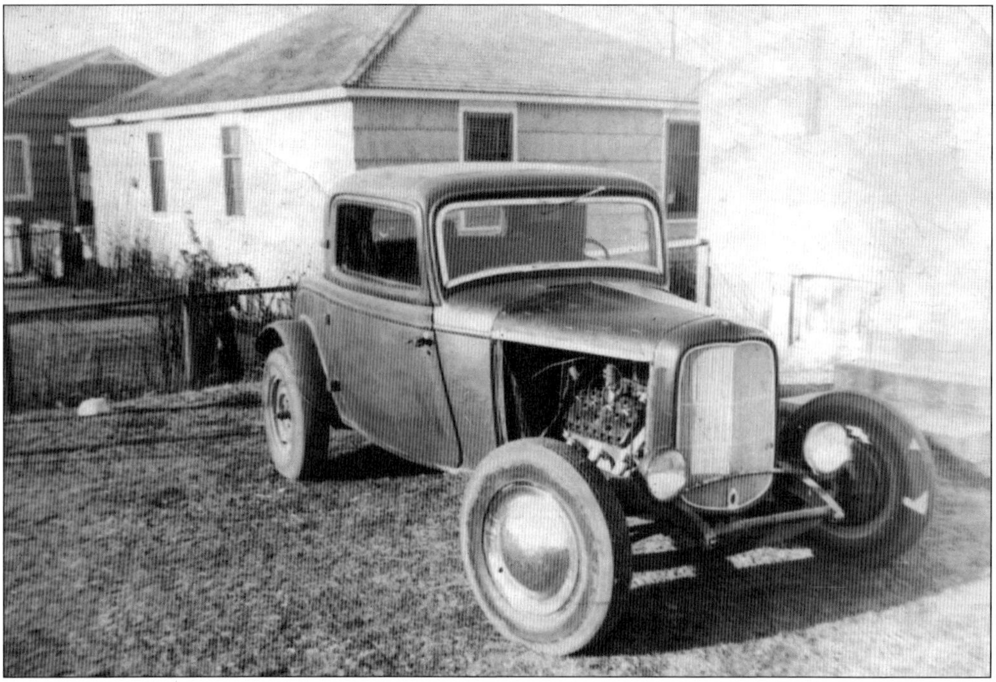

Ken Kelly's 1932 Ford three-window sits in his mom's backyard on Olympic Avenue. Kelly's car had a big channel and no chop, bobbed rear fenders, and a red oxide primer. The grille has been cut down to match the channel, and the insert is painted white. The motor is basically a stock-looking 24-stud flathead with custom exhaust. (Brian Kelly.)

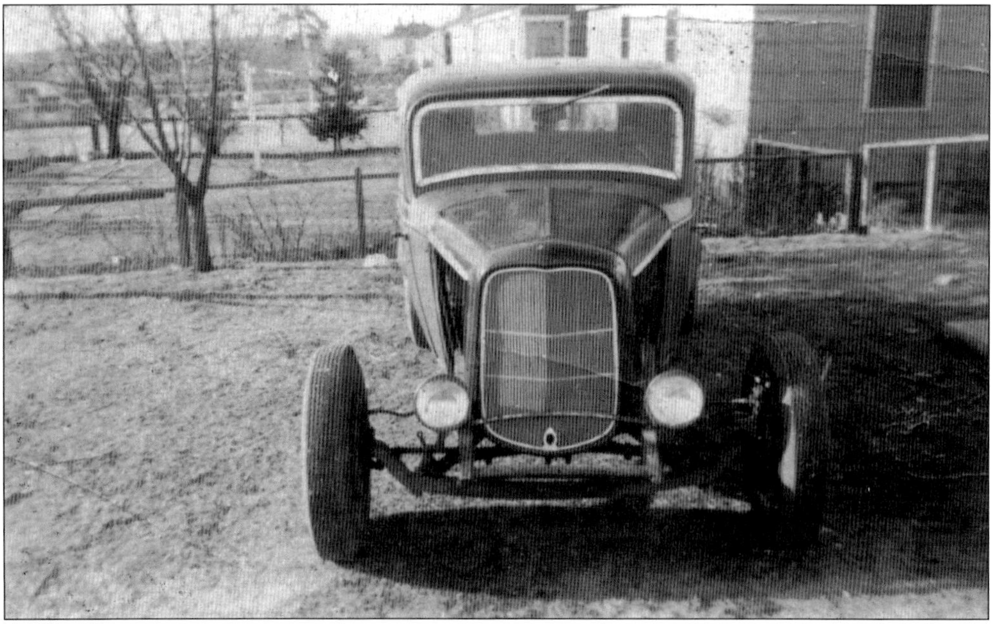

This front view shows just how far the '32 grille shell has been cut down to match the body on Ken Kelly's coupe. The headlight bar, made from a stock '32 and with a matching set of small lights, is probably lower than legal. But it is an amazing look for the time. The front suspension is running the shocks off of the perch pins, with an unsplit wishbone and dropped axle. (Brian Kelly.)

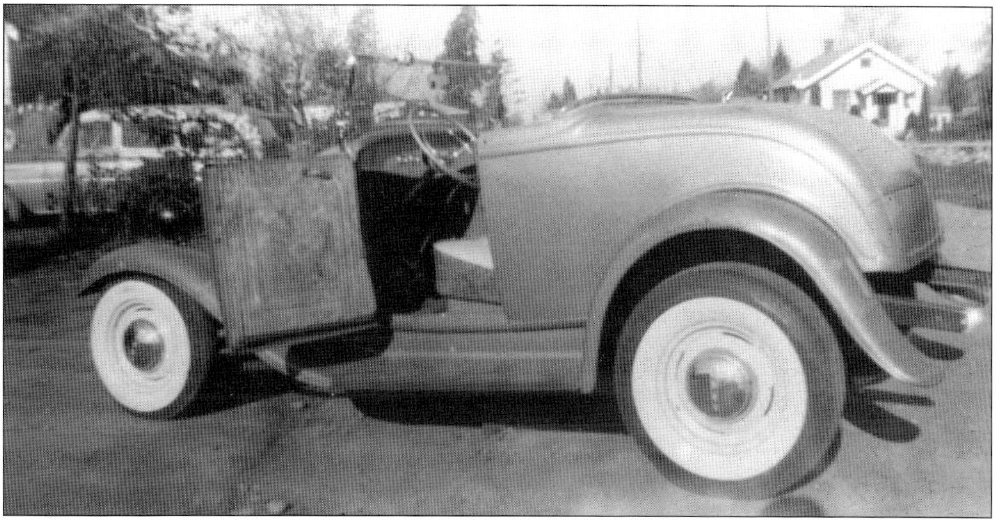

In 1957, Jack Henderson bought a blue 1932 Ford full-fendered roadster in the five-mile area of Spokane for $250. The car, already a hot rod, was brought from California to the Northwest. Henderson purchased the deuce without a motor and remembers that the front suspension was out of a '35-'40 Ford, with the spring in front of the axle. He replaced that setup with a set of split wishbones and a dropped axle that he bought at Thrifty Auto Supply. However, he did not like the way it handled, so he took it back to an unsplit 1932 wishbone. (Frank Moyer.)

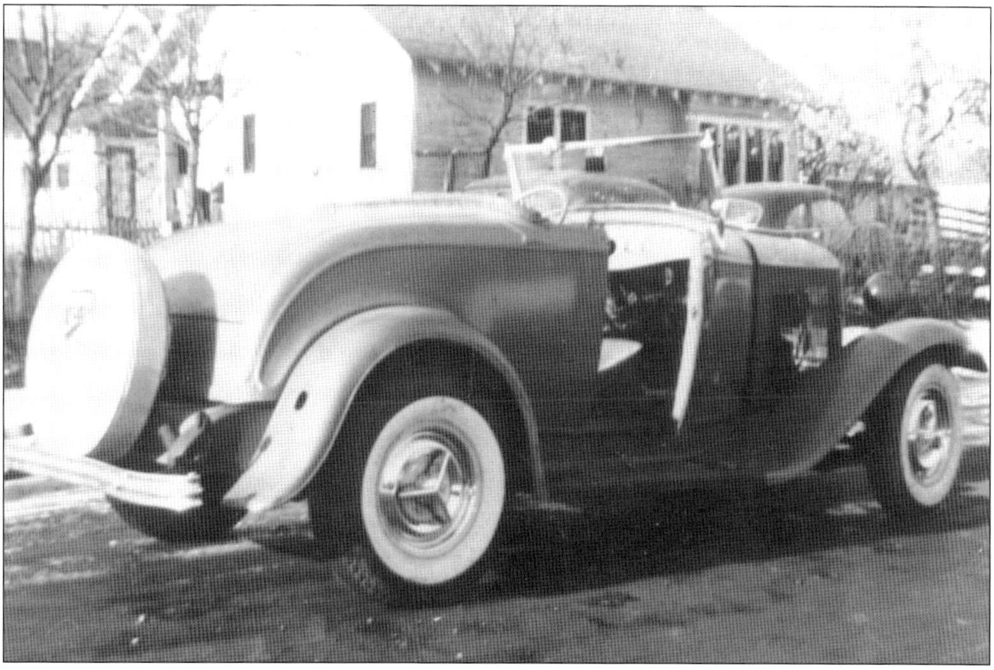

Jack Henderson, a member of the Dragins Auto Club, installed a 1956 small-block Chevy crate motor and mated it to a '39 Ford tranny with Zephyr gears. Buddy Brannon was tasked with stitching the new interior—cream color with a gold diagonal stripe. After tearing up the original '32 Ford rear end while drag racing, Henderson put a '46 Ford rear end in the roadster. Don Audel pinstriped the 1956 Packard opal amethyst body in 1958 and added the "I EAT CORVETTES" cereal character to the passenger-side cowl. (Frank Moyer.)

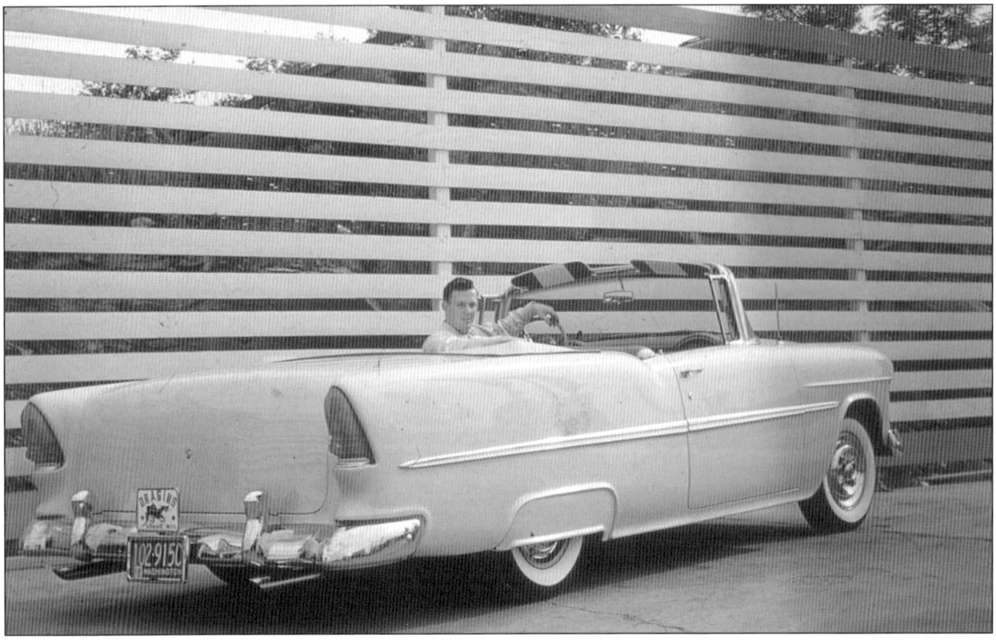

Bill Bongers sits in his full custom 1955 Chevrolet convertible at the Payleast gas station. Custom Auto Body did the work on the Chevy, which later graced the cover of *Hot Rod* magazine. The car was named "My Blue Heaven," but here, it is not blue yet. It is a light pink, with blue-and-white interior. The car looked just as pretty in pink as it did in light blue. (Roger Domini.)

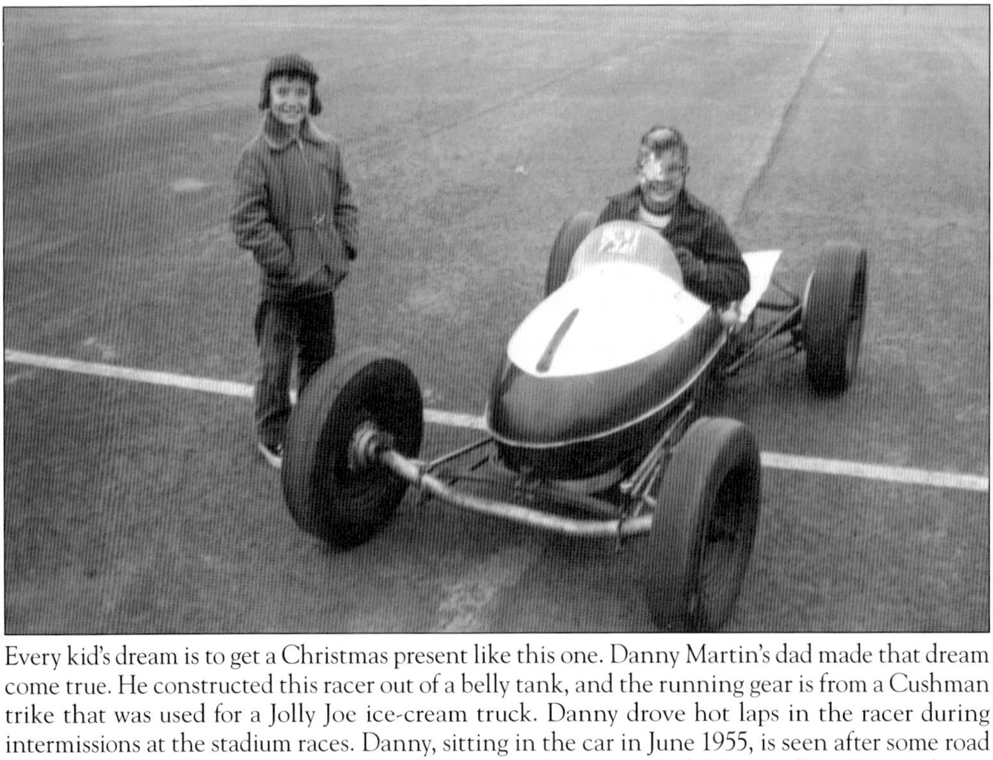

Every kid's dream is to get a Christmas present like this one. Danny Martin's dad made that dream come true. He constructed this racer out of a belly tank, and the running gear is from a Cushman trike that was used for a Jolly Joe ice-cream truck. Danny drove hot laps in the racer during intermissions at the stadium races. Danny, sitting in the car in June 1955, is seen after some road debris hit him in the eye. Standing beside the car is his cousin Jack Martin. (Dan Martin.)

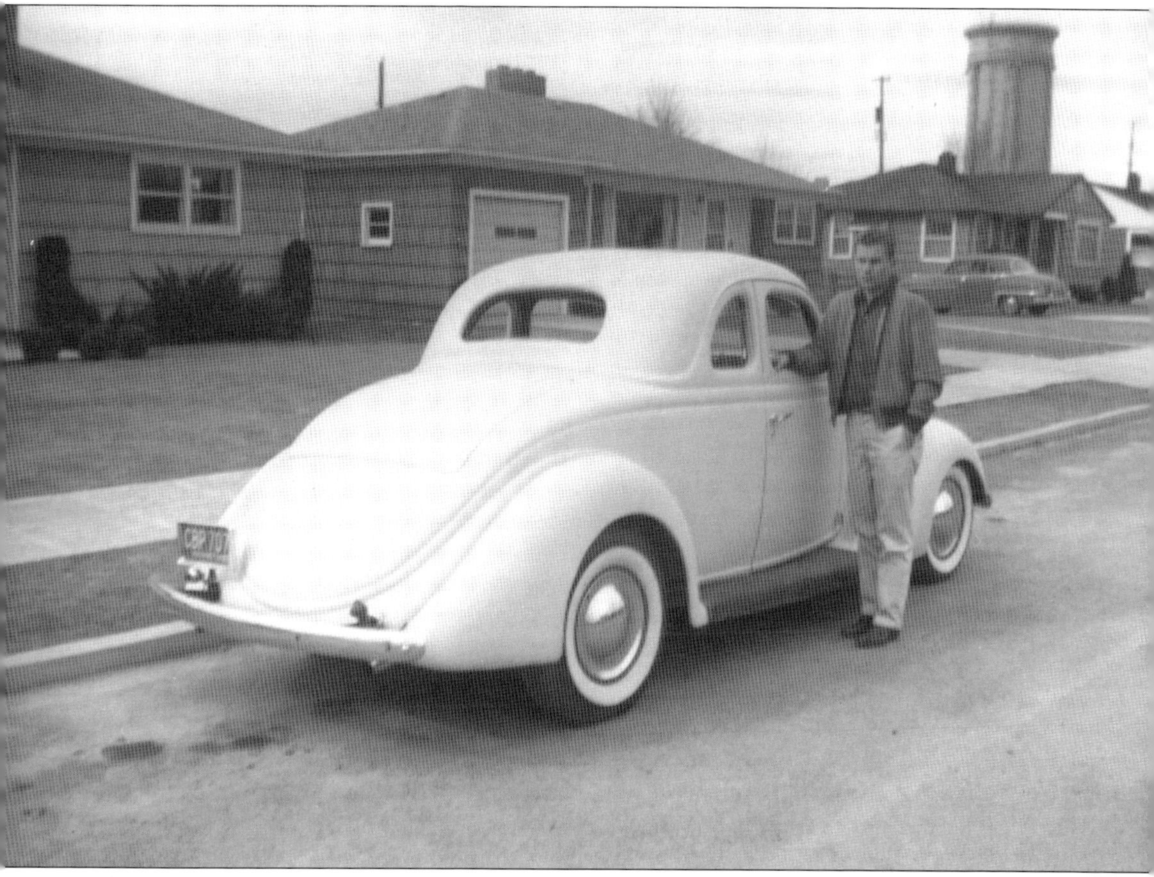

Dukes member Danny Martin stands next to his 1936 Ford five-window in 1959. The coupe was previously owned by Bobby Austin, a member of SRRA, and had been a Spokane hot rod since the early 1950s. The car featured a LaSalle grille, '40 Ford bumpers, and a chrome dash. Visible above the bumper is a pair of Harley Davidson lights, common in early Spokane hot rodding. Martin had fellow Dukes member Don Audel tint yellow primer for the coupe, and Martin sprayed it in his dad's garage. His father was not pleased with Danny's lack of understanding of overspray. (Dan Martin.)

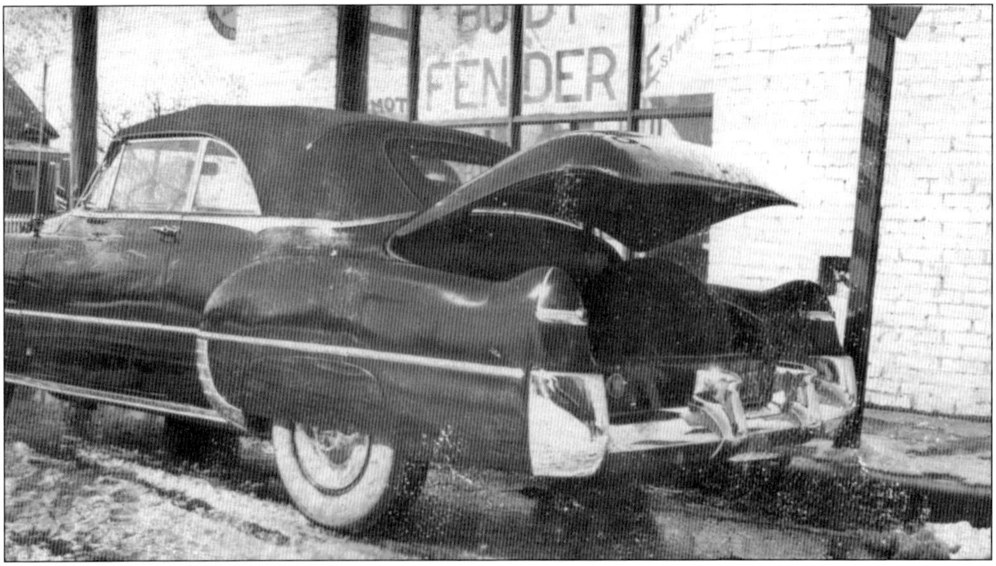

Some of the best customs in Spokane were created by Don Hustad and Nam Name at Custom Auto Body, 3104 North Monroe Street. This photograph from Custom's archives shows a 1950 Pontiac convertible sitting just outside the shop in the snow. The back end of the car is restylized with '49 Cadillac quarters, taillights, and bumper. (Gary Hustad.)

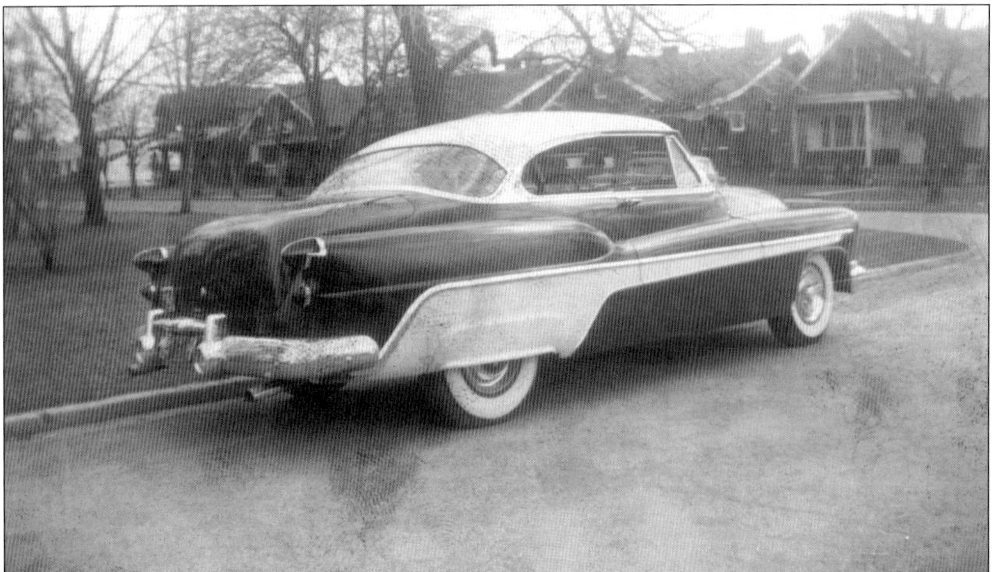

Another great photograph in Custom Auto Body's collection is this one, of a 1953 Buick hard top sitting next to Corbin Park on Spokane's north side. The '55 Desoto side trim, Fiesta hubcaps, and Oldsmobile taillights were added to the Buick. (Gary Hustad.)

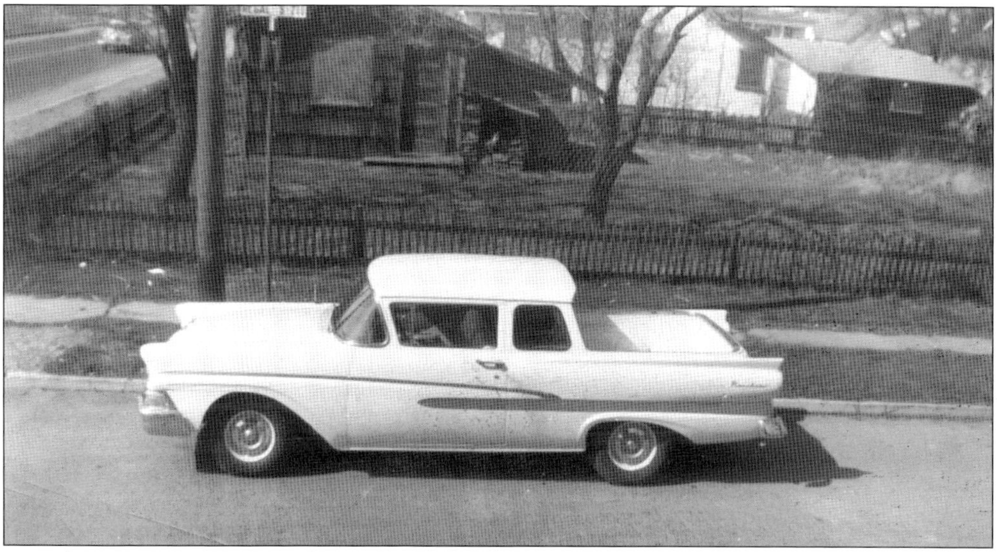

Not all custom projects were show cars. This 1958 Ford Ranchero was reworked by Custom Auto Body. The car has the appearance of being stock, except for the lengthened interior space, which housed jumper seats behind the factory seat. Custom Auto Body was well known for creations like this. It even showed a hand-built '55 Chevy station wagon that was converted into a pickup. (Gary Hustad.)

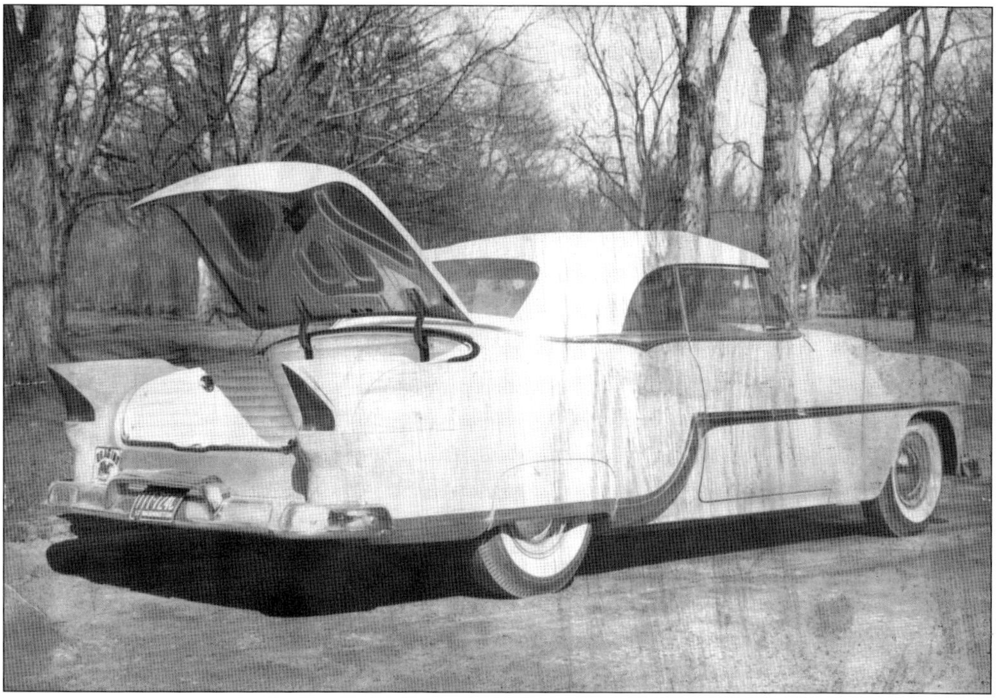

Dragins member Don Stockman's 1954 Pontiac convertible, the "Orchid Lady," sits next to Corbin Park. This photograph came from the archives of Custom Auto Body, where the bodywork and paintwork were done. The convert is still running the stock straight eight, and body modifications include Packard taillights. The pinstriping was done by Jack Currie in Seattle, when Stockman took it to the Sea Fair Show. Inland Auto Upholstery did the interior. (Gary Hustad.)

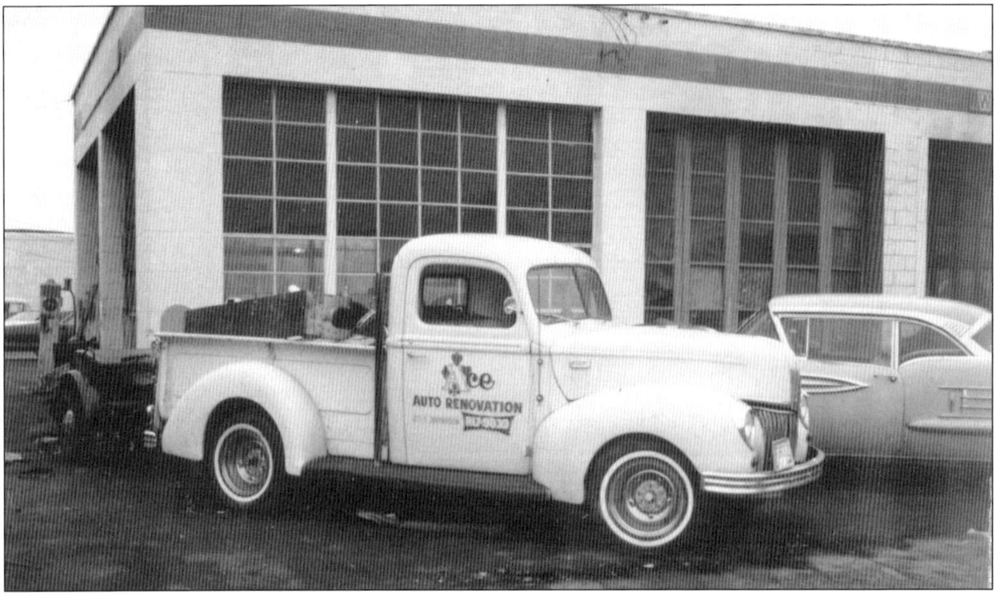

Ace Martello's custom 1941 Ford work truck is seen at 221 South Jefferson Street, between First and Second Avenues. This was the former location of Stoddard-Wendell Ford; Martello now ran an auto renovation shop from here. The truck had 1949 Plymouth bumpers added to both ends, along with 1940 chrome headlight rings and a louvered hood. The exhaust is run through the running boards behind the cab, like stacks. (Frank Moyer.)

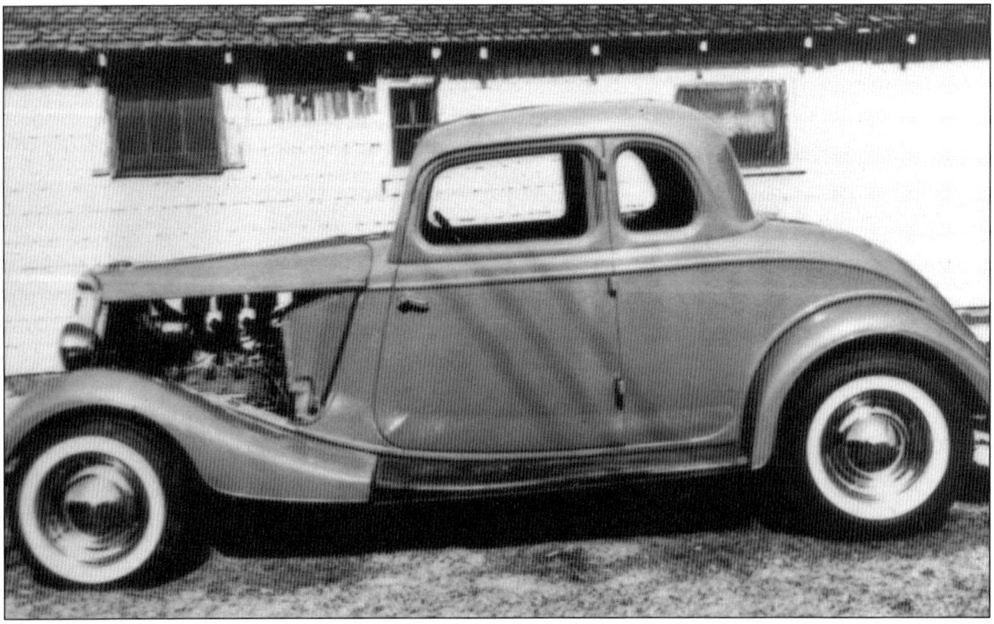

Fred Felice's 1934 coupe is the perfect example of a car started by one guy and finished by another. The five-window was begun by Wayne Freeman, a student at SCC. He bought it in 1959 at Fairchild Air Force Base for $300 and started to tear it apart to build a hot rod. He painted it matador red at Spokane County College. Unfortunately, Freeman was killed in a car accident before he could finish the project. Felice bought the coupe and made it into a full show car by the early 1960s. He was a member of the Dukes Auto Club, along with his son Joe. (Tim Hein.)

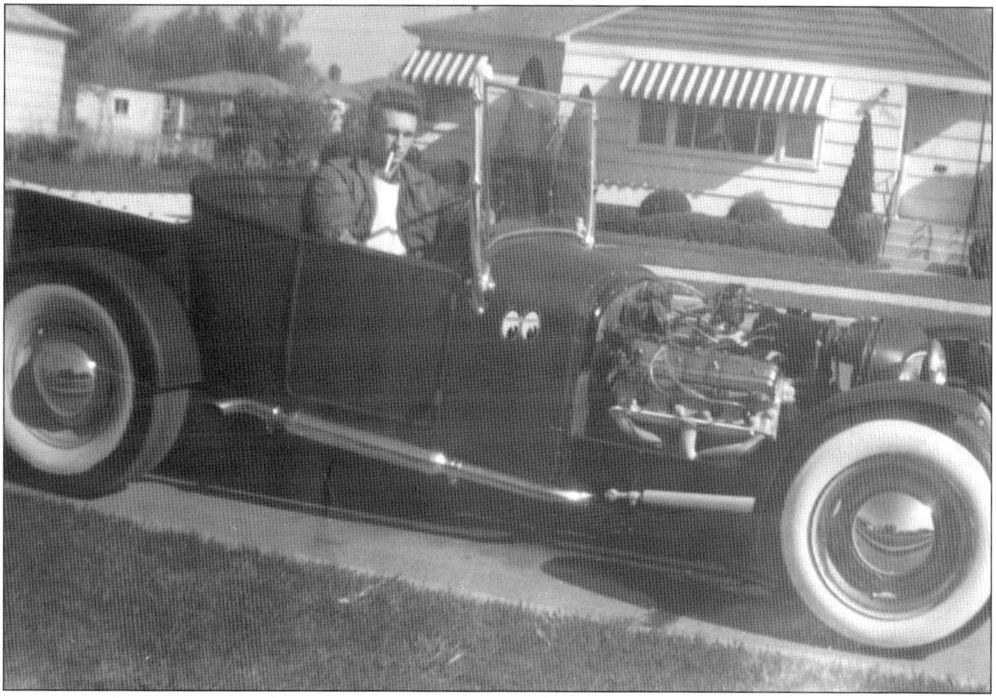

Larry Smith sits in Jim Tipke's Studebaker-powered T roadster pickup. The T was a stalled project that Tipke found by Rogers High School, minus the motor and box. There is very little seen in this photograph that he did not change from the original car, except the body. At first, Tipke was running a flathead out of his 1948 convertible, but he pulled it out for a more powerful Stude motor. The frame is a 1932 Ford with a banjo rear and a Ford three-speed. Don Audel painted the car in gray primer. Tipke added the pickup box, cut down a '32 Ford grille, and made the exhaust using Harley Davidson mufflers. Then, he made the fender out of spare tire covers. (Jim Tipke.)

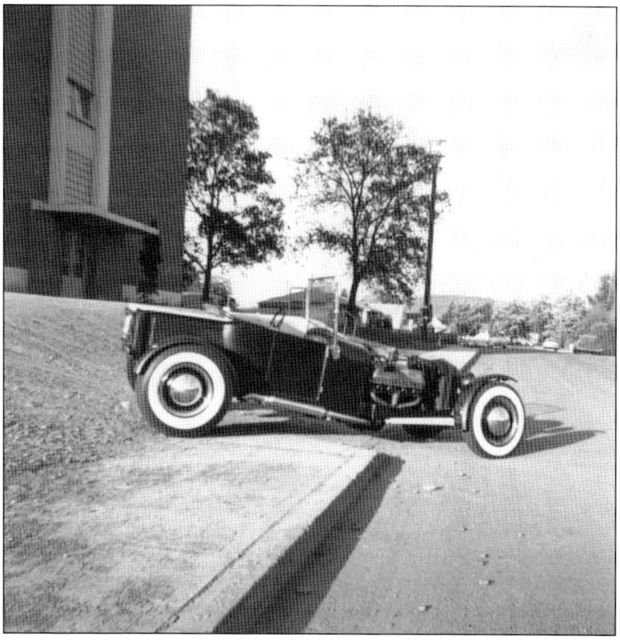

This photograph was taken after Jim Tipke sold the roadster to Larry Smith, who added the white interior to the car. Don Audel sprayed it Tahitian red in Larry's basement. In payment for the paint job, Audel was given a Model T body that became the "So Tuff Toy." Smith also put the tall windshield on the car. (Frank Moyer.)

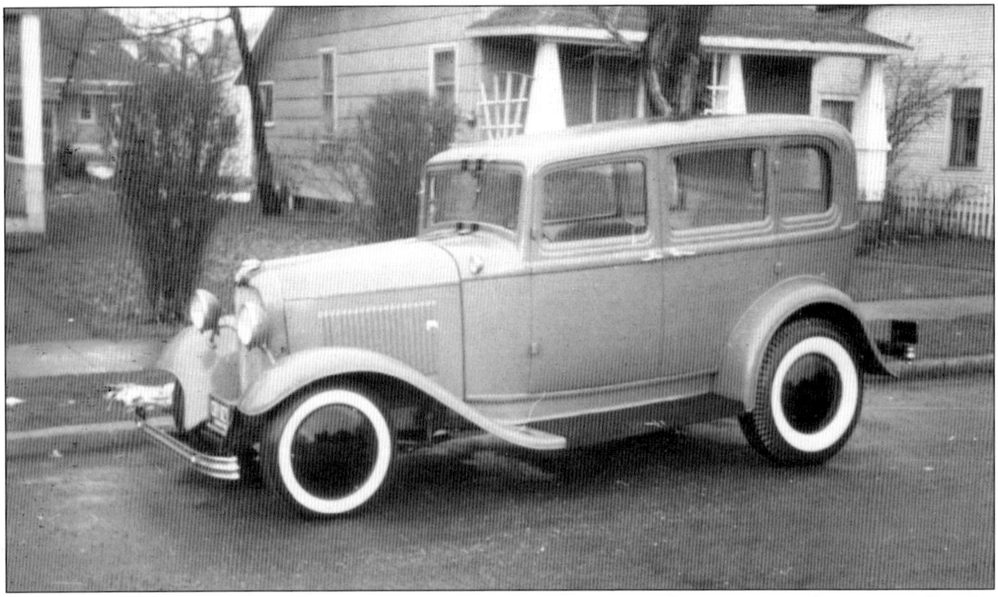

Don Audel's 1932 Ford four-door is parked in front of his mom's house on Spokane's north side. Audel traded a '40 Ford coupe to Henry Proctor for it. Proctor had received the four-door from Dan Kroetch. Audel painted the deuce Lincoln matador red, a color that is more bright orange than red. Next, he added dual black racing stripes and painted the moon discs gloss black. (Don Audel.)

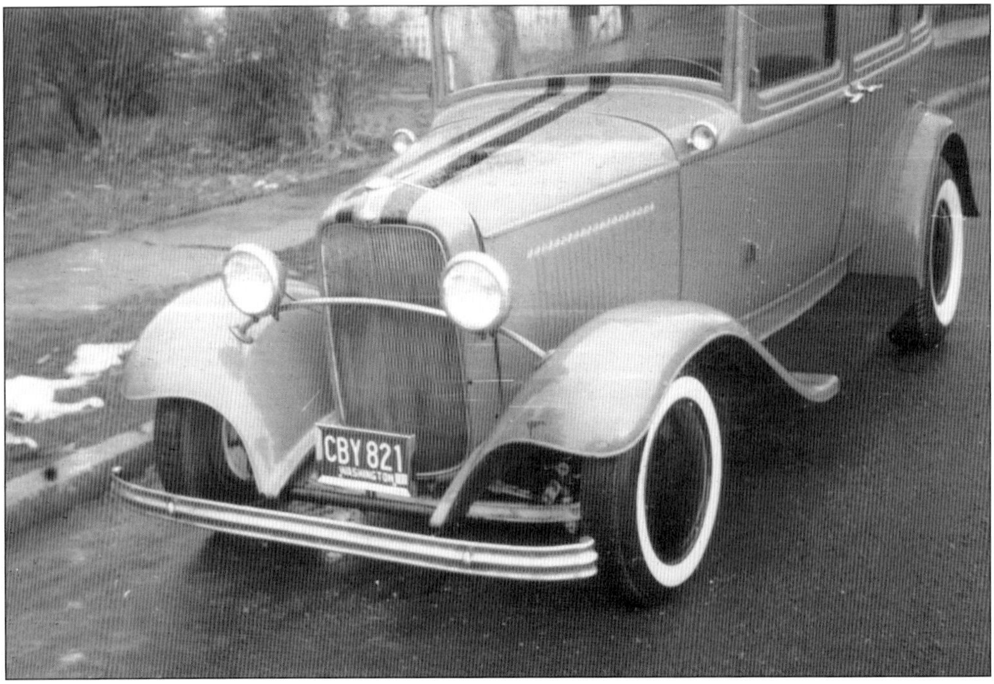

"Small lights and wide whites," as Dick Page would say, finish the look on Don Audel's car. The motor, which came from Chuck Crowley, was a 59 AB out of a 1940 Ford. A member of the Dukes Auto Club, Audel became the pinstriper of choice in the region. He also painted cars, did show signs, and helped promote Spokane hot rodding all over the Northwest with his showmanship. (Don Audel.)

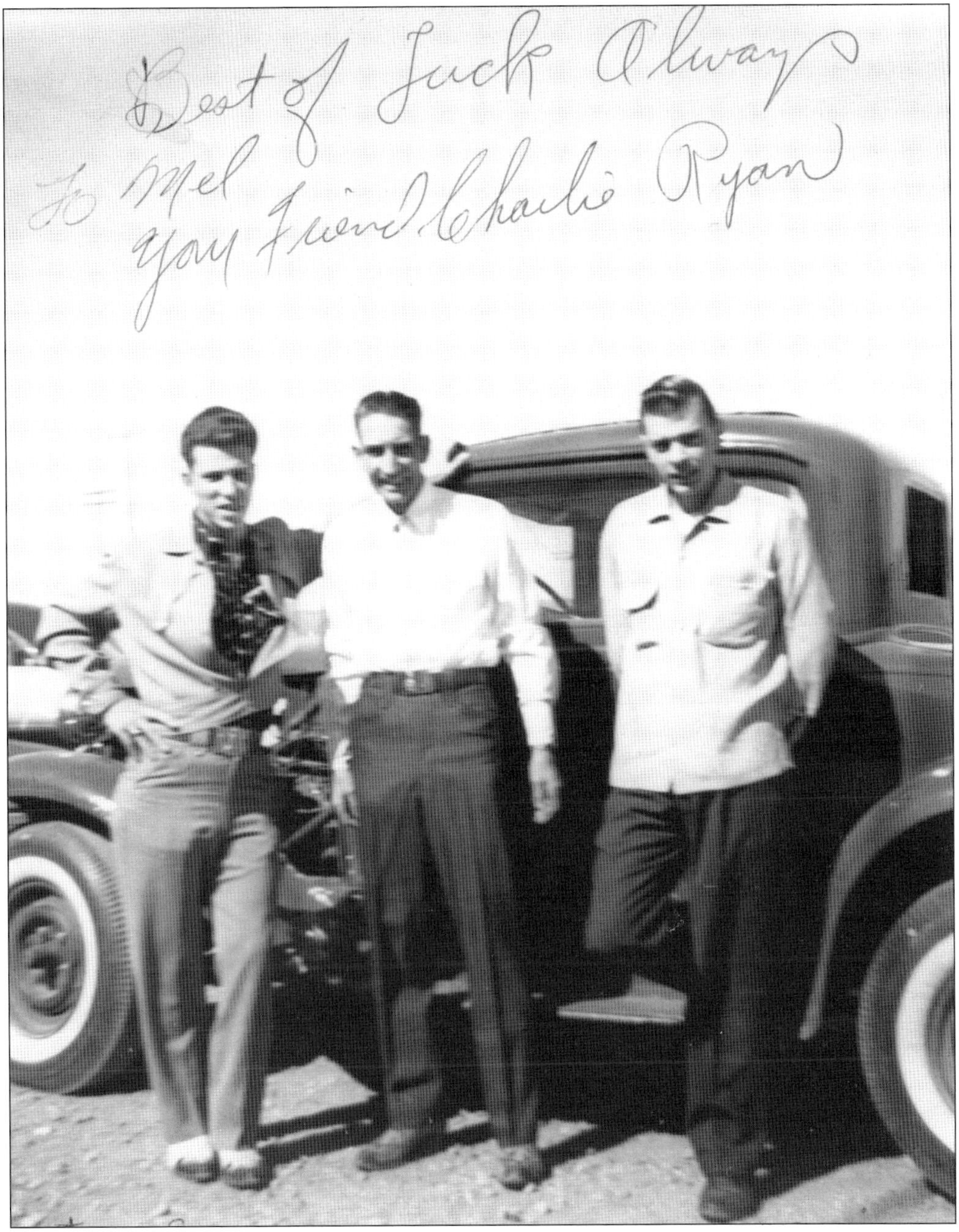

"You're gonna drive me to drinkin' / If you don't stop driving that hot rod Lincoln." Charlie Ryan wrote the song "Hot Rod Lincoln" based on the model A Ford with a Lincoln motor, as seen here. Ryan (center) poses with Jack Stanley (left) and Gary Stewart. The author found this photograph at a swap meet in Portland in the mid-1990s. Ryan was a member of the Dukes Auto Club and an active member in the Spokane hot-rod community.

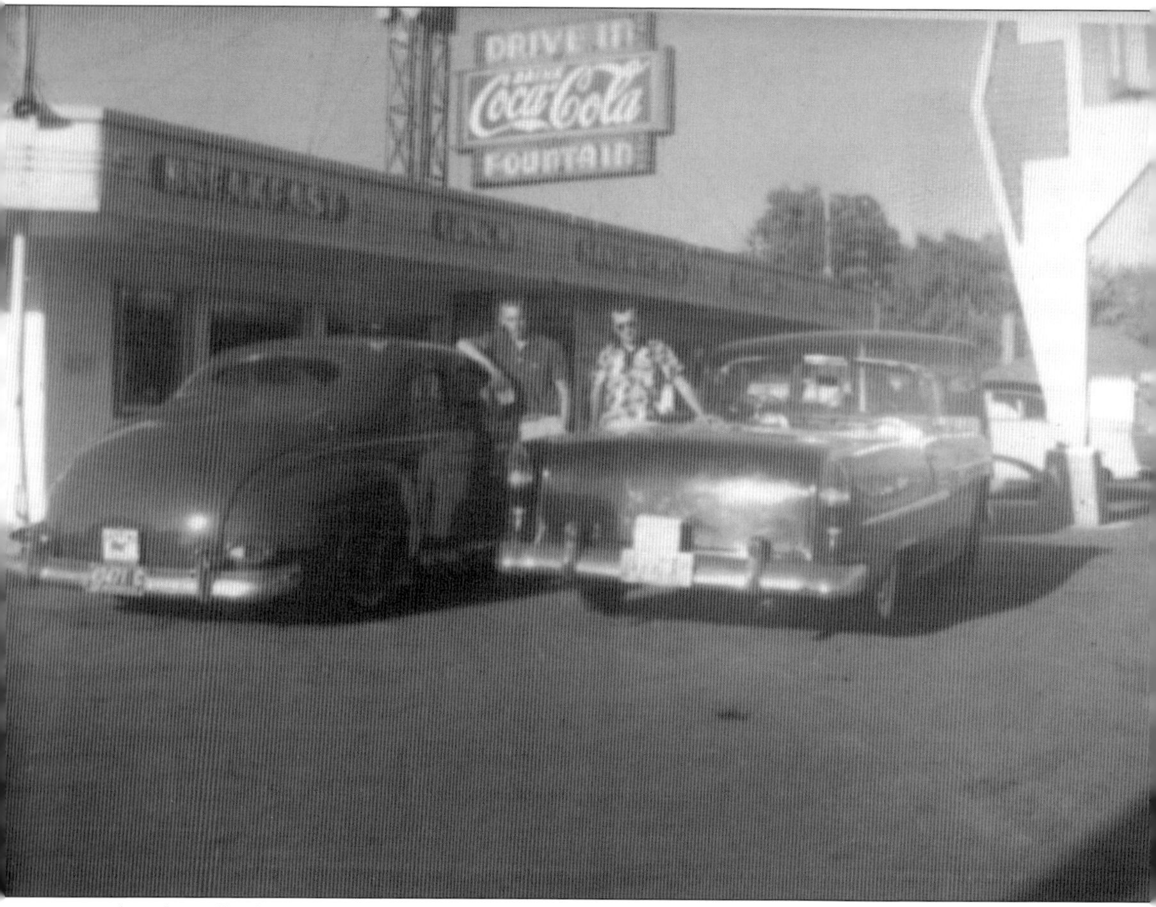

Bob Adams (left) poses with his 1942 Ford custom, and Bill Vandouris stands with his 1955 Chevy convertible in front of the Tower Drive-in on East Sprague Avenue. Both men were members of the Dragins. Adams's car was in primer when he got it, so he had Humrick's Body Shop on Sprague Avenue paint it purple for him. Don O'Neill Z'd the frame and added the Chevy tail lights to the fenders. Joe Kostelecky chopped the car behind his house just off of Division Street and Ruby, and Adams customized the grille. The car was powered by a flathead that was pulled out of the Calori coupe when Bill Bongers owned it. (Bob Adams.)

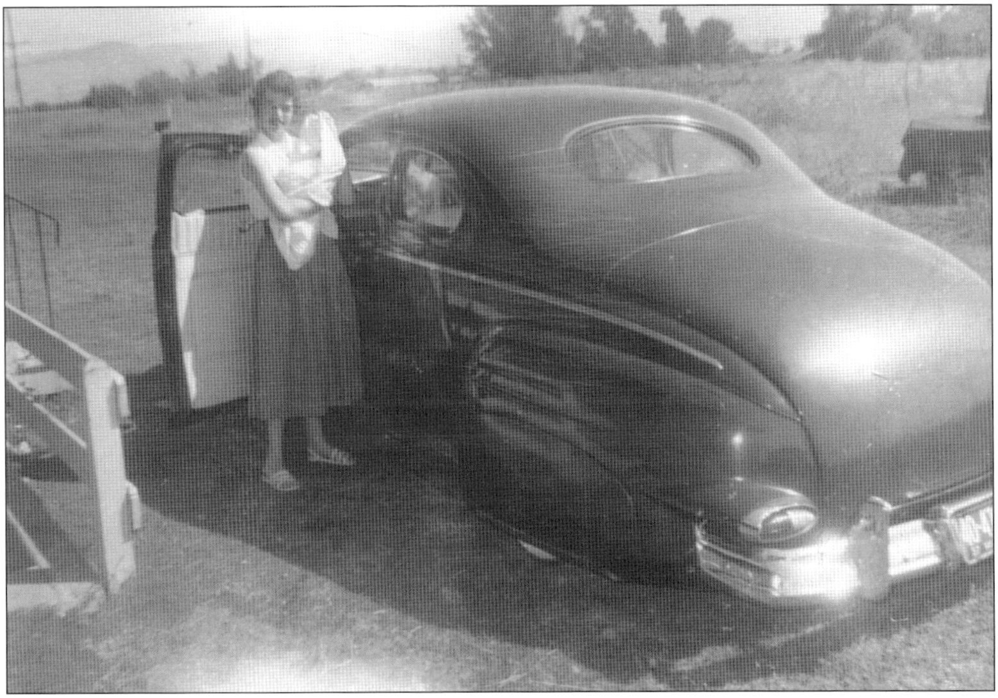

Shirlie Adams holds Loreen on the day she and Bob brought her home from the hospital. They had met each other while Shirlie worked at the Tower Drive-In. Here, they are taking their newborn for her first ride in a custom. This appears to be the second paint job, a candy red, done by Stevenson's Auto Body on East Sprague. (Bob Adams.)

Like lots of hot rods, this little '32 five-window passed through many hands in a short time, so it is hard to pinpoint who actually owned it at certain times. When Dusty Rhodes owned it, the car was powered with an Oldsmobile. Jack Henderson put a small-block Chevy in it. Finally, an Olds went back in it when Don Zundel had the car. At the time of this photograph, the car, part of the Pacers Car Club of Spokane, is painted '55 Ford canary yellow, with pinstriping by Joe Burnett. (Frank Moyer.)

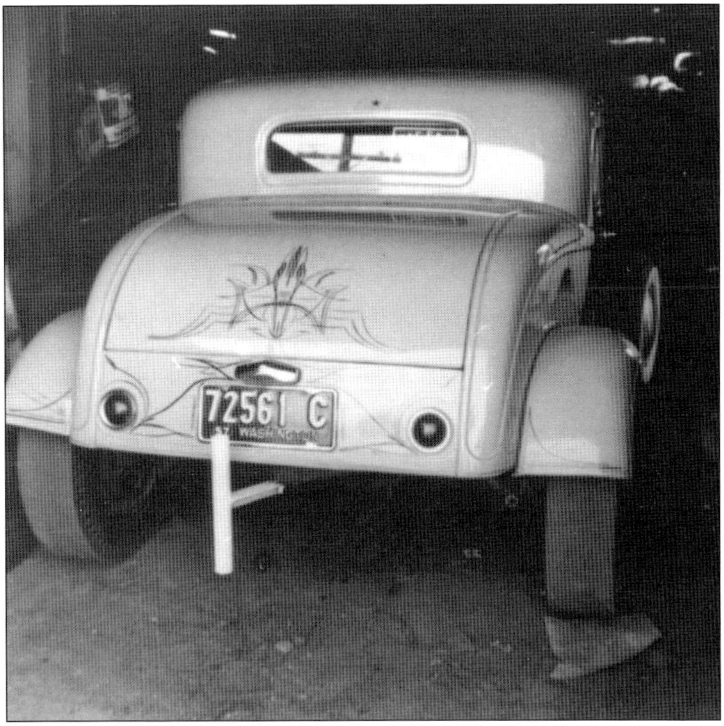

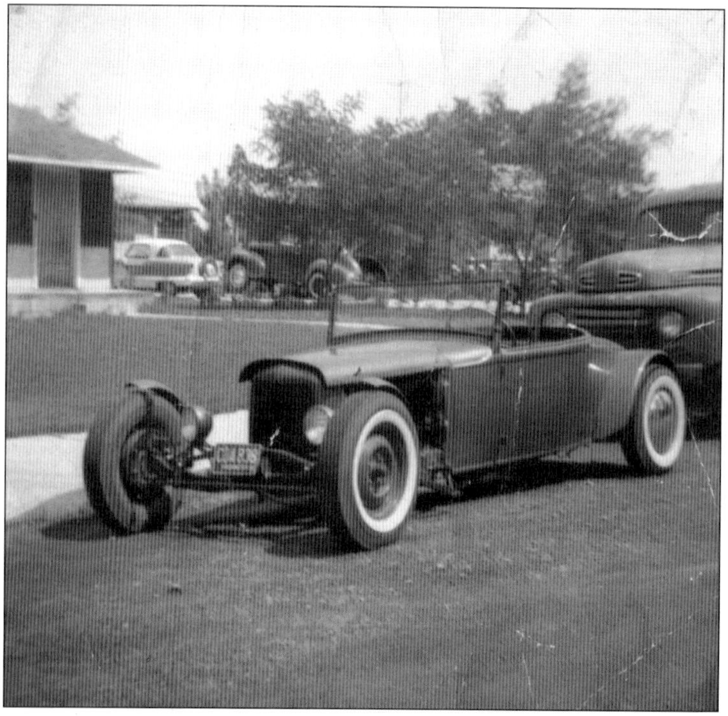

Dick Nimmer's metallic-blue Model A roadster is seen here in 1958. The odd hood is just covering the engine compartment while the transmission is being fixed. The transmission was blown up in a bet between two police officers who had to find out if the hot rod was faster than their new police car. They borrowed the A from Nimmer, but brought it back being towed behind the cruiser. The car was painted limefire gold after it was back on the road. (Frank Moyer.)

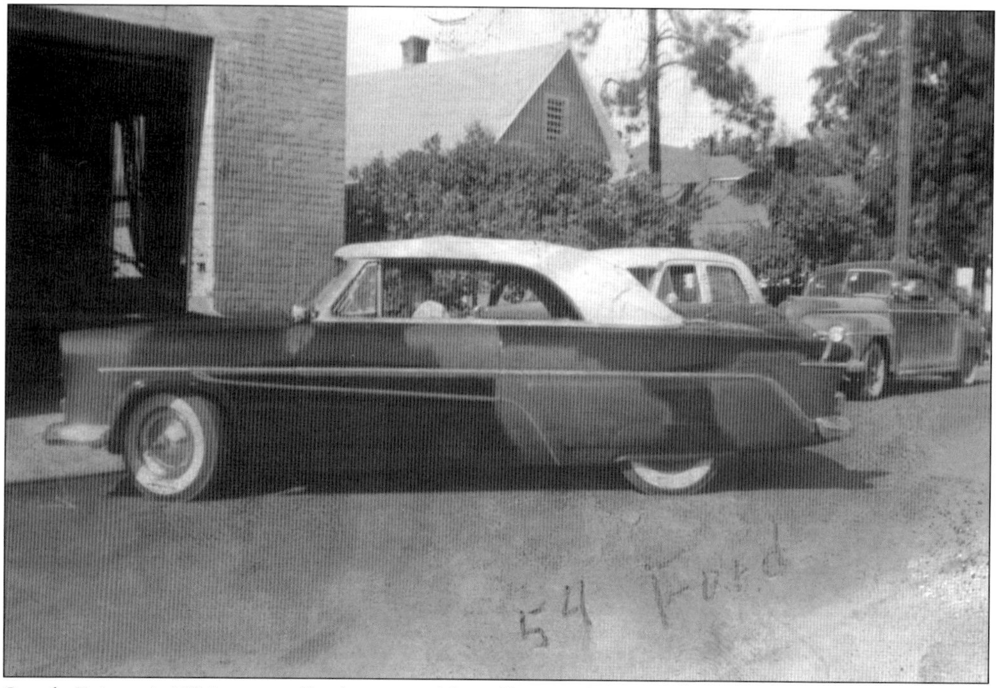

Swede Ericson's 1954 custom Ford convertible pulls out of Custom Auto Body on Monroe Street. Ericson was a member of the Dragins Auto Club from the Spokane Valley. The motor in the convertible was the stock Y-block Ford, but Custom Auto completed several body modifications to it. Kaiser taillights were added to the car, along with Desoto side trim and Buick headlights. The interior was stitched with white tuck and roll. (Richard "Speedy" Gunsaulis.)

Nothing looks better than customs in the snow! This is Road Knights member Bob Burn's 1952 Ford Victoria, a very mild custom. Spotlights and a shaved deck lid and hood were some of the only modifications to the exterior. Later, the car was repainted black and given lake pipes and custom taillights. The Road Knights, based out of Davenport, Washington, participated in all Spokane functions and held shows that Spokane clubs participated in. (Don Wilbur.)

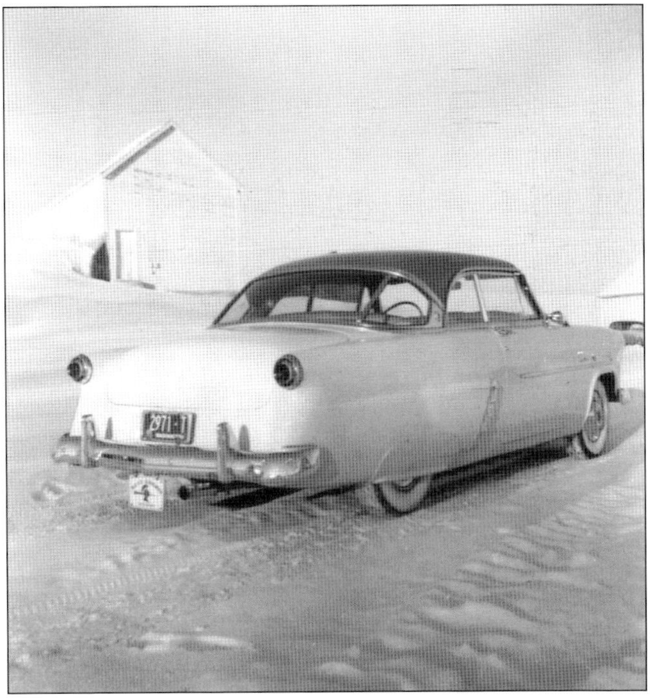

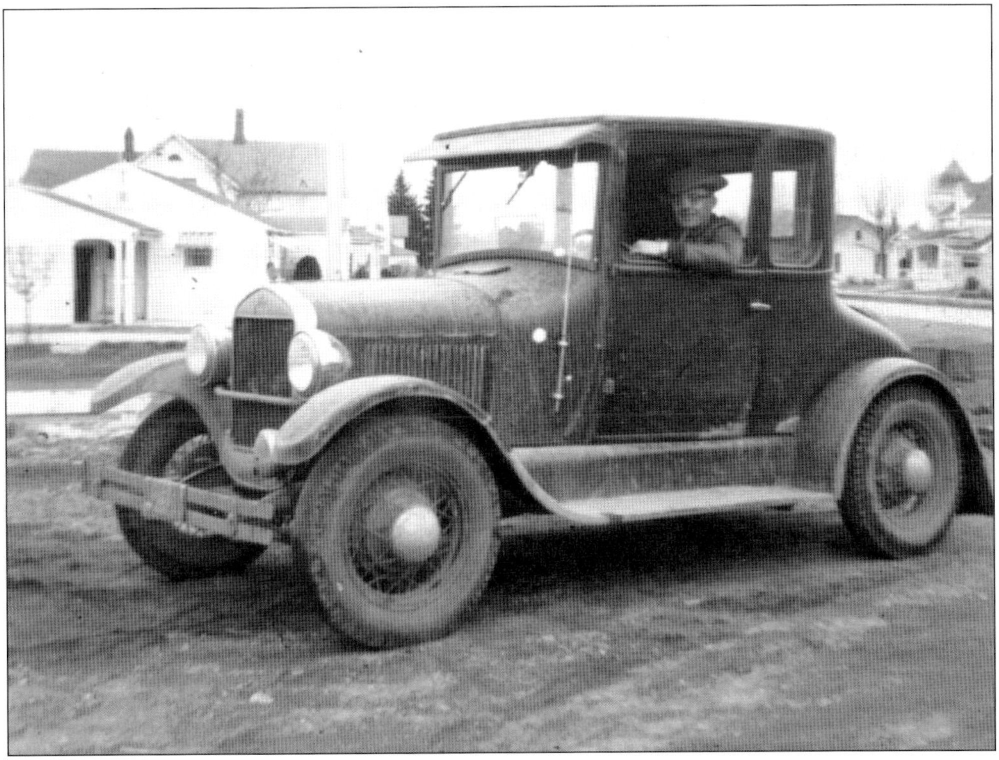

Early sleeper? This fairly stock-appearing 1926 T coupe belonging to Gene Stuckle was far from stock. It featured a full race 1941 Merc flathead, 1934 Ford running gear, V-8 Ford wire wheels, and, later, headlights. (Don Wilbur.)

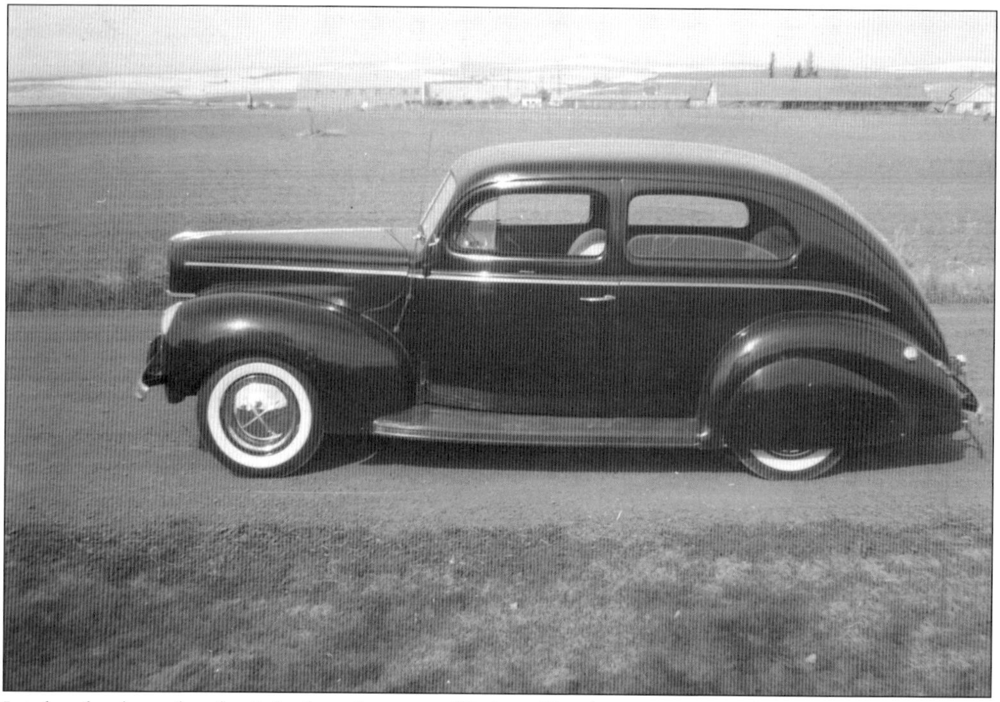

It is hard to beat the classic look and stance of Robert Henderson's 1940 Deluxe sedan. It is dropped in the back with fender skirts set off by full-wheel hubcaps. The '40 is just slightly de-chromed, with the Ford Deluxe emblems shaved off the hood. Though difficult to see from this angle, the car has 1941 Ford Super Deluxe bumpers, which replaced the stock set. (Don Wilbur.)

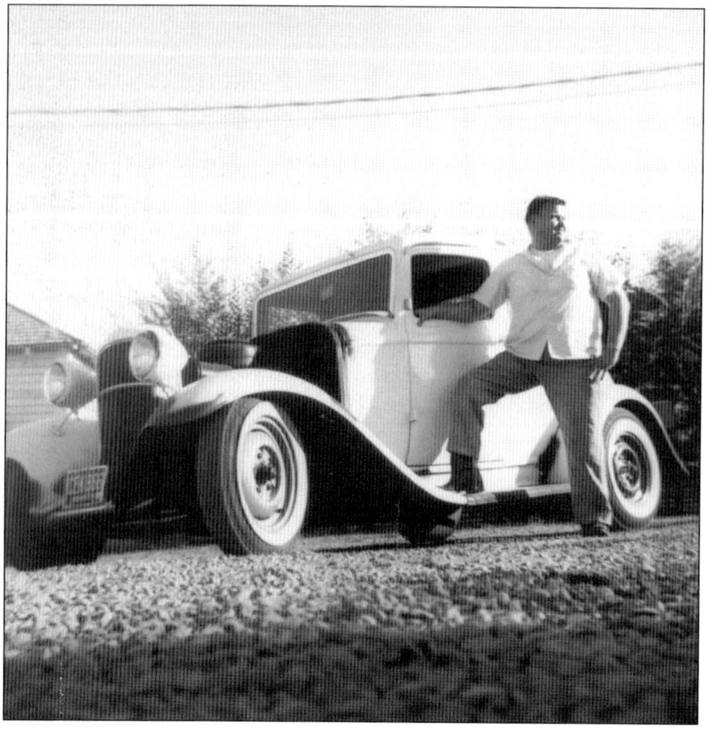

Richard "Speedy" Gunsaulis poses with his Chrysler-powered '32 Ford five-window at Sprague Avenue and Evergreen Street in the Spokane Valley. Gunsaulis, a member of the Road Knights of Davenport at this time, owned a record store, the Record Rack, in the valley. The car was painted white, and the interior was white Naugahyde. The car was later owned by Tom Cunningham and Danny Martin. (Richard "Speedy" Gunsaulis.)

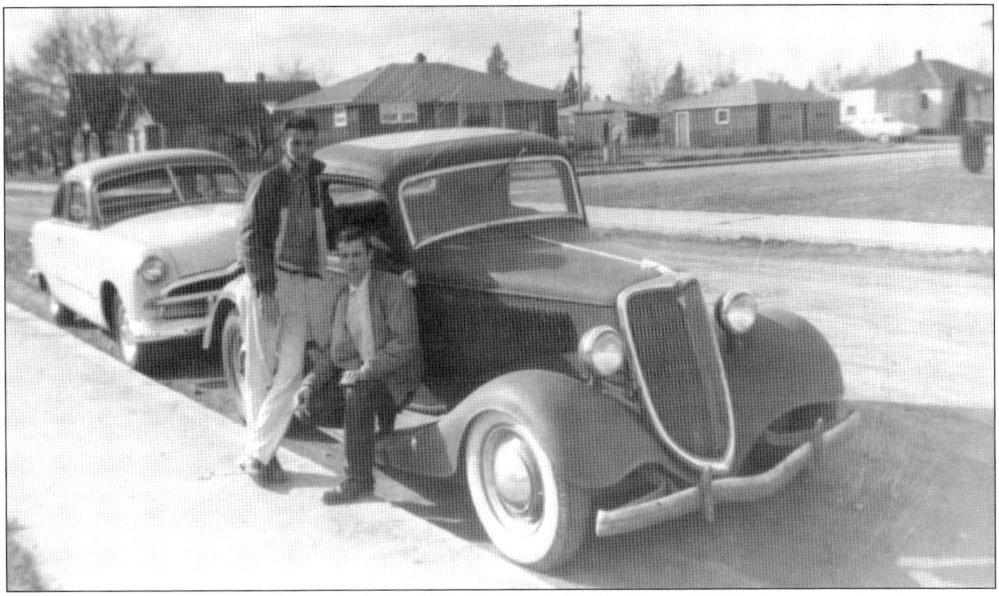

Tom Ryan found his 1934 Ford three-window coupe for sale at a service station on North Monroe Street in 1955. The car, powered by a 1950 Mercury motor, had a four-inch dropped axle and bone stock interior, except for a Stewart Warner "Hollywood" instrument cluster. The coupe had a price tag of $125, and soon, it belonged to Ryan. Bob Ryan (left) and Ron Nielson lean on the coupe, with mismatched tires and '40 Ford wheels. Ryan enlisted Art Santa Rosa to do some light bodywork to the rear panel and to primer the car gray. In the background is Nielson's 1949 Ford coupe. (Frank Moyer.)

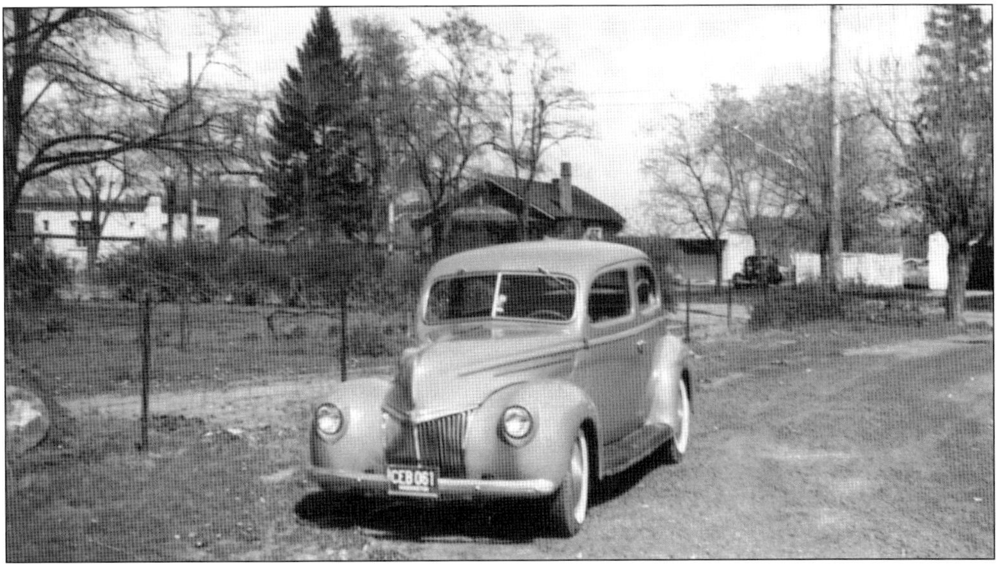

It is easy to spot where a car came from in Washington State by its license plate. This is a photograph of an unknown 1939 Ford sedan that a local hot-rodder, Josh Scott, picked up at an estate sale. The letter C, the third letter in the alphabet, stands for Spokane County, which ranked third in population at that time. King County plates are labeled with the letter A, and Tacoma plates have a B. The sedan looks to be mostly stock, with moon discs and aftermarket headlight conversions. (Josh Scott.)

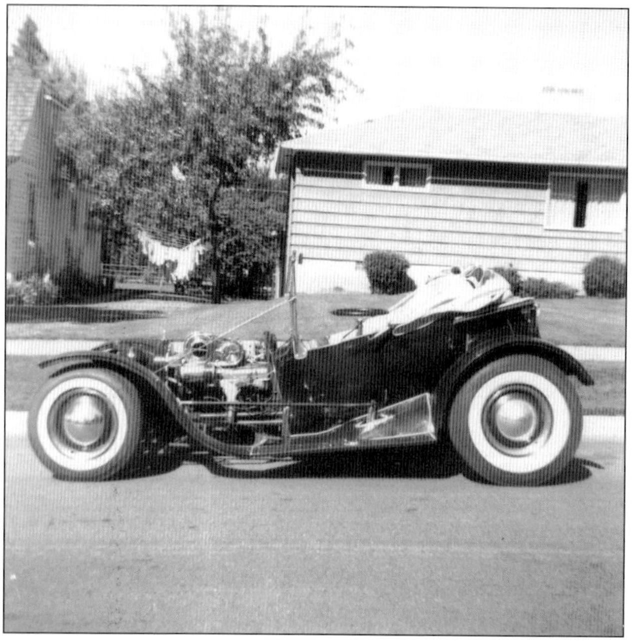

Buddy Wickstrom's 1925 Model T is seen here when Robert Hein owned it. Hein, a member of the Eliminators Car Club, showed the car at one of Tacoma's armory shows. The fuel injection setup is off of Lee Sherman's 1957 Chevy convertible and was the same one used on the Dukes dual-engine dragster driven by Earl Wham. The fenders for the T came from the Antique Auto Ranch in Spokane, and the frame is built out of round tubing. An odd space created between the running boards and the body was finished off with upholstery that matched the body color. (Richard "Speedy" Gunsaulis.)

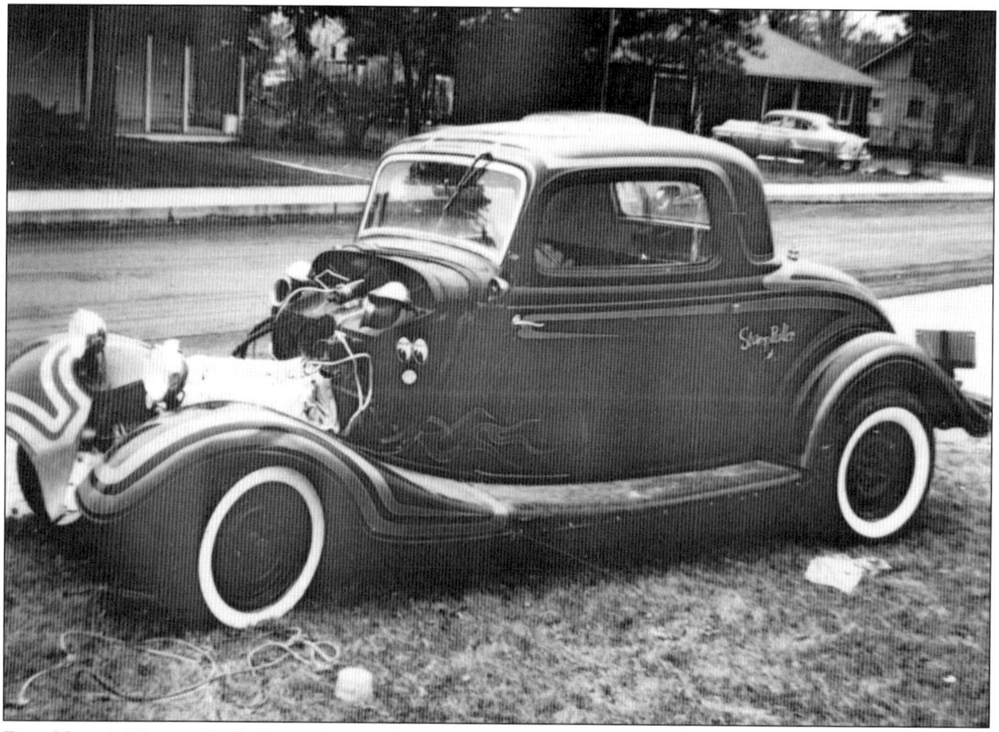

Don Hurst's "Stump Puller" was featured in *CARS* magazine, in an article written and photographed by Allen Carter of Tacoma. Hurst was a member of the Dukes. The '33 coupe was powered by a 1956 Olds motor backed by a '37-'38 Packard transmission, later changed to a Chrysler motor when it was owned by Frank Moyer. The interior was done in black-and-white Naugahyde and had white running-board covers (not installed in this photograph). Don Audel sprayed the scallops on the coupe in his mom's backyard. (Frank Moyer.)

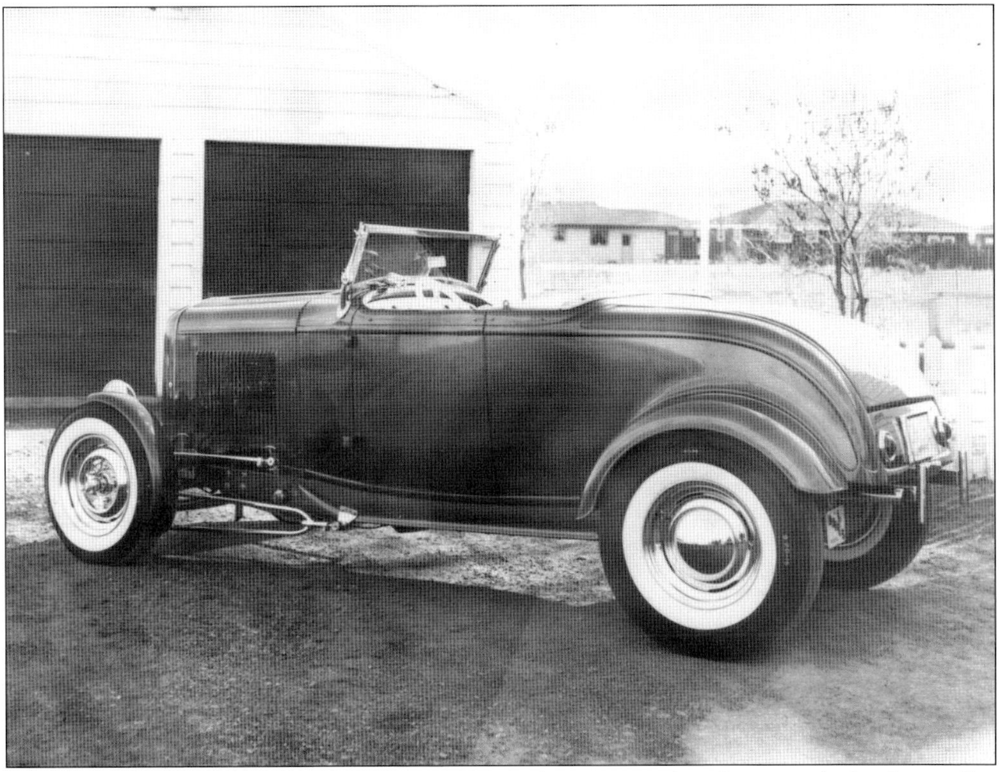

Dukes Auto Club member Richard "Speedy" Gunsaulis's 1932 Ford roadster is parked in front of his garage in the Spokane Valley. The '32 also had Portland history. Bob Knowles bought a 1932 full-fendered roadster in the mid-1950s and was set to make a "California Highboy" out of it. He enlisted the help of Stan Diets, who worked at Dee Westcott's shop, to do the bodywork and paintwork. Diets bobbed the back fenders and rolled the bead back on. (Richard "Speedy" Gunsaulis.)

This view from the front shows the custom headlight bar and rolled frame horns from the original Bob Knowles build. The roadster was finished in this way in 1957 for the second-annual Portland Roadster Show. After that, Knowles pulled the flathead out and installed a Y-block Ford out of a '54 Ford truck. Soon after that, he traded it in for a 1955 Austin Healey 104 at Bob Jones Used Cars in Portland. The roadster went through the Portland auto auction and somehow ended up in the hands of Max Allen in Wenatchee, Washington, where it was the subject of a *Rod & Custom* feature in November 1959. (Richard "Speedy" Gunsaulis.)

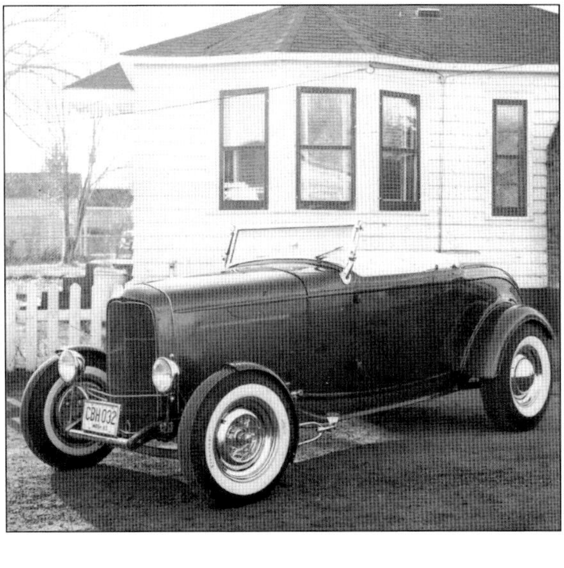

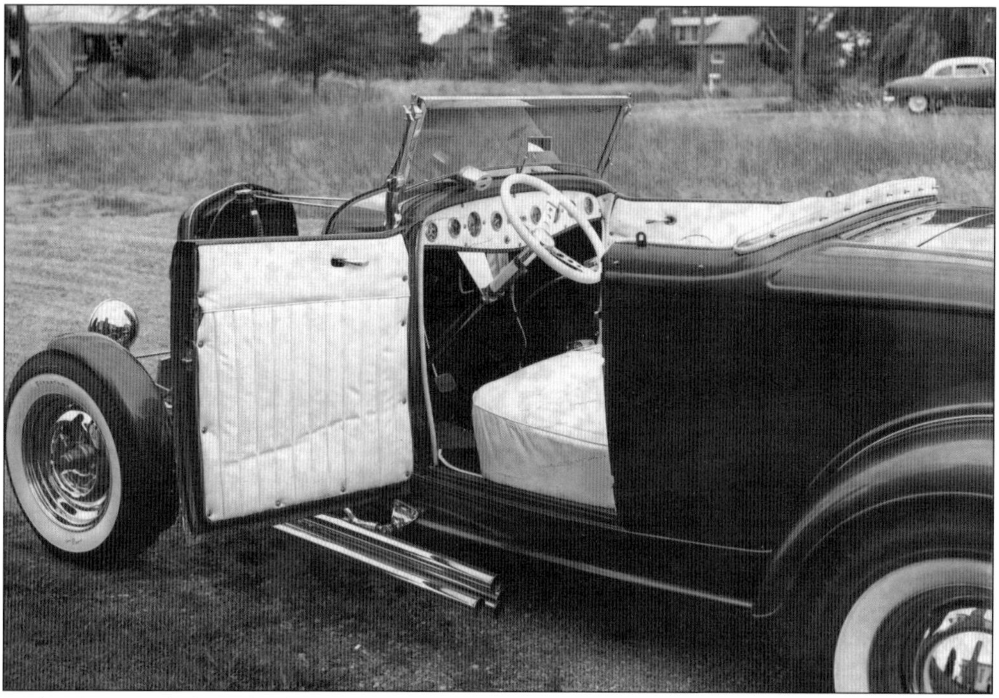

Richard Gunsaulis brought the '32 to Spokane with the help of Joe Yates. As the show circuit started changing in the 1960s, so did the car. This photograph shows the beginning of those changes, with the addition of custom chrome headers. Gunsaulis could not drive the car with his leg braces, which he was forced to wear as a result of polio. During the early 1960s, this car was the everyday driver for Richard and his wife, Barbara. Richard won the Ford Motor Company's outstanding achievement award in Portland at the 1963 Roadster Show. (Richard "Speedy" Gunsaulis.)

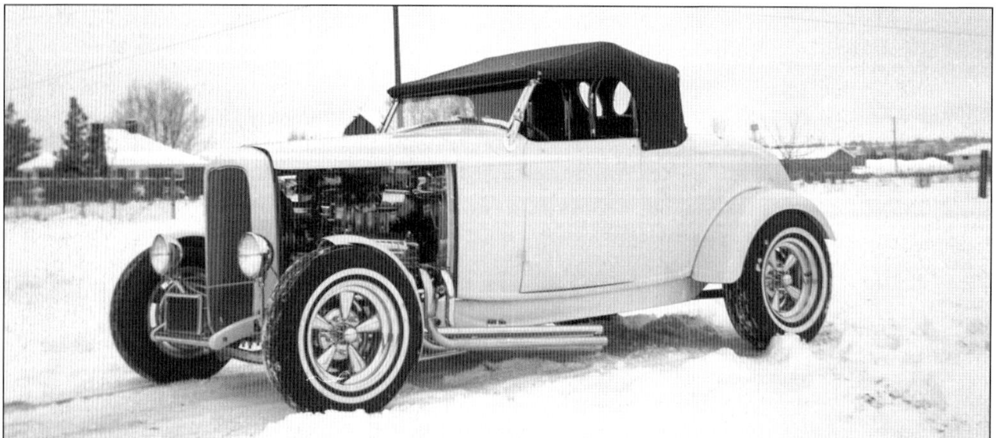

Here is Speedy's roadster in the mid-1960s full show in the snow. The car is bright yellow, with a blown Y-block, chrome roll bars, and a new top. The original platform that Bob Knowles started was now polished into a show machine by Richard Gunsaulis. The car was painted four times in four years, and the back end ended up with a roll pan and handmade taillights by Custom Auto Body of Spokane. The roadster hit the show circuit, scooping up sweepstakes awards all over the Northwest. In 1965, it was featured on the front of the Seattle Roadster Show program, and was the subject of a full feature in *Car Craft* in November 1967. (Richard "Speedy" Gunsaulis.)

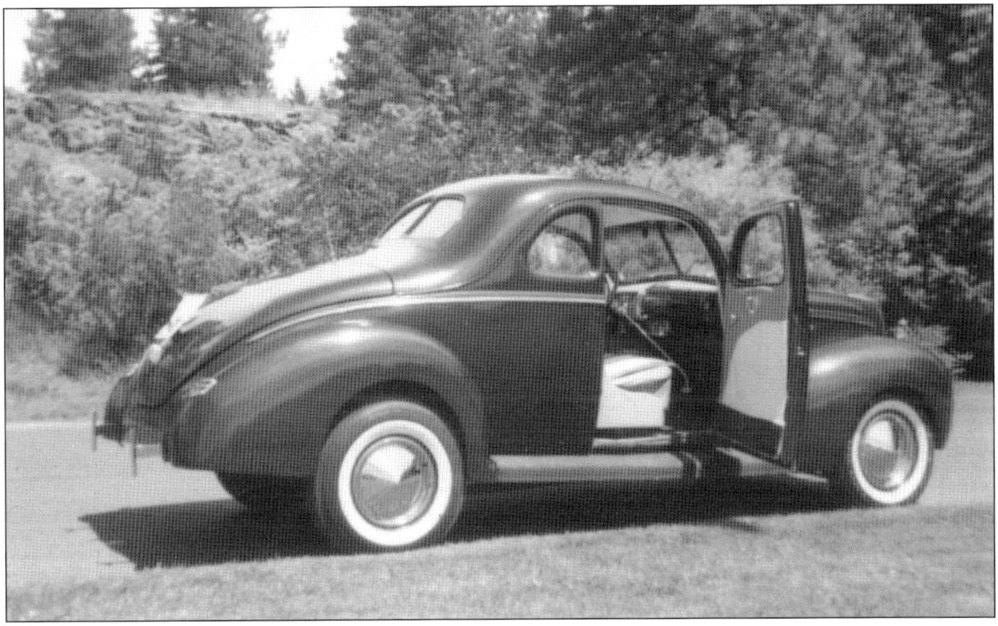

A great big rake is shown here on Dukes member Don Gorman's 1940 Ford Standard coupe. The dark blue Ford had a white tuck-and-roll interior, a two-toned dash, and custom nerf bars. Gorman's coupe was powered by a 265 Chevy motor. The '40 three-on-the-tree transmission was removed, and a top-loader '39 tranny replaced it. (Don Gorman.)

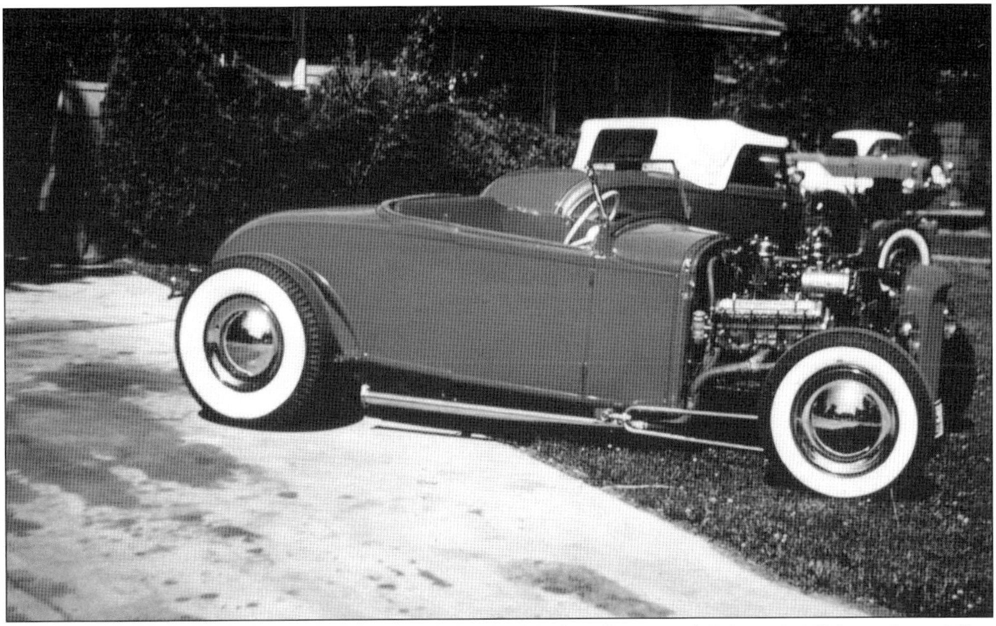

Shown here are Joe Felice's Model A roadster and, behind it, Frank Moyer's 1932 roadster. This is when Felice's car still had the Oldsmobile motor in it. The A came in a partial trade deal with Ned Kelly. Felice gave Kelly a mid-1910s Dodge roadster that was Olds-powered in return for the A roadster. The car is orange/red with a '40 Ford dash in it. Felice had the interior installed when it was his. Moyer's car is painted metallic purple, with white top and cycle-style fenders all the way around. (Frank Moyer.)

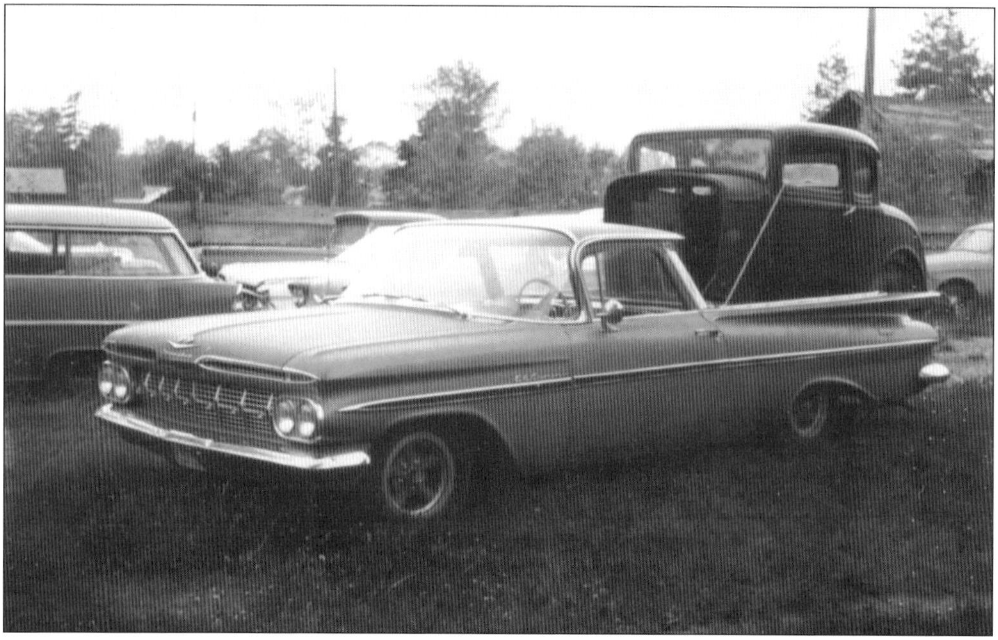

Frank Moyer brings his newly purchased '32 five-window home in the back of his 1959 El Camino. He worked the night shift at the railroad during this time, and so had a head start scanning the car advertisements in the morning paper. By 5:00 a.m., he was calling the owner and, by midmorning, he was hauling it home. Dusty Rhodes originally owned the coupe. The guy Moyer bought it from was going to make a stock car out of it if he could not sell it. (Frank Moyer.)

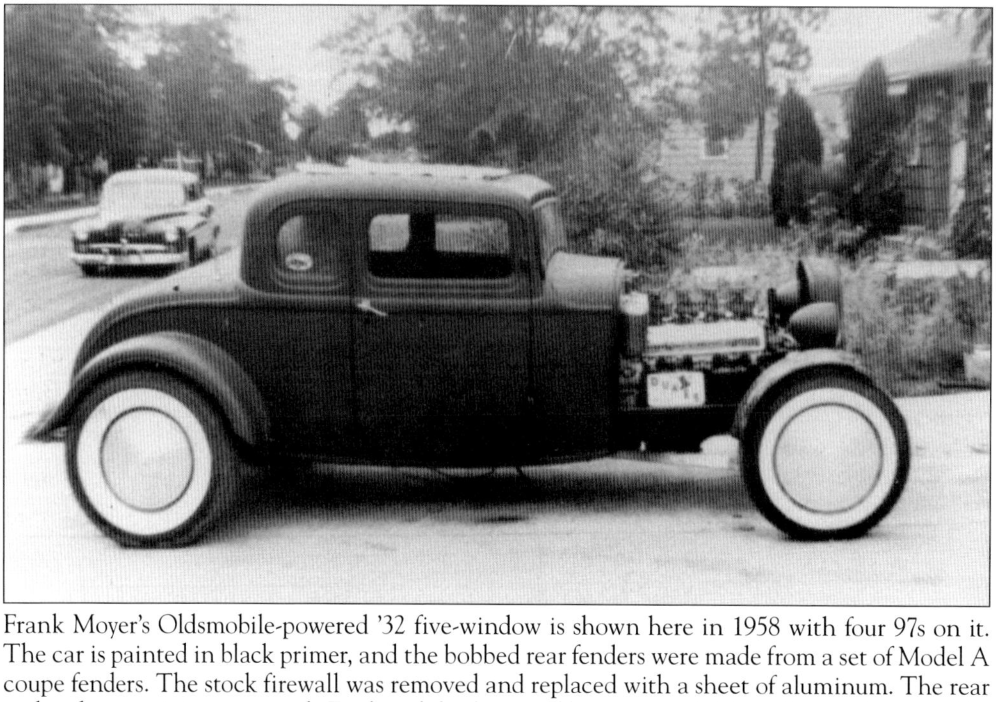

Frank Moyer's Oldsmobile-powered '32 five-window is shown here in 1958 with four 97s on it. The car is painted in black primer, and the bobbed rear fenders were made from a set of Model A coupe fenders. The stock firewall was removed and replaced with a sheet of aluminum. The rear end and transmission were early Ford, and the front end has an unsplit '32 wishbone that straddles the Oldsmobile motor. Moyer joined the Dukes in 1958 with this coupe. (Frank Moyer.)

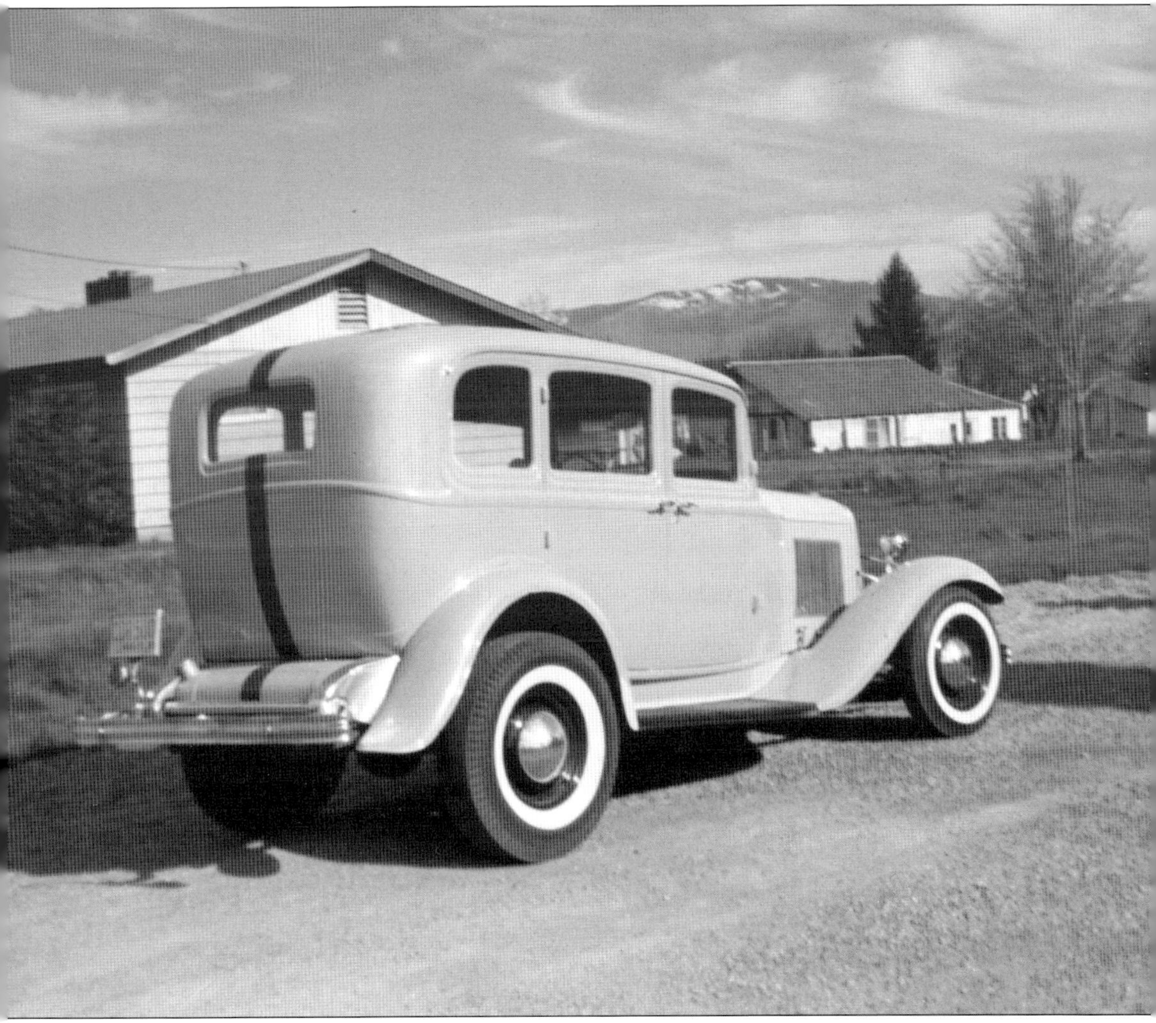

Dukes member Lloyd Johnson's "Many Doors" sits at Speedy Gunsaulis's house on Broadway in the Spokane Valley. Johnson bought this 1932 Ford four-door in 1960 for $400. It had a complete stock interior, but was missing the motor. Johnson quickly installed a 283 mill, '39 trans, chrome frame horns, a '48 rear end, and a black racing stripe. This car began its life as a hot rod at a Flying A station in Hillyard, when it was owned by Johnny Martin. He and his brother Leon put a built flathead in it and painted it a neon orange color that came from the Army surplus store. They had repainted it yellow before selling it to Johnson. The four-door was later owned by three other Dukes members: Danny Martin, Colonel Walker, and Frank Moyer.

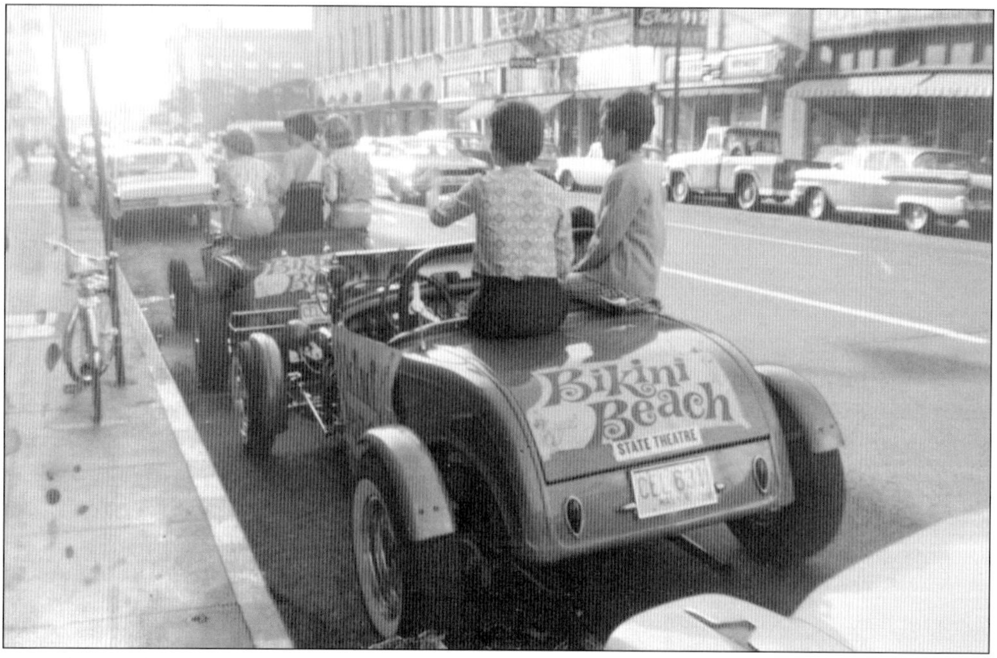

Joe Felice and Frank Moyer's roadster sits in front of the State Theatre (now the Bing Crosby Theatre) at 901 West Sprague Avenue. The theater hired Felice and Moyer (both members of the Dukes) to drive around Spokane and advertise the release of *Bikini Beach* (1964), staring Annette Funicello and Frankie Avalon. The ladies were members of the Royal Court, part of the Spokane Lilac Festival. (Frank Moyer.)

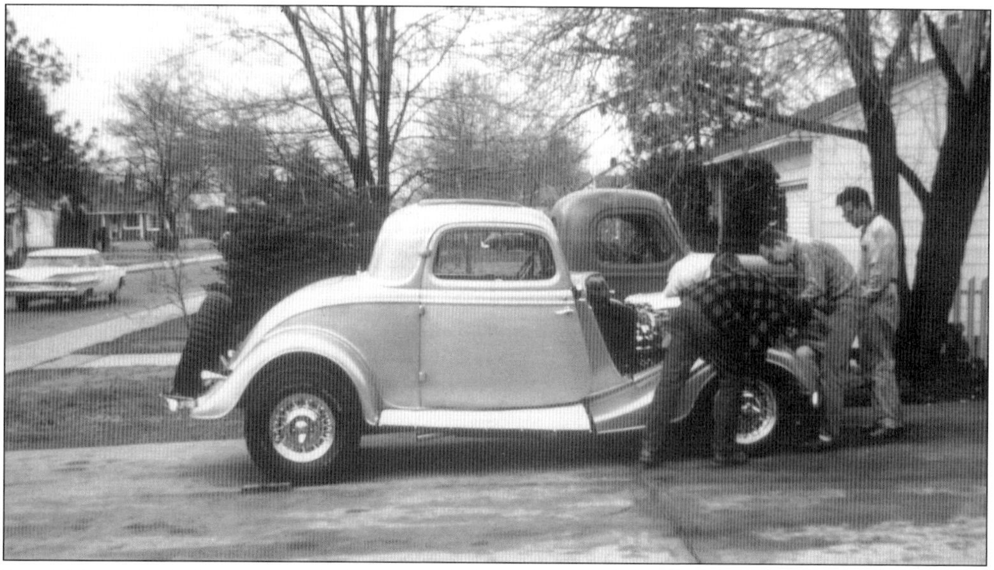

Frank Moyer, Mike Hiens, Bob Holmes, and Bob Lockin get "The Stump Puller" ready for the 1965 show season. The 1933 three-window had been a show/street car in Spokane since the mid-1950s, but here it is getting a 1960s makeover. The motor is a 413 cross ram out of a 1962 Chrysler, and the coupe is sitting on a set of Chrysler wire wheels. The paint was a custom gold metal flake, mixed by George Barris, which he delivered to the airport to be flown up just in time for Moyer to paint it for the show. (Frank Moyer.)

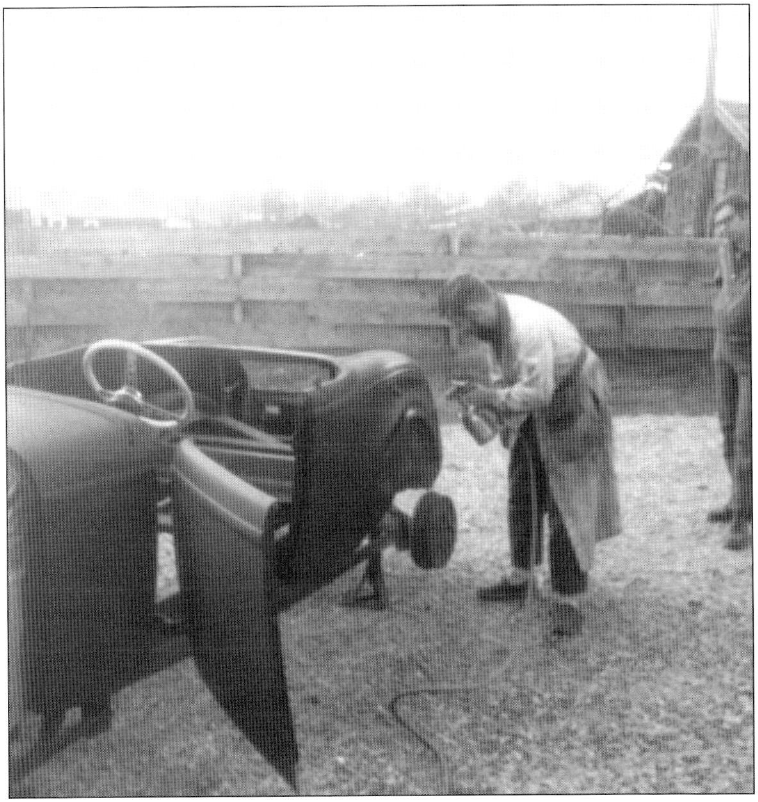

Bob Holmes watches Frank Moyer apply a new color to Ron Corkum's 1932 Ford roadster at Moyer's house in Hillyard. The car was a Studebaker-powered hot rod when Corkum bought it, but he switched it over to a Pontiac motor. Corkum has owned the car for over 50 years and it can still be seen wandering the streets of Spokane. (Frank Moyer.)

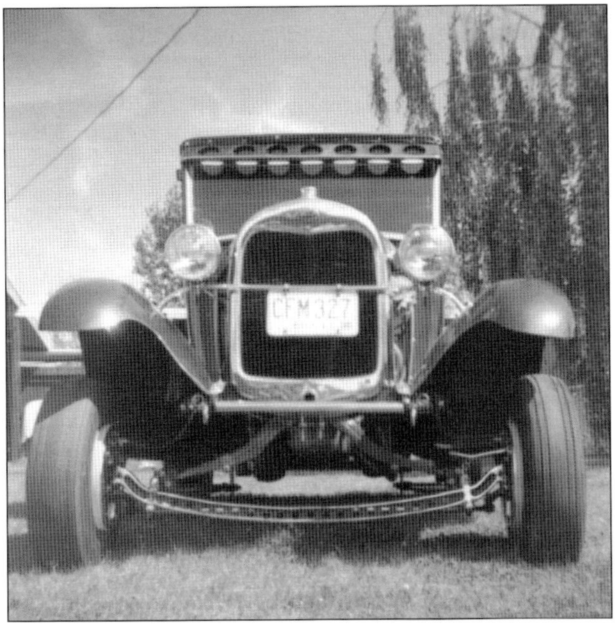

The 1929 Model A coupe of brothers Mark and Dan Weaver, built for both street and strip, was powered by a 327 Chevy engine with an Oldsmobile rear end. The coupe was basically stock when they traded for it, giving Darrel Larson a '32 five-window project in exchange. They boxed the frame, put one-fourth elliptical springs on the back, then took the car's factory rear A spring and used it on the front end. Paul Dixon did the interior work in black tuck and roll; the body was painted Pontiac cordovan brown, and the windows were amber plexiglass. The car ended up in *Rod & Custom* after it was shot by famed Northwest photographer Peter Sukalac. (Dan Weaver.)

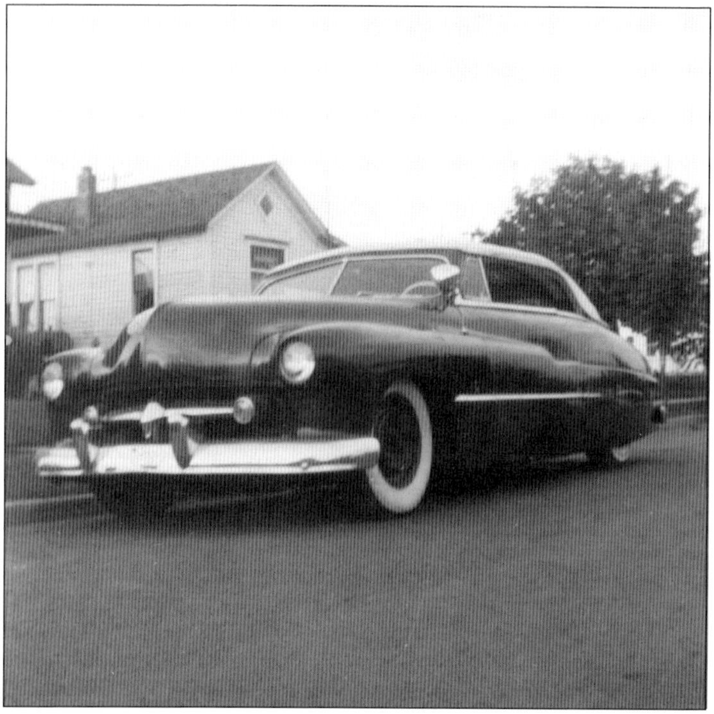

The Ralph Testa 1950 Mercury built by Barris sits on the 1500 block of East First Avenue in Spokane in September 1957. The car was featured in many magazines in the early 1950s when it was in Los Angeles, but it was Bobby Lantman who bought the car on the coast and brought it to Spokane. The Merc was painted Honduras metallic maroon when it showed up, and Lantman ended up trading it to Dragins member Buddy Brennan for a 1948 Chevy coupe. Brennan also ended up owning the Calori coupe. (Glen Harbison.)

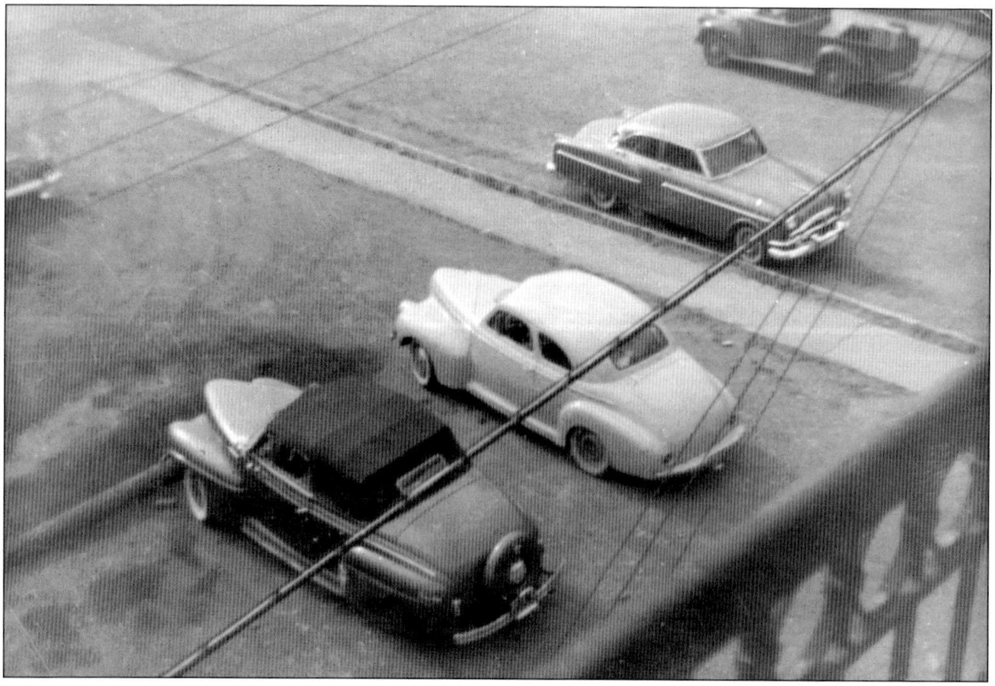

This photograph looks down on two mild customs from The Daniels apartments on Sinto Avenue and Howard Street in 1954. The '41 Chevy coupe (right) had its deck lid shaved and a pair of baby Lincoln taillights added by its owner, Gary Mitchell. The '41 Ford convertible (left) was owned by a friend and was dolled up with a Continental kit, dual spotlights, and fender skirts. (Glen Harbison.)

The Calori coupe now owned by Buddy Brannon is seen behind Custom Auto Upholstery on Sprague Avenue around 1957. Brannon, a member of the Dragins Auto Club, did the upholstery work on numerous Spokane hot rods. He bought this car, minus the fuel-injected Chevy motor, from Bill Bongers, who replaced the flat motor with the Chevy. Jack Calori was known for his avid hatred of white walls, but this car is resting on a set of wide whites. Lake pipes were added at some point during this time. (Glen Harbison.)

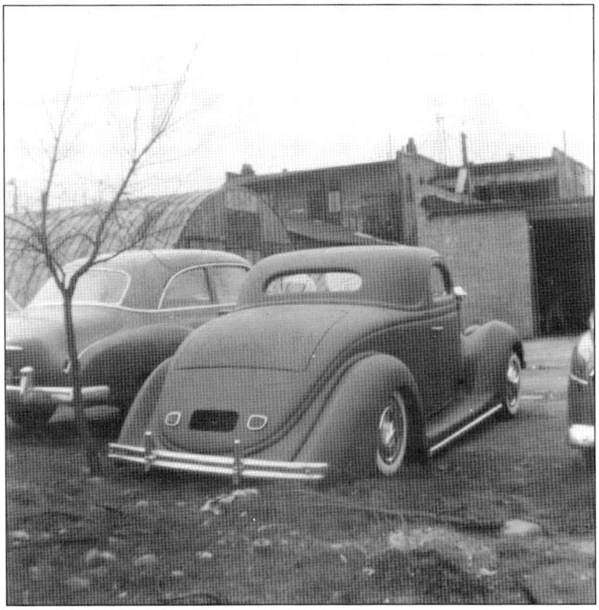

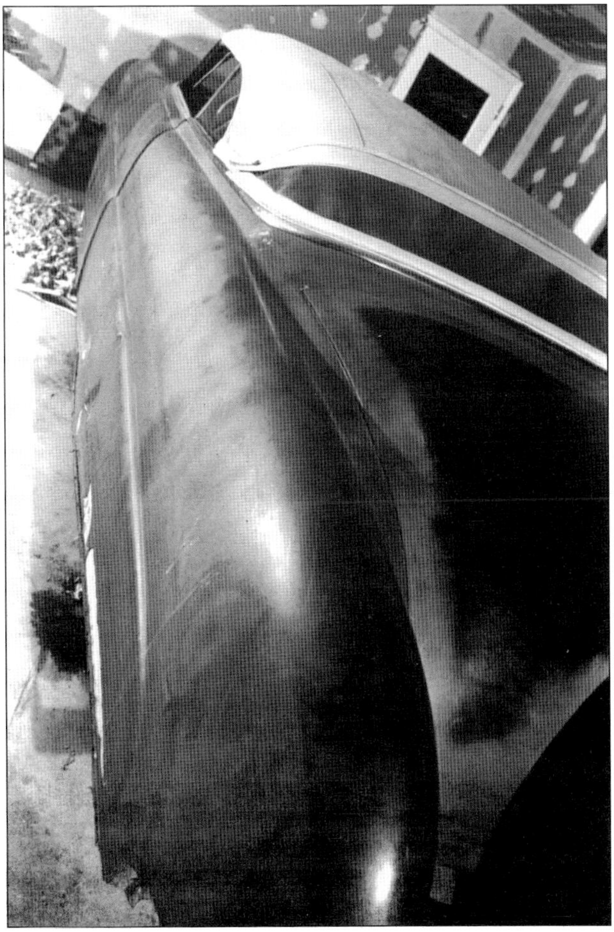

Jack McClesky worked at Paris Cleaners in the 1500 block of East Sprague Avenue. He was lucky enough that his employer would let him and his friends work in a small garage attached to the back. Many cars were painted and customized in that little shop, including this 1950 Hudson convertible. The rear was lengthened by 15 inches with the use of four sets of quarter panels. Next, the tailings were shaved and Harley "Buddy" lights were added to the rear of the car. McClesky built the Continental kit, and Buddy Brannon did the interior and padded top in pink. The side damage was the result of some street racing up the Lewiston grade. (Roger Domini.)

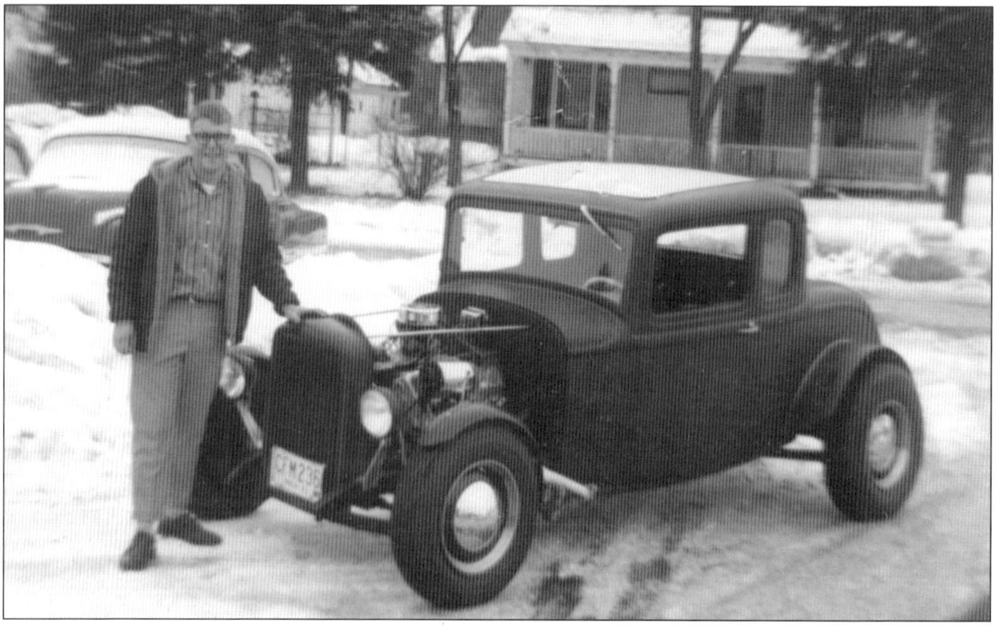

Darrel Larson stands next to his 1932 Ford five-window coupe. He acquired the car in an early 1960s trade with the Weaver brothers, giving them a 1928 Model A coupe. He replaced the Oldsmobile motor that came with the coupe with a better-running Olds motor he got from Larry Bozarth. That motor came in another trade deal, when Larson and Bozarth swapped the Olds mill for a 50cc motorbike. He made the seats by cutting the legs off of fiberglass patio chairs. Larson became a key player in the look of Spokane hot rodding, with his illustrations and logos for speed shops, clubs, and shows. (Darrel Larson.)

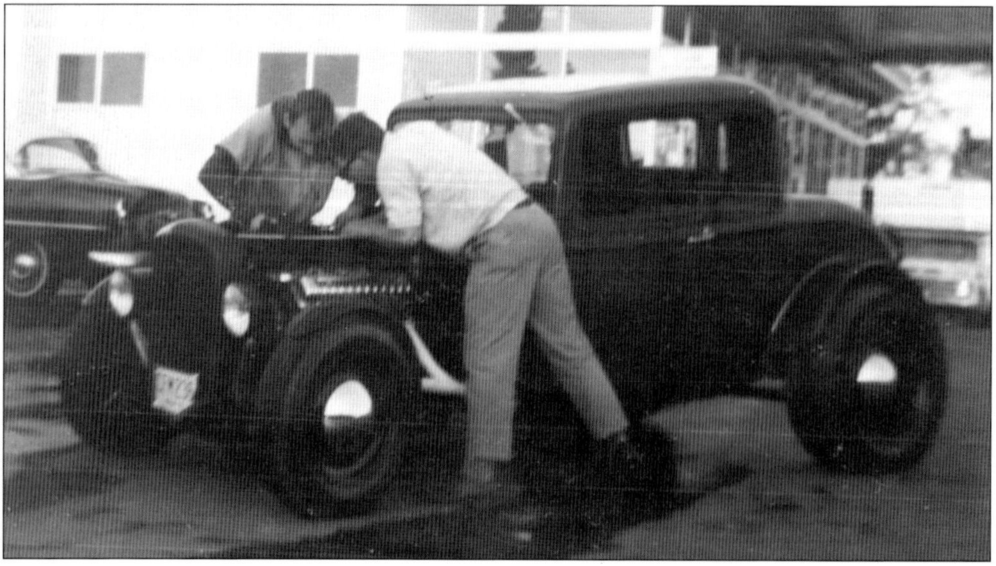

Stan Porter (left) and Darrel Larson work on the coupe at the Chevron gas station on Mission Avenue and Napa Street, where both men were employed. Larson became a member of the Dukes with the car. He painted it yellow before he did the final trade with fellow club member Dave Callahan. This time, Larson traded the coupe to Callahan for a 1940 two-door sedan and $275. (Darrel Larson.)

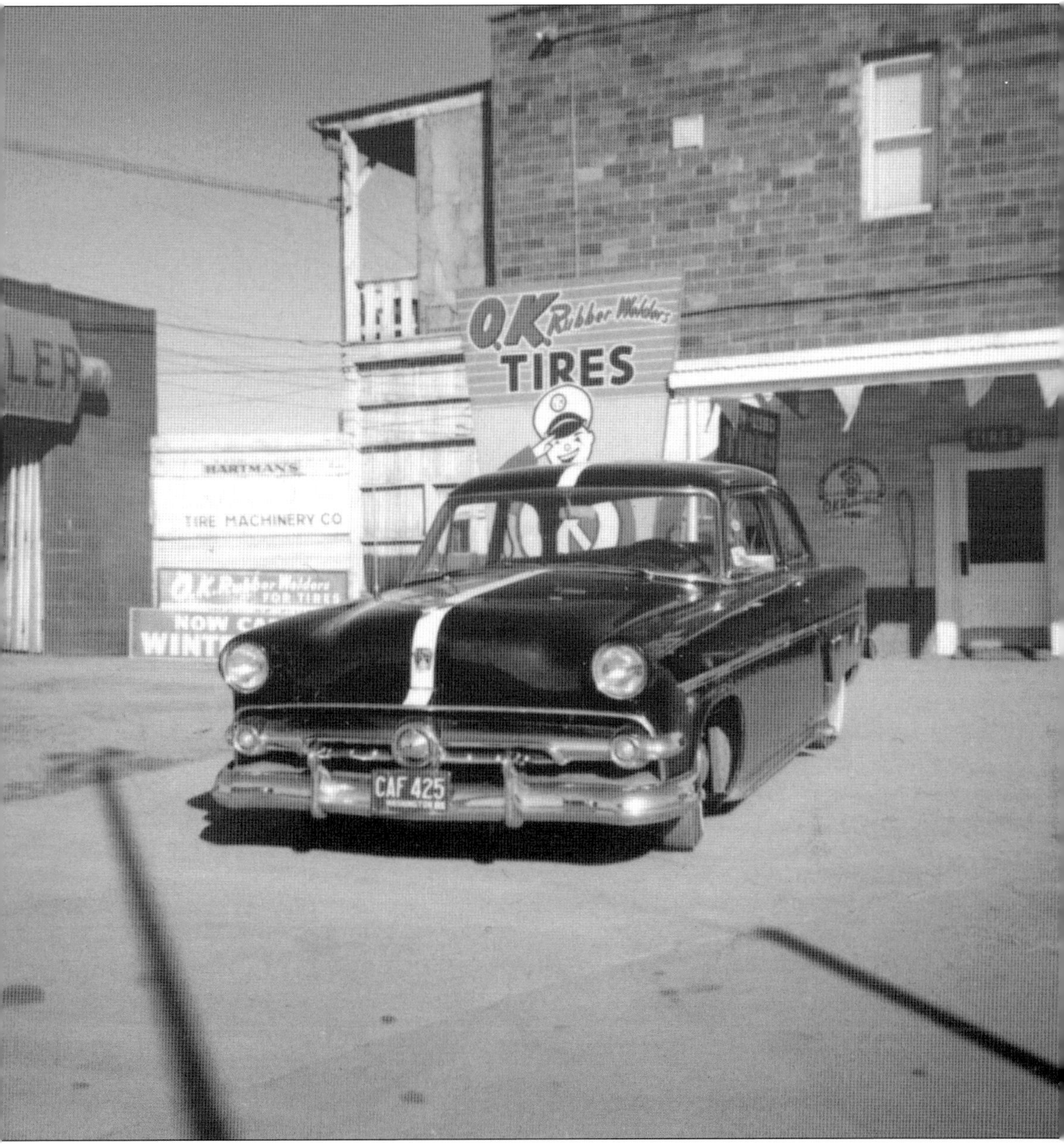

Larry "The Muffler Man" Taylor's 1954 Ford two-door sedan sits in front of Magic Muffler, 806 West Sprague Avenue. This is where Taylor learned the muffler business from Lloyd Scott and Jack Rose. The sedan was black, with lake pipes and Chrysler wire wheels. Slow Annie did the upholstery in white Naugahyde, and the white racing stripe was painted by Chase and Dalbert Auto Body. Taylor became a fixture in drag racing in Spokane and built some great cars, including a '31 Ford pickup that made it into *Hot Rod* magazine in April 1970. (Larry Taylor.)

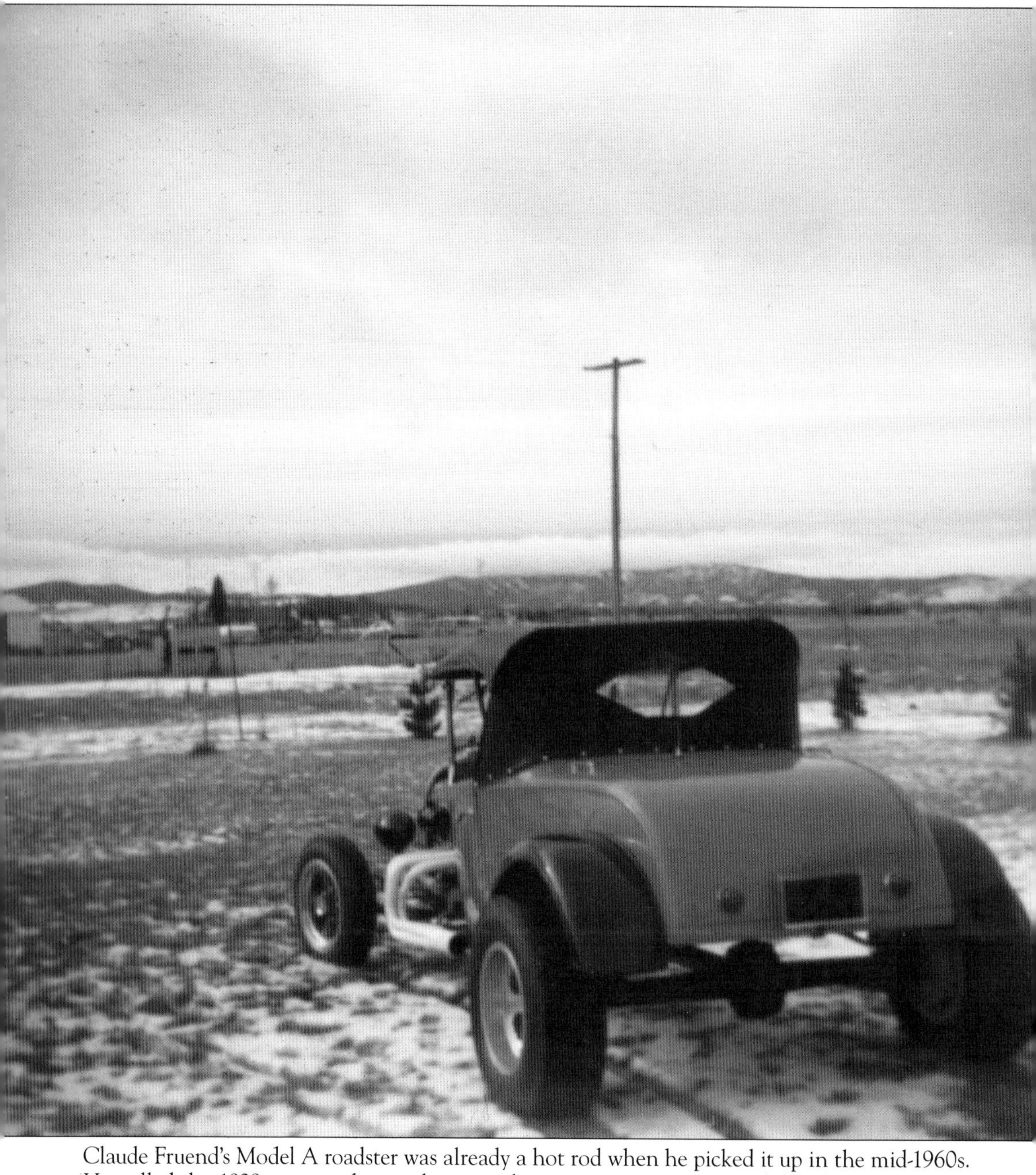

Claude Fruend's Model A roadster was already a hot rod when he picked it up in the mid-1960s. He pulled the 1929 apart and started to rework it, painting it orange with black fenders in the rear and installing black upholstery. The car was powered by a small-block Chevy, with an early Ford three-speed and a banjo rear end. (Sue Fruend.)

Two

SHOW

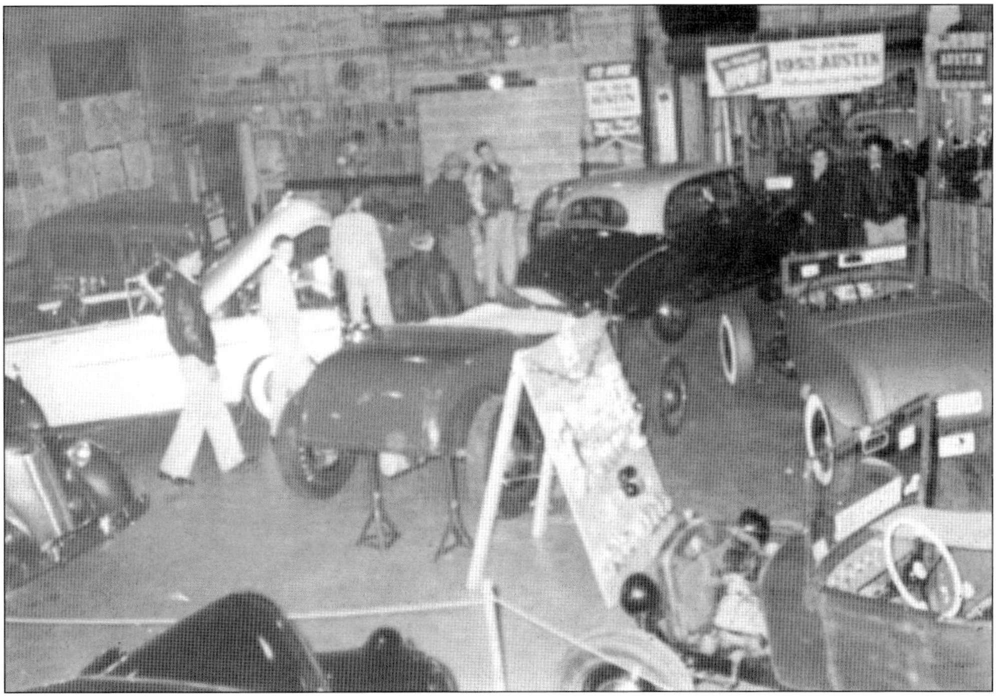

The Dukes Auto Club held the first indoor hot-rod show in Spokane, at Jaremko Motors, 2020 North Monroe Street, in 1953. At upper left is Dusty Rhodes's ARDUN-powered '32 Ford sedan. Bobby Austin's purple 1936 custom with the LaSalle grille is partially visible at far left. At top center is a brand-new Austin on display for Jaremko, and to the lower right of it is the 1932 Cabriolet owned by Jack Curry. It later evolved into Art True's car. In the center is the Model A that Gary Harms and Tim Rochlitzer brought to Spokane from California, and at lower right is Gary Harms's V-8 60-powered T. The sandwich board is advertising for the Evans speed equipment that Rochlitzer was bringing to Spokane. (Gary Harms.)

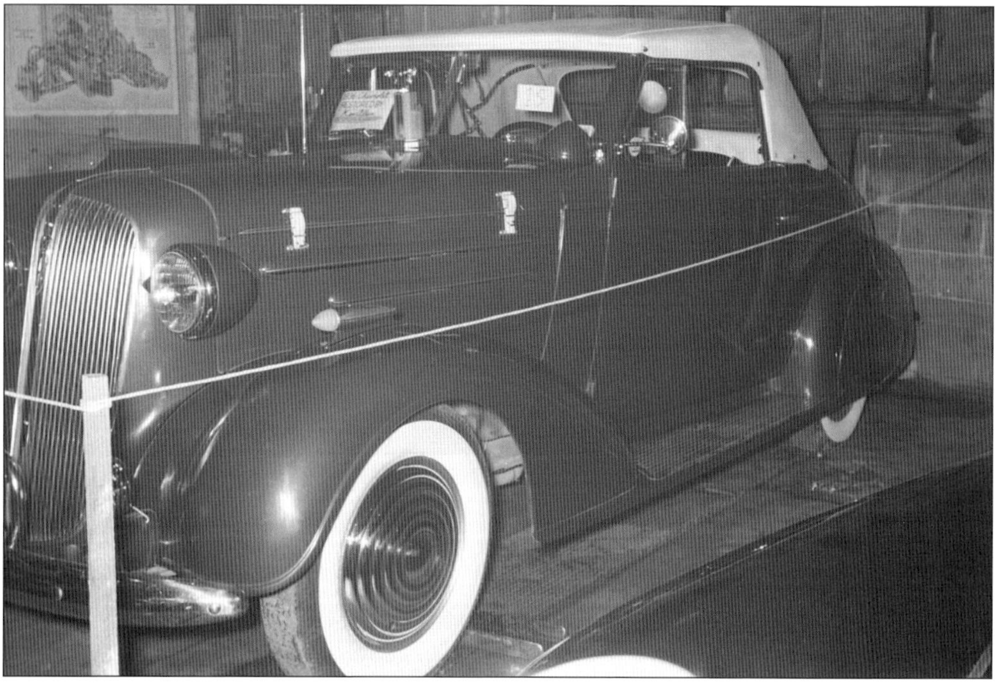

One of the cars at the Jaremko Motors show was this mild custom 1936 Chevrolet Cabriolet. (Harry Prouty.)

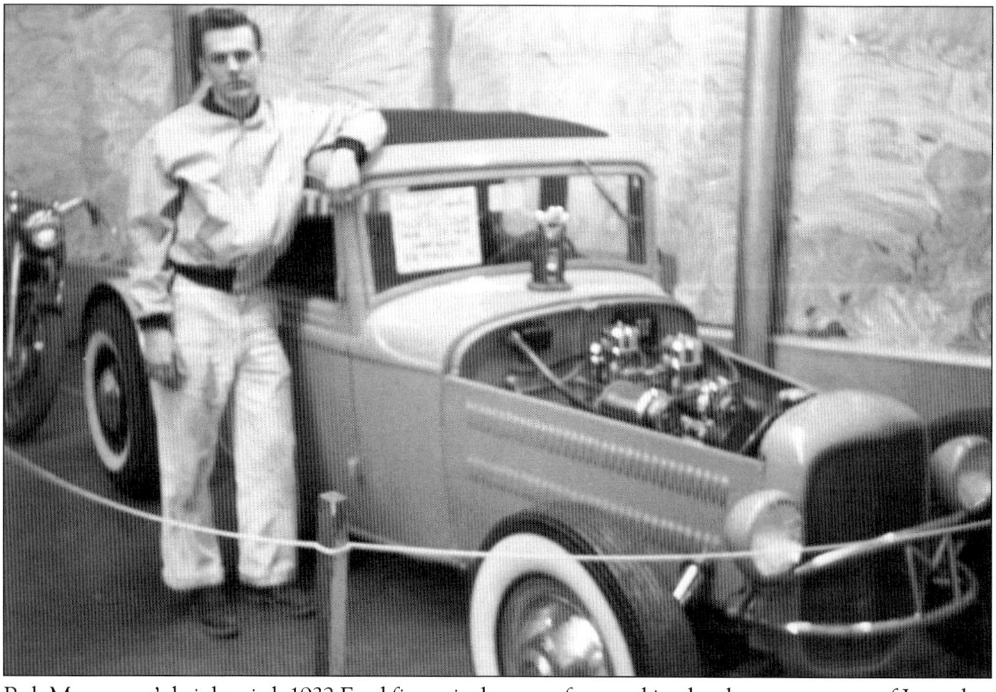

Bob Magnason's bright pink 1932 Ford five-window was featured in the showroom area of Jaremko. Windows in the showroom were whitewashed to attract spectators. The coupe is channeled over the frame, with homemade fenders in the back. Custom-louvered hood sides were made so that the grille could be pushed forward and cover the '35-'40 Ford suspensions. (Harry Prouty.)

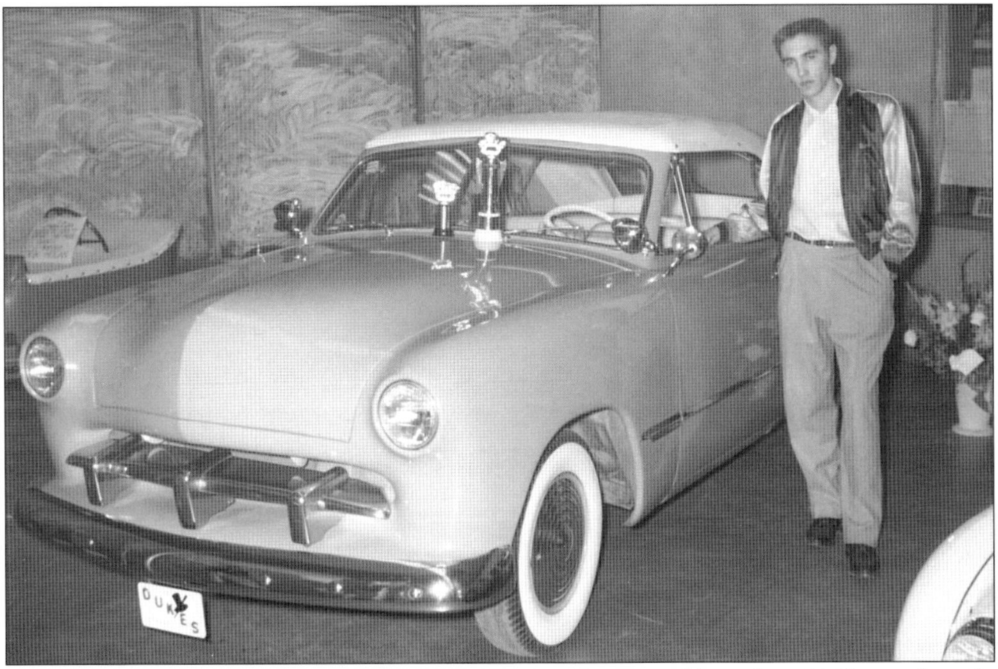

Dukes member Bob Goodwin poses with his 1950 Ford convertible with a '52 Plymouth grille and a '49-'50 Mercury grille opening. By 1953, as seen here, the Dukes Car Club had switched to cast aluminum plaques. In the background is Dick Hogan's Model T, which became Bob Coutts's car. (Harry Prouty.)

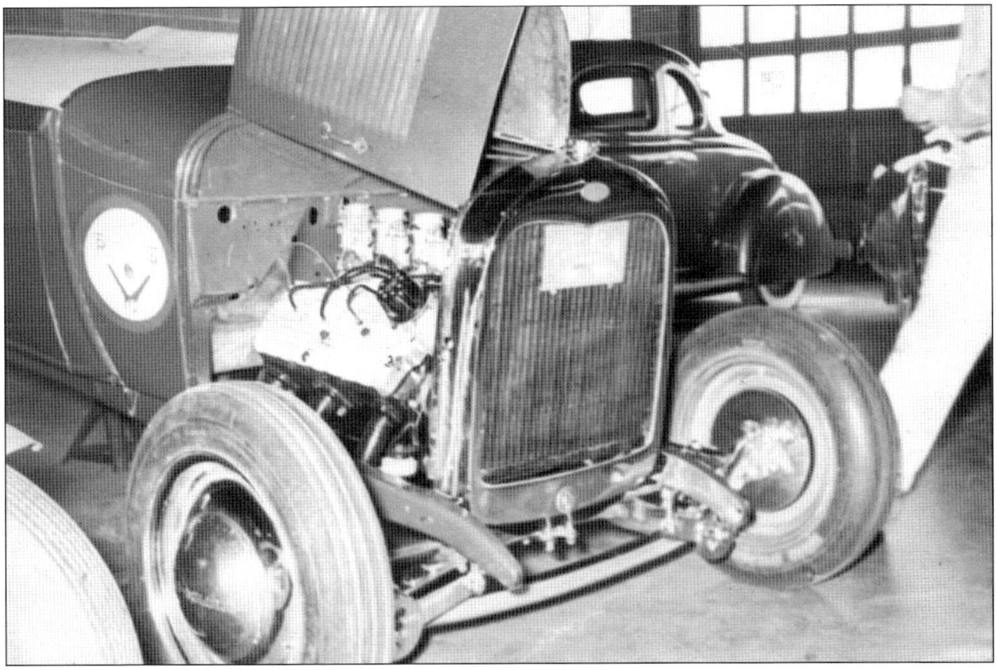

The plaque on the front of Gary Harms's Model A was for the SRRA, of which Harms was a member. In the background is Bobby Austin's 1936 Ford five-window, which had a flocked dash. The new art over the old Bob Joehnck's logo is for R&R, or Rochlitzer and Rogers. (Gary Harms.)

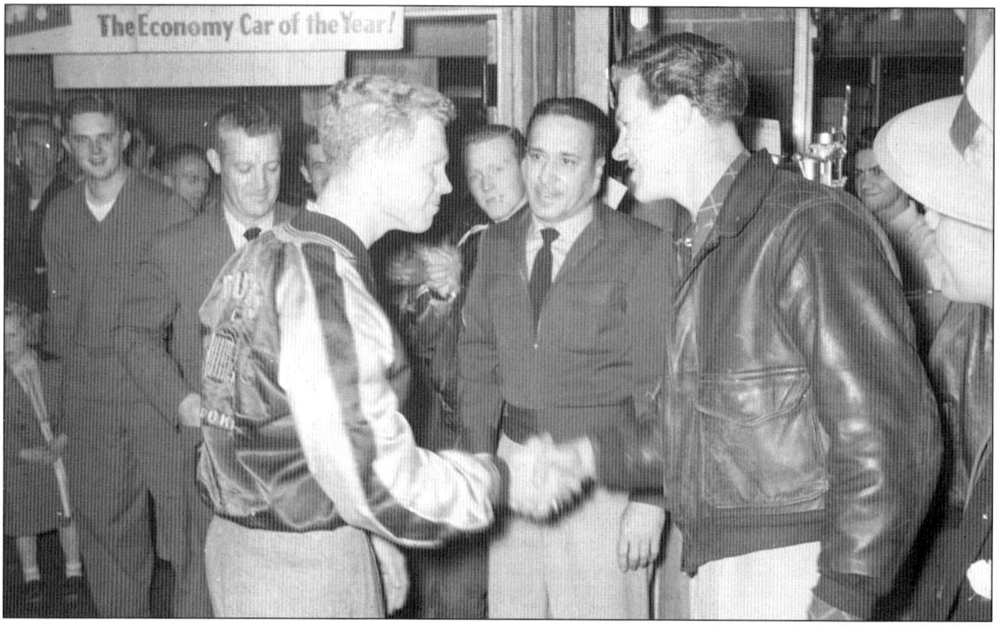

Dukes member Ron Jolley (left) accepts the award for his 1936 five-window from Ed Sneva (right). Jolley worked at Jones Engines in Spokane, and his '36 five-window was flathead powered with filled quarter windows. Bud Falico, who promoted midget races and owned a Signal gas station on Division Street, is standing between Jolley and Sneva. (Harry Prouty.)

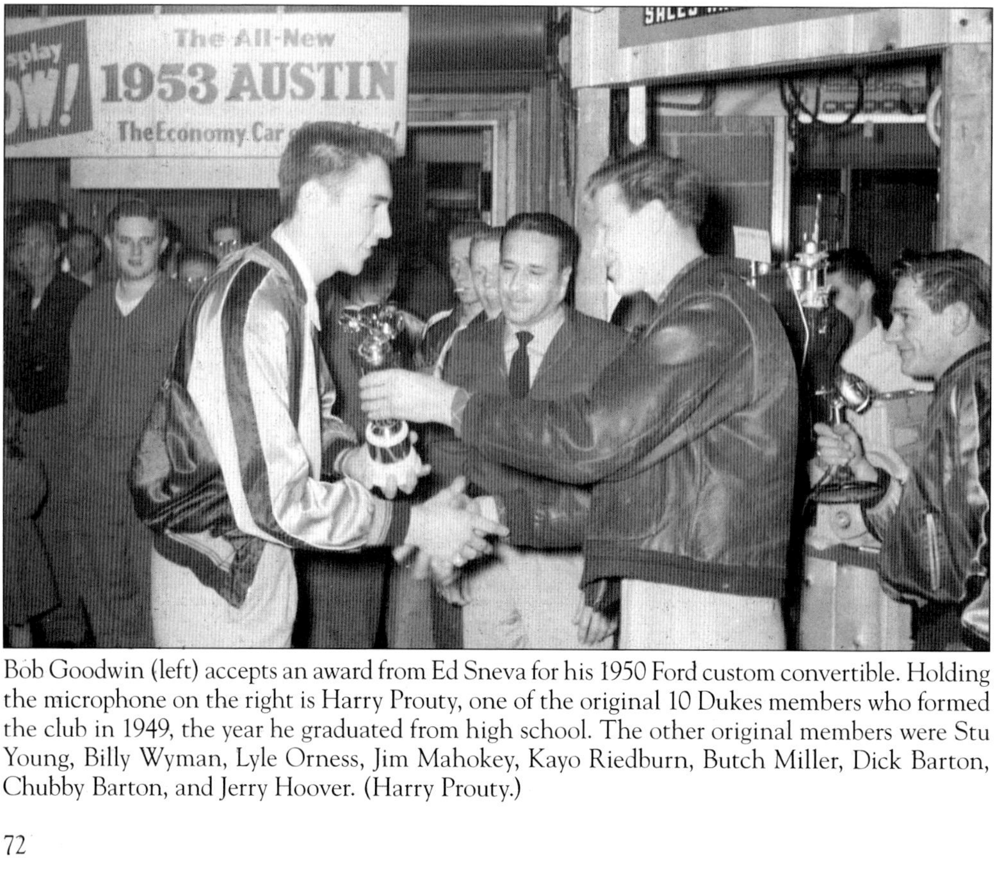

Bob Goodwin (left) accepts an award from Ed Sneva for his 1950 Ford custom convertible. Holding the microphone on the right is Harry Prouty, one of the original 10 Dukes members who formed the club in 1949, the year he graduated from high school. The other original members were Stu Young, Billy Wyman, Lyle Orness, Jim Mahokey, Kayo Riedburn, Butch Miller, Dick Barton, Chubby Barton, and Jerry Hoover. (Harry Prouty.)

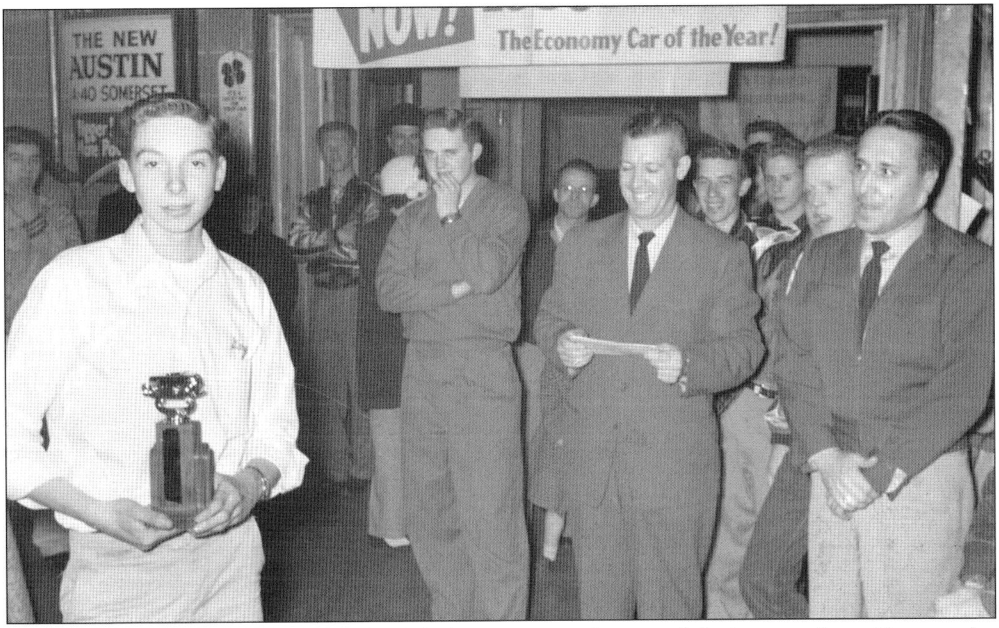

A very young Gary Harms, in his SRRA shirt, accepts the award for best roadster. He won the category with his Model A. In the background is Ron Jolley, and to the right of the man holding the card with the big smile is Dukes president Kayo Riedburn, who designed the Dukes logo. (Harry Prouty.)

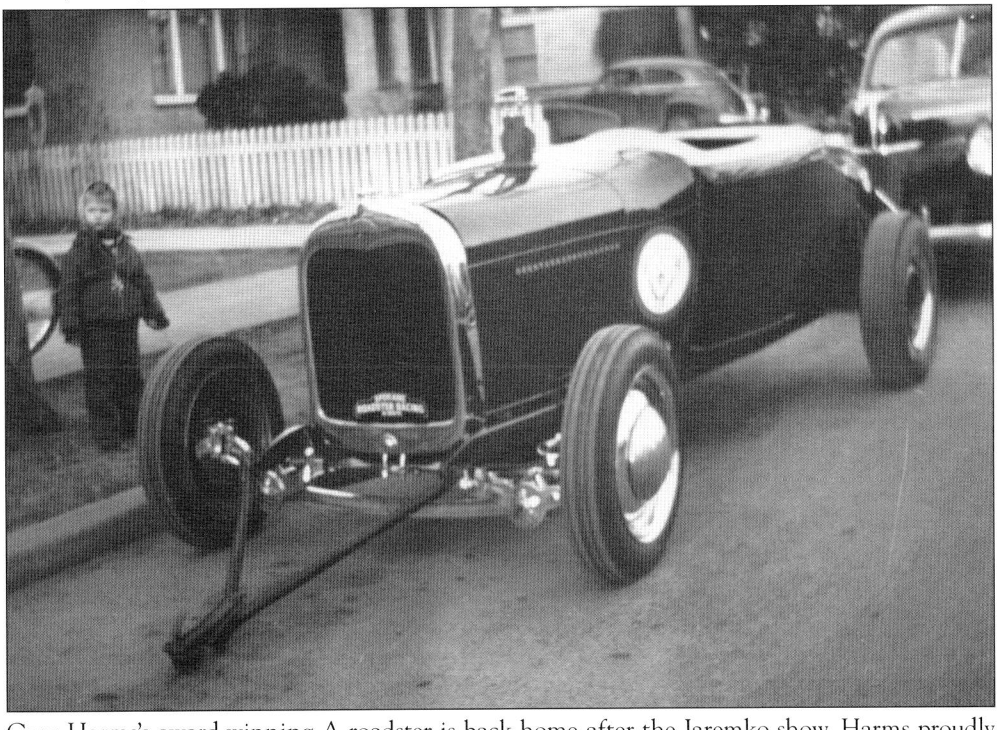

Gary Harms's award-winning A roadster is back home after the Jaremko show. Harms proudly displays his new trophy on the cowl. He switched out the SRRA plaque for a license-plate topper, tucked between the radiator and the grille shell. (Gary Harms.)

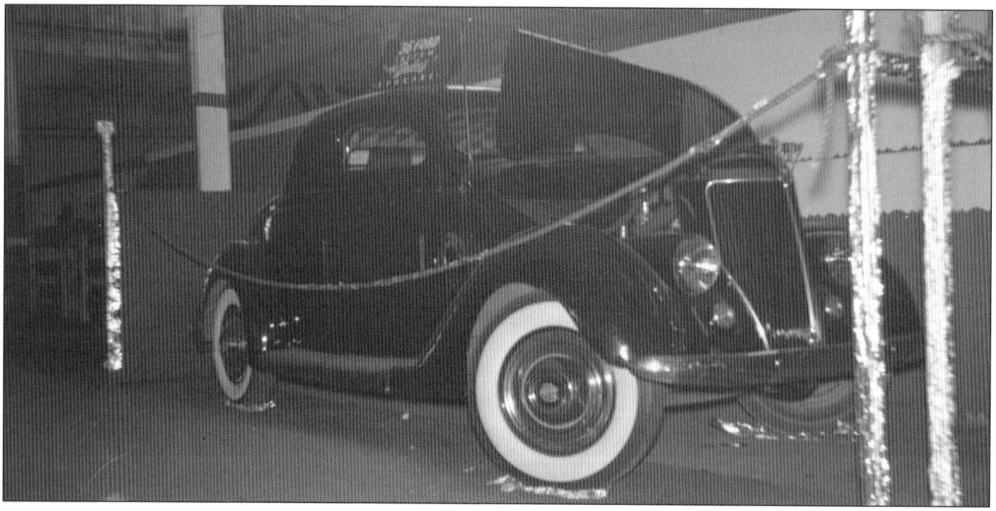

Ron Jolley's five-window custom is seen at the Portland indoor show. The Dukes drove down to participate in this event. The solid hood sides were made by Spokane Tin, the headlights are 1940 Chevrolet, and the quarter windows are filled. The interior features include an argyle pattern in the headliner, and the horn grilles are replaced with marker lights. (Harry Prouty.)

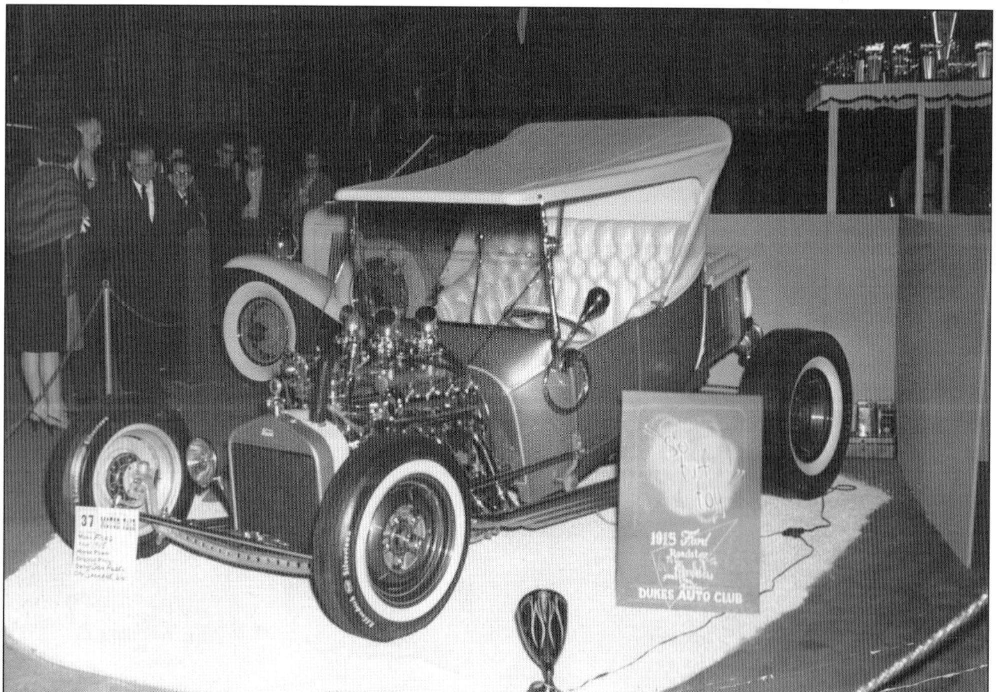

Seen here is Don Audel's 1915 Model T, dubbed the "So Tuff Toy," at the first Motor Fair at the Spokane fairgrounds. The T is running a fully detailed Studebaker motor, with a later 1930s Packard top-loader transmission adapted to work with the Ford torque tube. Audel used his pinstriping skills to add subtle details to the wheels, the front hubs of the T, and to parts of the show display. Audel must have been working at the show, as his pinstriping kit is tucked behind the rear tire. The Dukes Auto Club, along with the HASSIE Club, helped put on the Motor Fair. (Don Audel.)

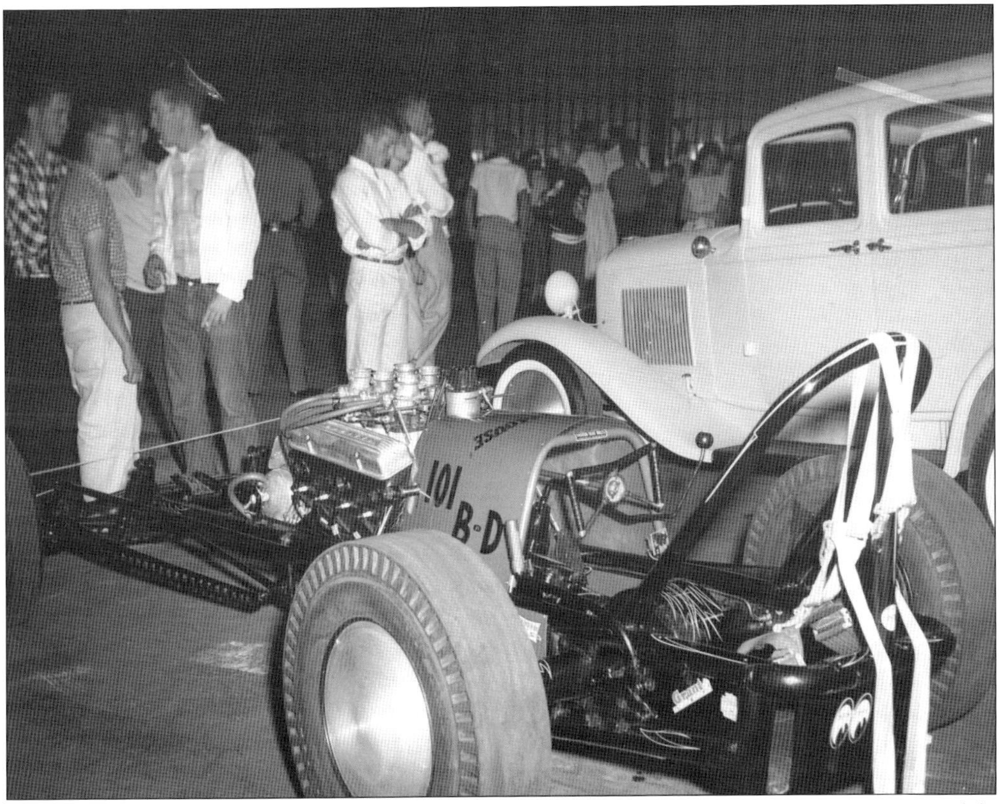

The Mickey Mouse dragster, owned by Dick Morphy, was also at the first Auto Fair. Don Audel's 1932 four-door is in the background. The dragster, built by Morphy, was powered by a 265 small-block Chevy. Audel did the paintwork on the rail; from this angle, all of his brushwork can be seen. Audel's four-door is in light blue primer and is being propped up in the rear by a cement block to make the car look like it had a bigger rake than it did. (Don Audel.)

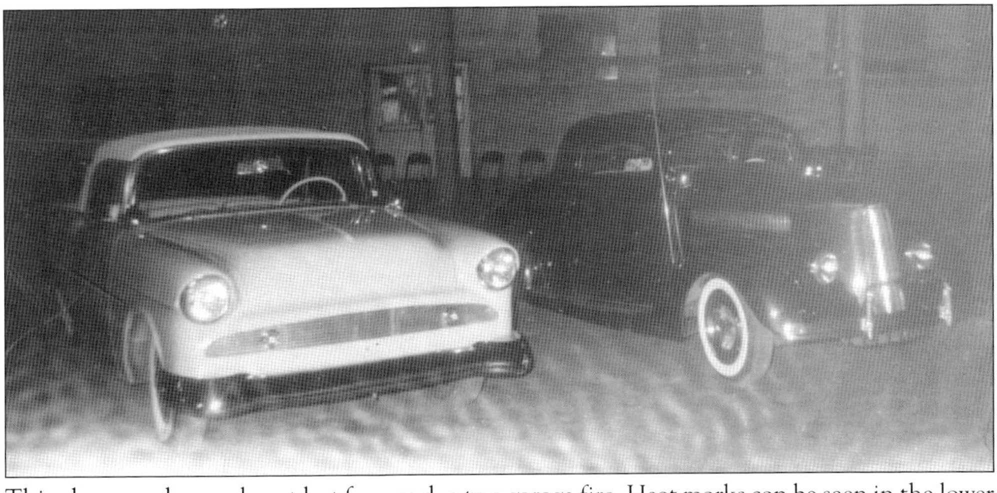

This photograph was almost lost forever due to a garage fire. Heat marks can be seen in the lower part of the image. Bill Bongers, from the Draggins Auto club, owned both of these customs. Here, he is getting ready for the Auto Fair. Both cars had graced the cover of *Hot Rod* magazine: "My Blue Heaven" (left) in November 1957 and "the Calori Coupe" in November 1949. (Bob Adams.)

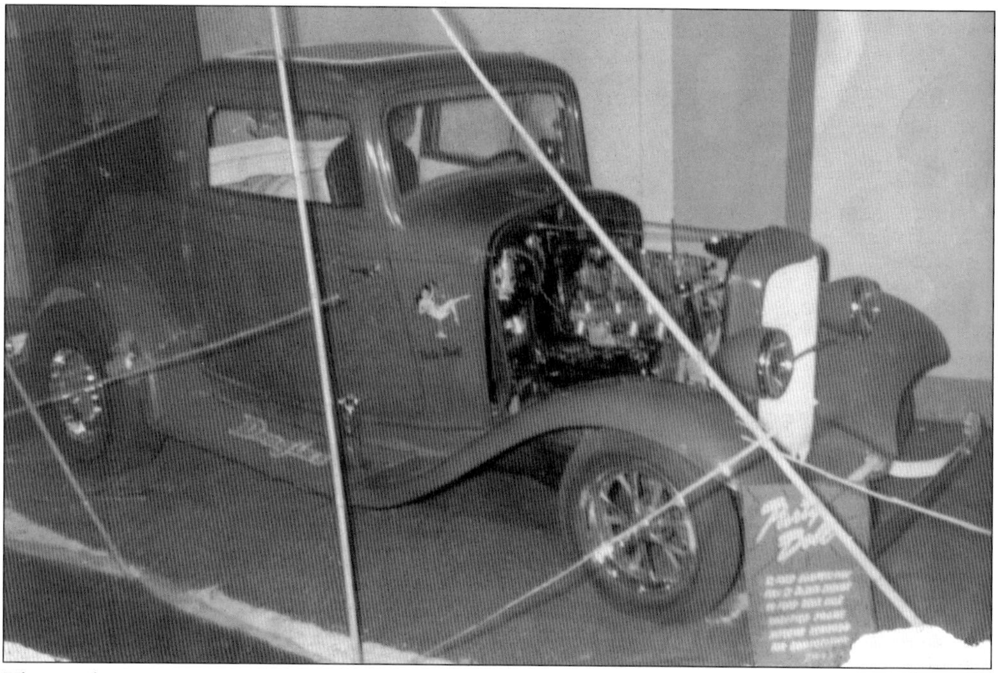

This is the same 1932 coupe that was previously owned by Jack Hordemann and Dick Flynn. Swede Erickson, the new owner of the deuce, turned it into a show car named the "Party Doll." The factory interior is gone, and the car is now upholstered with white tuck and roll, including a white insert on the top. The grille shell is now completely filled and peaked on top, a detail that is still on the car today. (Bob Adams.)

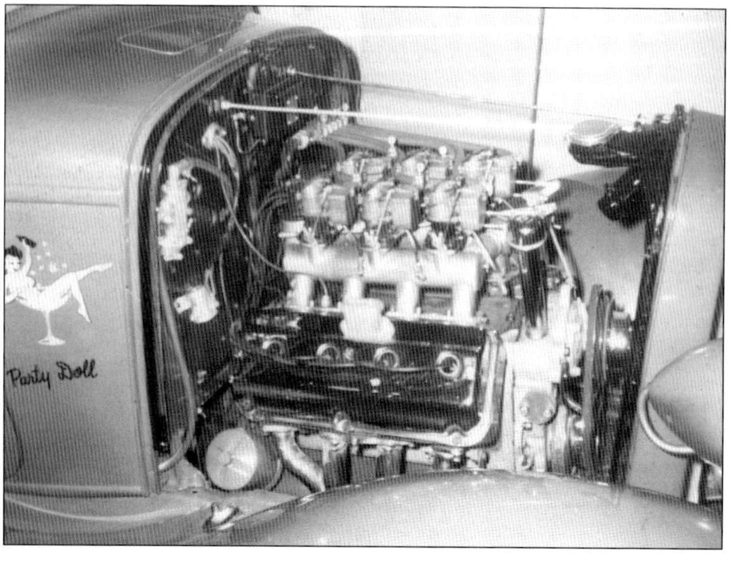

The "Party Doll" is still Desoto-powered, but it is a mix between a motor that Swede Erickson built and parts that he bought from Dick Flynn, such as the headers. Don Audel painted the party doll logo. This is the motor that ended up in the Allstate that Erickson and Vern Massie built. (Frank Moyer.)

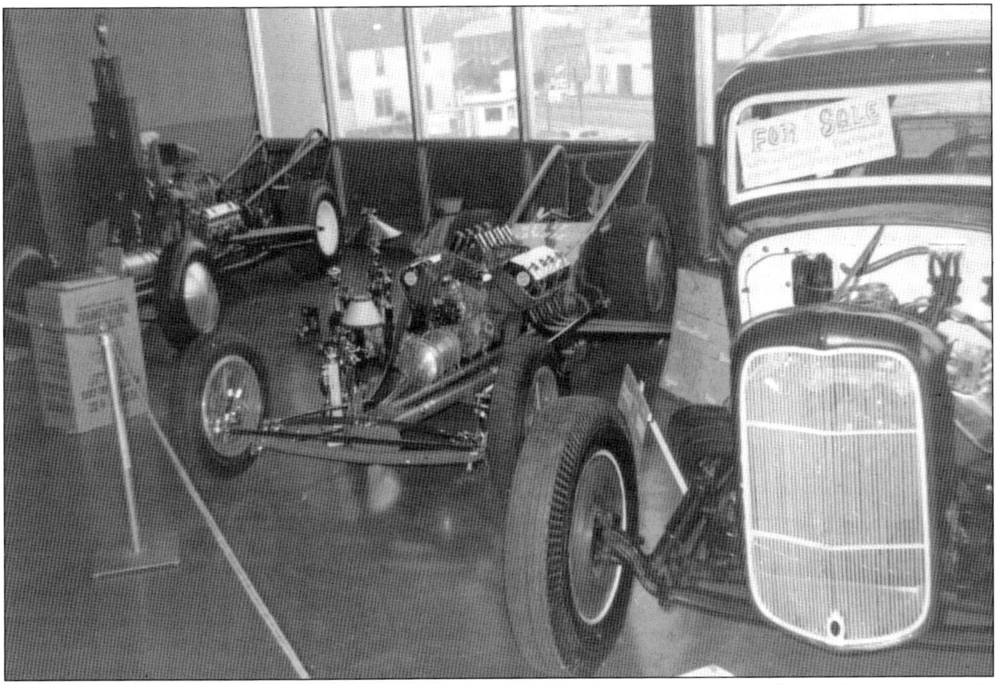

It was not an easy task to get the cars upstairs in the Spokane Coliseum, where this photograph was taken. Cars were pushed up the pedestrian ramps, which had a 180-degree switchback halfway up. A floor jack was used to swing the car around the corner so it could be pushed the rest of the way. At center is the Kelly-Massie dragster, powered by a 354 Chrysler in a Chassis Research frame. The '32 coupe on the right has the same styled beak on top of the grille shell that is on Swede Erickson's "Party Doll." (Bob Adams.)

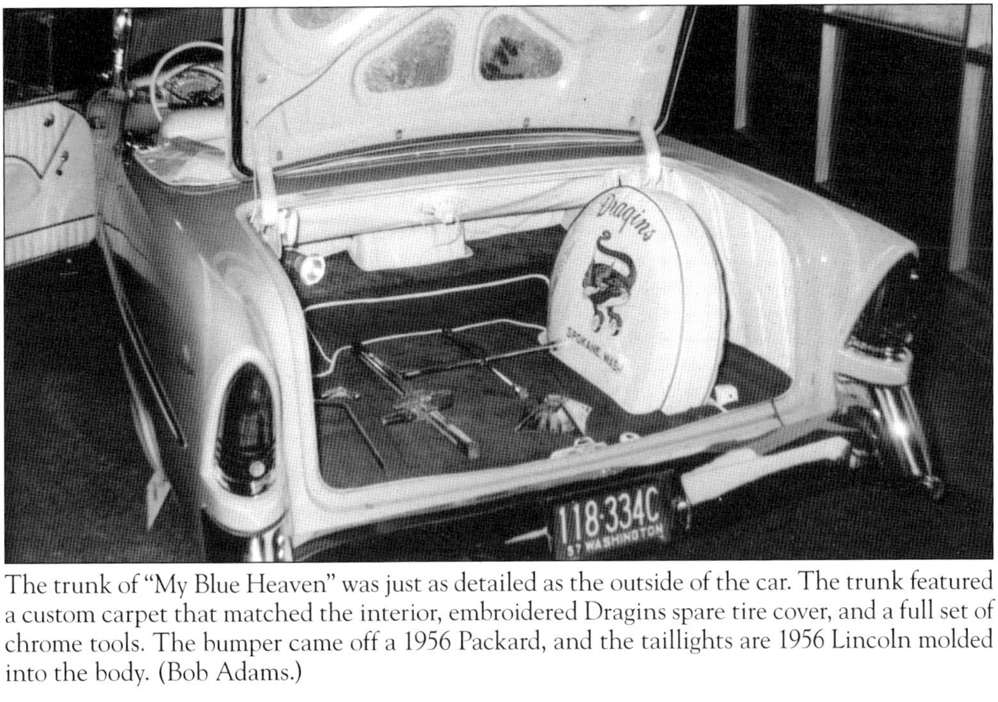

The trunk of "My Blue Heaven" was just as detailed as the outside of the car. The trunk featured a custom carpet that matched the interior, embroidered Dragins spare tire cover, and a full set of chrome tools. The bumper came off a 1956 Packard, and the taillights are 1956 Lincoln molded into the body. (Bob Adams.)

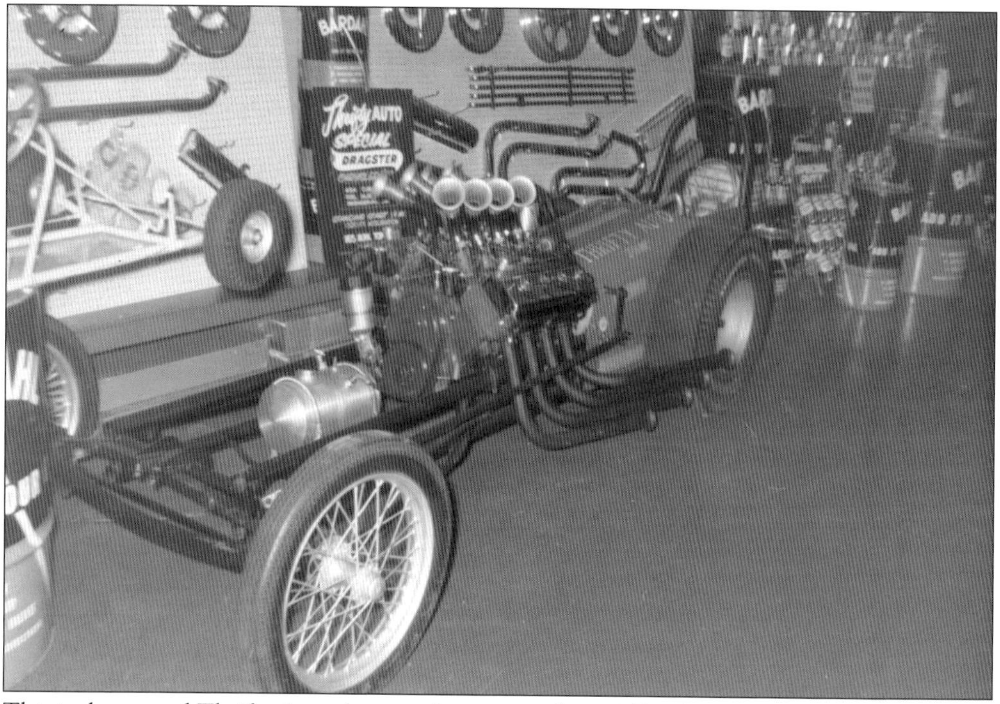

This is the second Thrifty Auto dragster. Its top speed was 165 miles per hour, powered by a 454 Chrysler that belonged to Dick Flynn. Butch Miller drove the car, Don Stortrden built the chassis, and Don Audel painted and lettered the body. The front wheels are from a Harley Davidson sidecar. Other members of the crew were Charlie Markley, Rod Cosgriffe, George Warsinski, and B.A. Spencer, president of the Inland Empire Timing Association. (Bob Adams.)

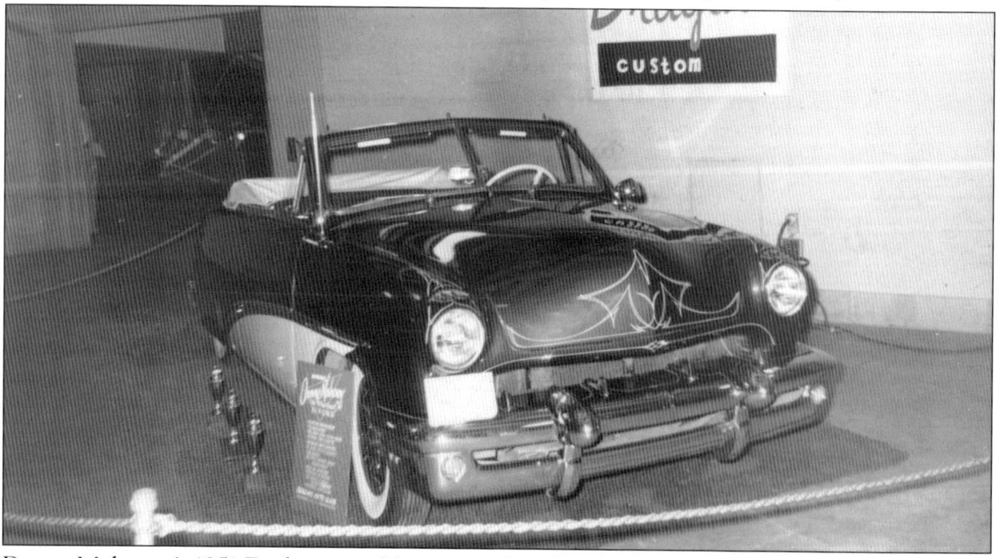

Denny Mahoney's 1951 Ford convertible was candy red and white, with dual spots and Buick side trim. The bumper and grille are off a 1953 Mercury, surrounded by an earlier '49-'51 Mercury grille opening. The front fender lips are off a '53 Mercury, so the body line would match up with the bumper. Custom scoops were added above the headlights. Mahoney ended up trading the car to Buddy Brannon for "Lil' Stinker," a '32 Ford five-window. (Bob Adams.)

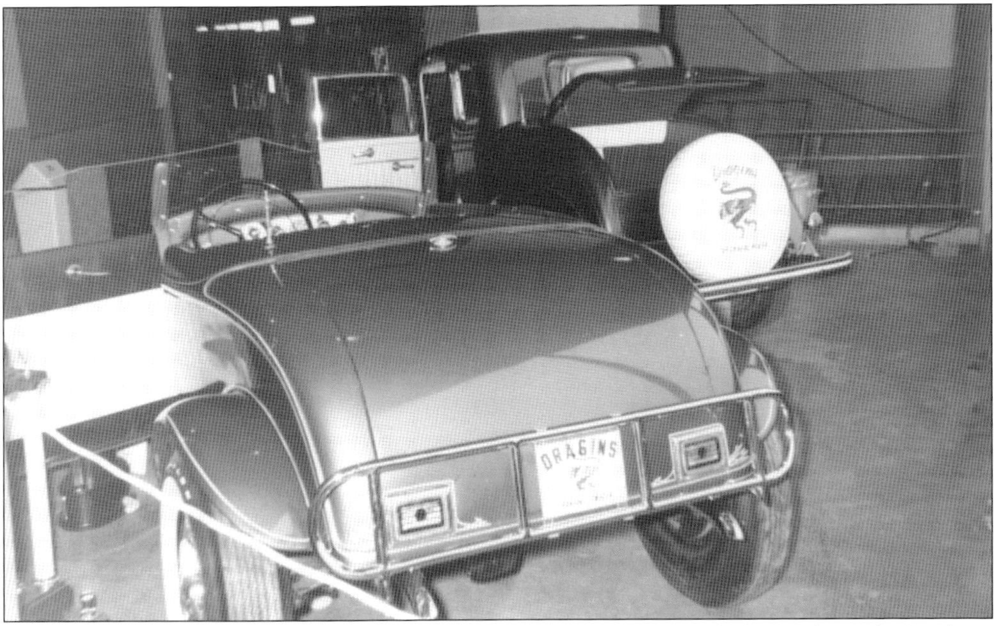

Shown here are Art True's 1932 Cabriolet (left), built by Joe Kostelecky, and "Little Stinker," owned here by Buddy Brannon. Both men were members of the Dragins Auto Club. Dusty Rhodes bought the '32 from an insurance agent who brought it up from California. It was orange when Rhodes bought it, but it is seen here after Art Santa Rosa painted it red. Brannon bought his car while it was parked at Kelly's gas station on Northwest Boulevard. It was powered by a flathead when he owned it. (Bob Adams.)

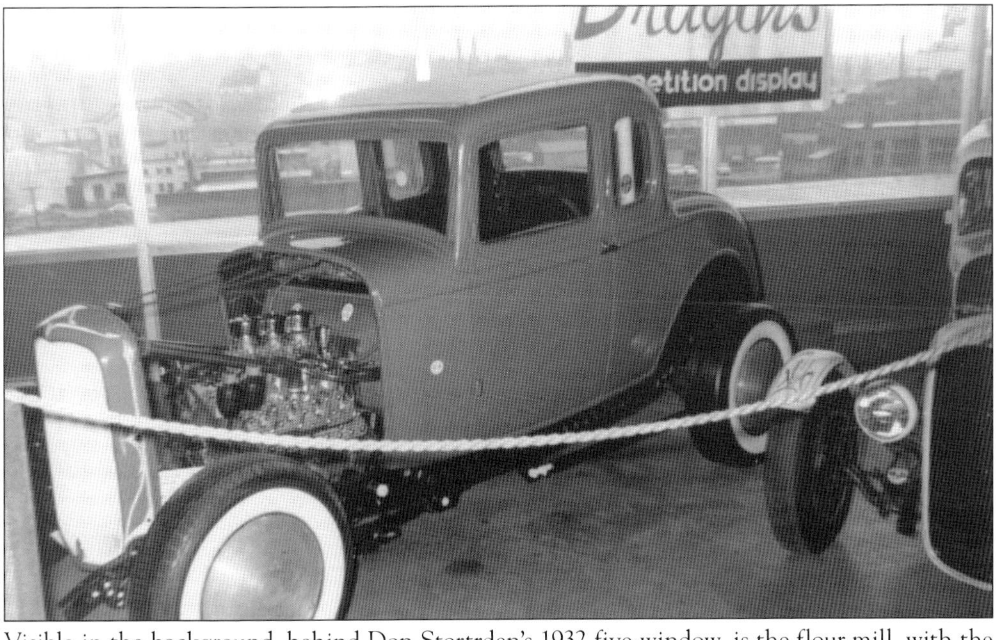

Visible in the background, behind Don Stortrden's 1932 five-window, is the flour mill, with the grain towers still standing. Jim Tipke did the hole saw work on the frame, and Don Audel painted the body light blue. Don Murock later turned the deuce into a stock car, and it was wrecked during a race. (Bob Adams.)

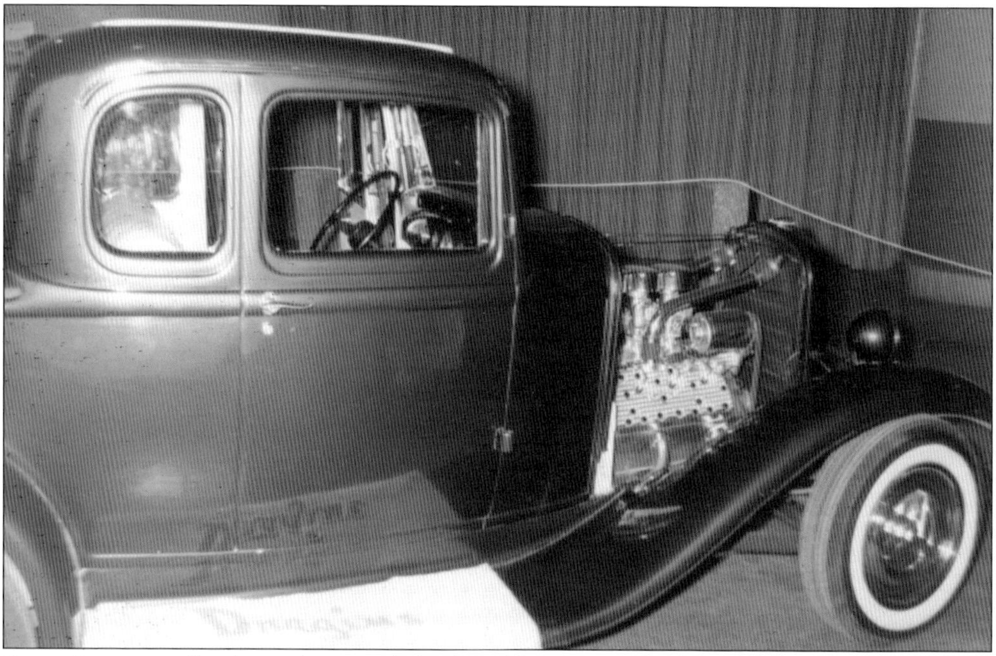

Roger Domini, still in his early teens, helped Buddy Brannon detail the flathead for the show by painting the bases of the 97s gold. The gauges in the dash are a full set of winged Stewart Warner, and the steering wheel is from a 1940 Ford. The outside of the body is Tahitian red. The edge of the white firewall can just be seen. (Bob Adams.)

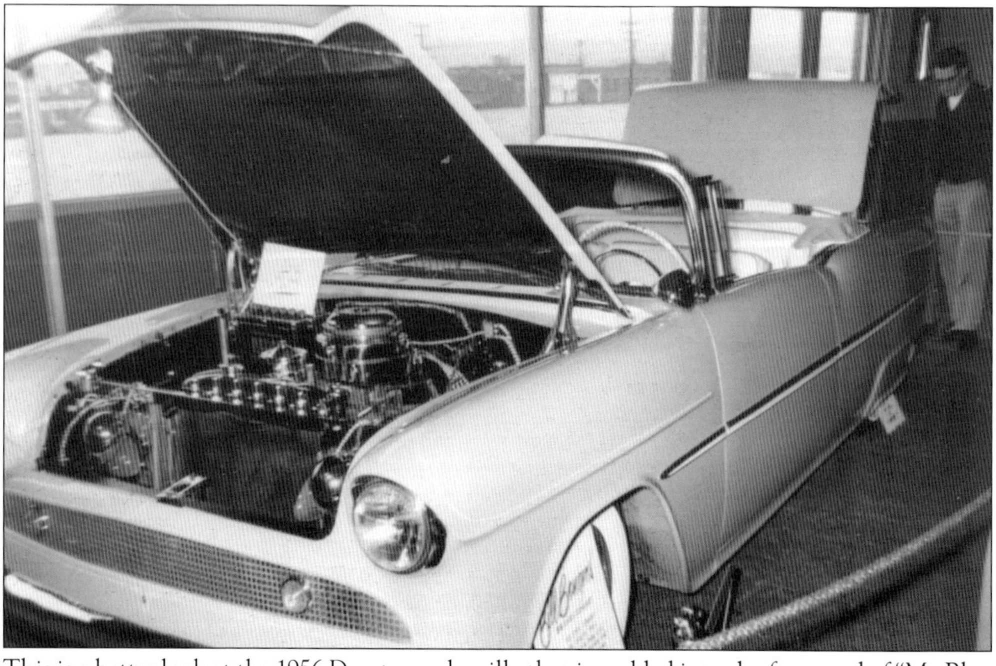

This is a better look at the 1956 Desoto mesh grille that is molded into the front end of "My Blue Heaven." Another piece of '55 Chevy quarter panel was flipped around with the point forward, to make the door and fender trim. Bill Bongers chrome-plated plenty of parts under the hood, too, from the air cleaner to the hood hinges and horns. (Bob Adams.)

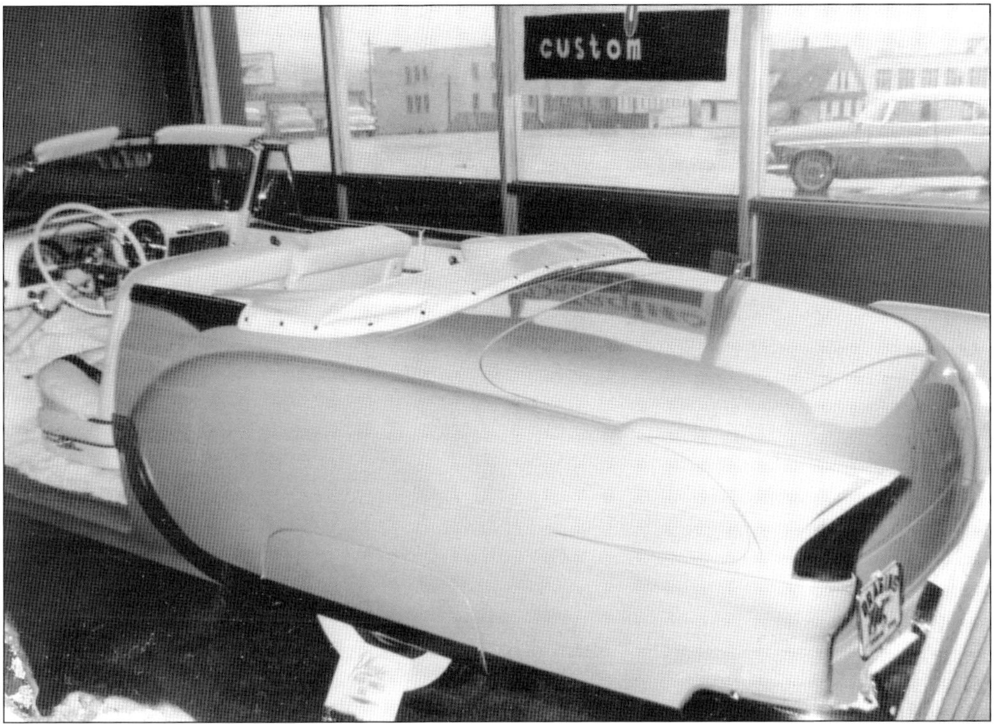

Before becoming a drag-race club, the Dragins were known for their customs. This is Don Stockman's "Orchid Lady" in the Dragins custom display. Inland Auto Upholstery did the white-on-white interior in the 1954 Pontiac convertible. The bump on the top of the Pontiac quarters was reshaped to accept the Chrysler taillight, and the deck lid has been shaved of all the stock trim. (Bob Adams.)

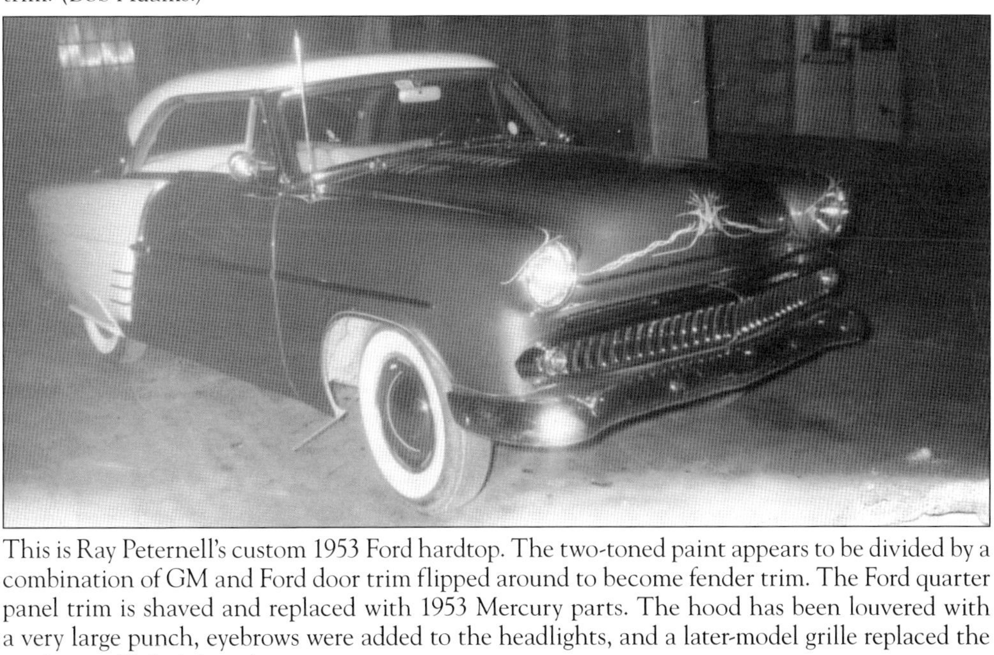

This is Ray Peternell's custom 1953 Ford hardtop. The two-toned paint appears to be divided by a combination of GM and Ford door trim flipped around to become fender trim. The Ford quarter panel trim is shaved and replaced with 1953 Mercury parts. The hood has been louvered with a very large punch, eyebrows were added to the headlights, and a later-model grille replaced the stock one. (Bob Adams.)

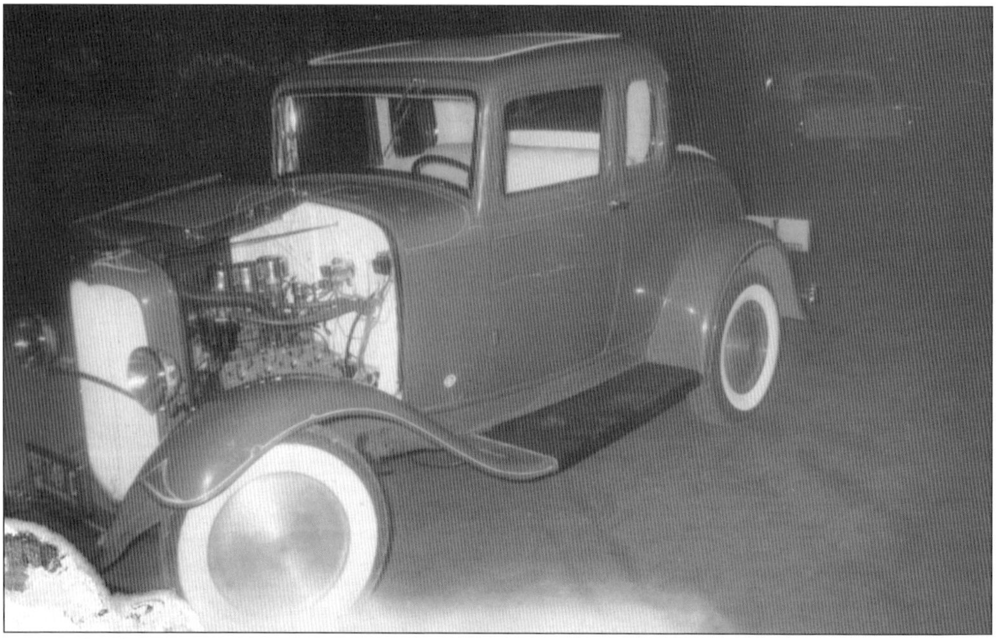

Dusty Rhodes's 1932 Ford five-window is still painted orange from when it came up from California. In Spokane, Larry Phelps added the pinstriping. The '46 Ford hubcaps were replaced with moon discs. This picture was taken before the running-board covers were added. This is the car that would later evolve into "Lil' Stinker" and end up on the cover of *Hot Rod* in June 2012. In the background is Bill Bongers's "My Blue Heaven," also a *Hot Rod* cover car. (Bob Adams.)

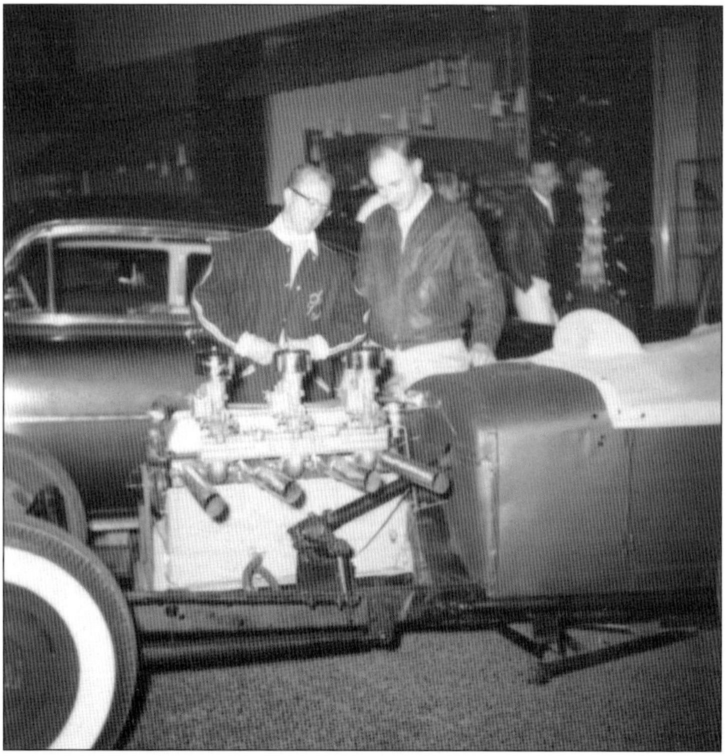

Carl Toombs and Dick Morphy look at Morphy's GMC-powered 1927 Ford. The T is still in black primer here, but it would later be painted bright white. Both men were members of the Dukes Auto Club. They were part of a show that was sponsored by the Orpheum Theatre, located at 118 North Howard Street. (Larry Taylor.)

Also at the Orpheum show was Darrel Pringle's 1940 Chevy coupe. Pringle worked at the GMC dealer. The car was painted in the back of a Scollard's Cleaners by fellow Dukes member Don Audel. The letter "E" on the coupe's license plate stands for Yakima County. (Larry Taylor.)

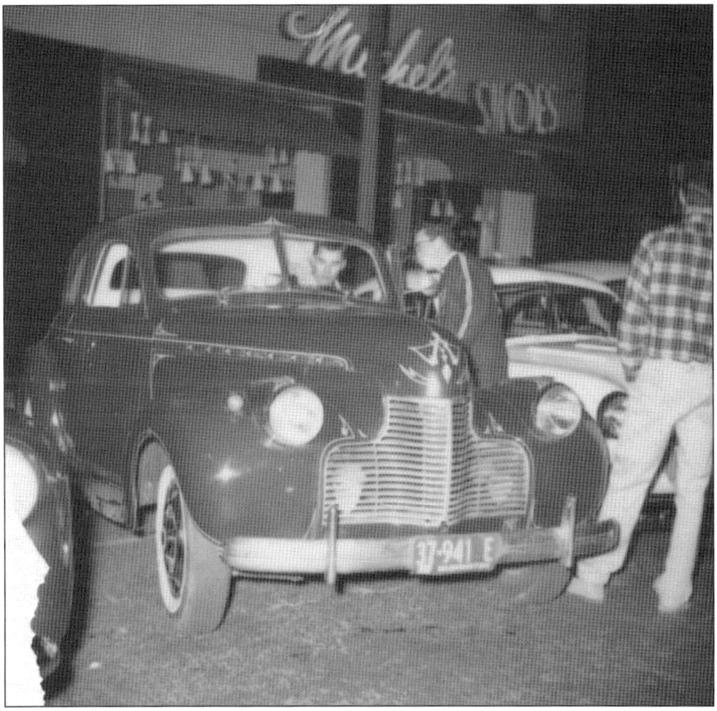

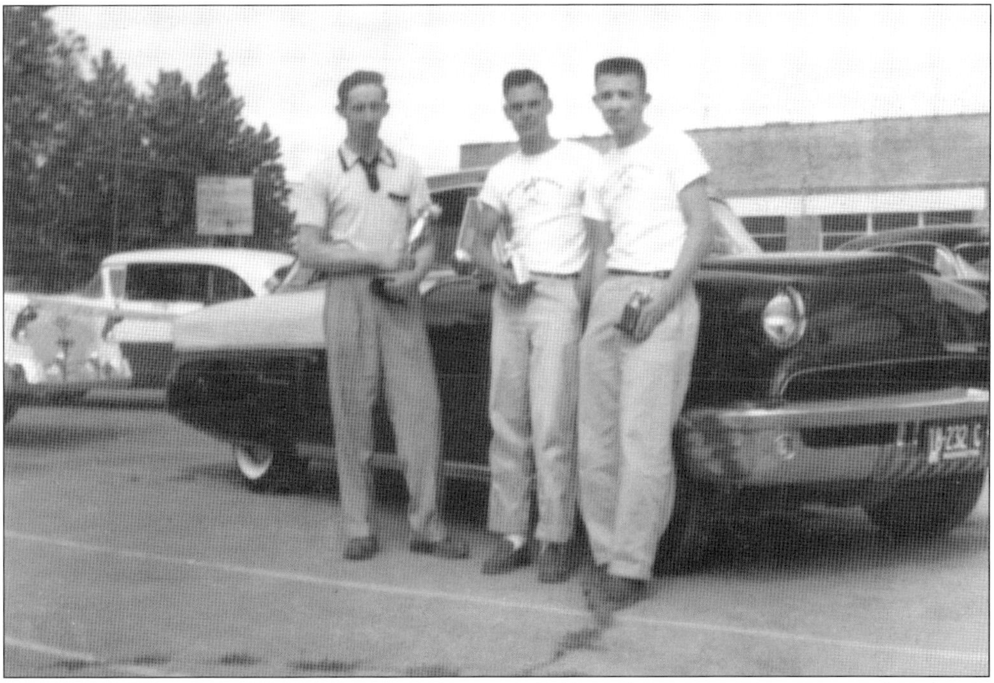

The first annual Lincoln County Auto Show was held outdoors, on Davenport High School's tennis courts. The Road Knights of Davenport promoted the show, and clubs like the Dragins drove out from Spokane to participate. Pictured here from left to right are Jack Iverson, Lyle Henderson, and Don Wilbur. They are posing in front of Iverson's 1952 Mercury, which took first place. (Don Wilbur.)

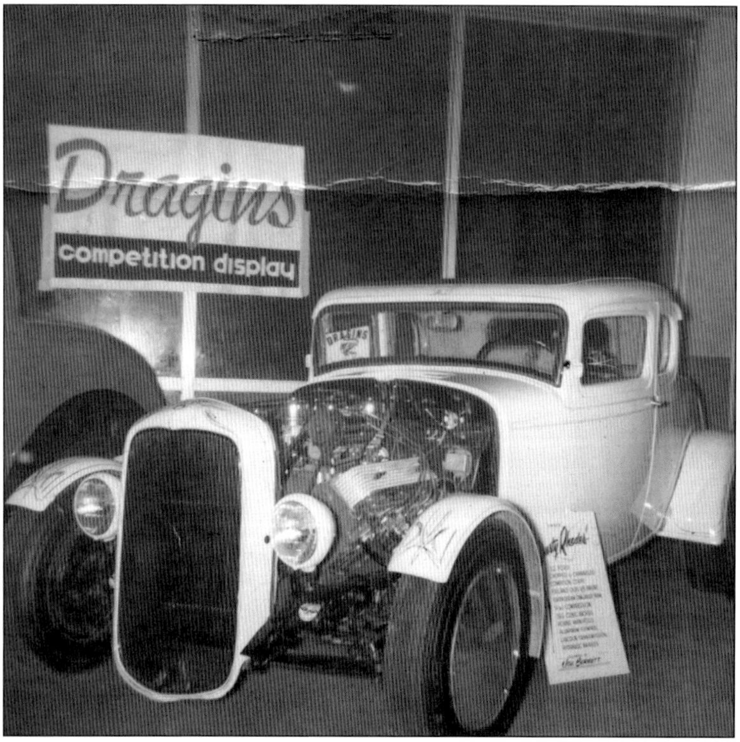

Dragins member Dusty Rhodes chopped and channeled the 1932 Ford five-window, seen here upstairs at the coliseum. This is the same bright-yellow coupe later owned by Jack Henderson and Don Zundel. When Rhodes owned the deuce, it was powered by a 355 Oldsmobile with a Horne manifold and Lincoln transmission. (Larry Taylor.)

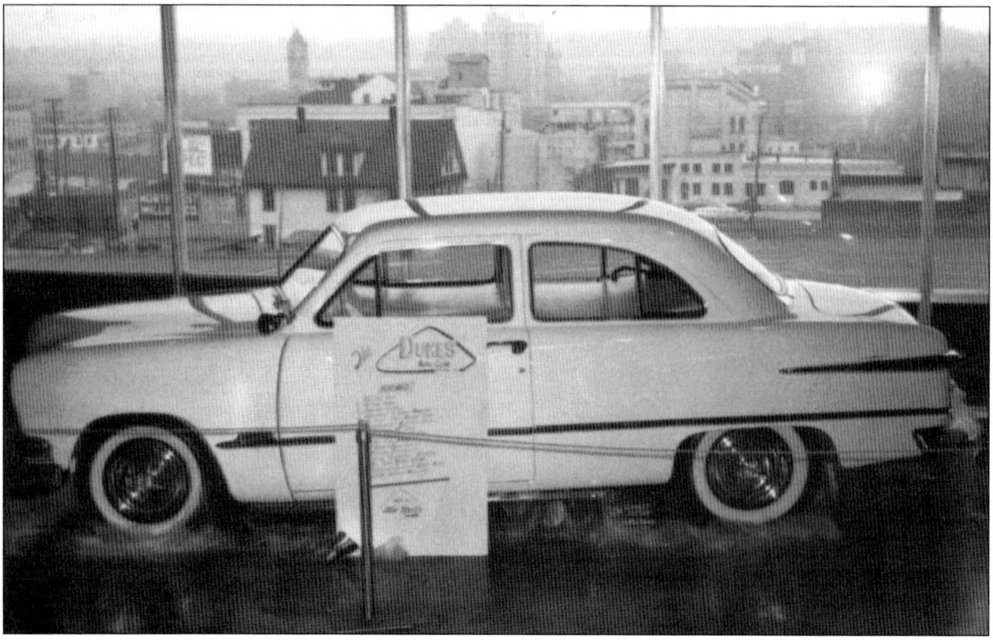

Downtown Spokane is seen behind Dukes member Dan Martin's Oldsmobile-powered 1950 Ford sedan. The exterior on the shoebox is basically stock, with 51 trim strips on the quarters and lancer hubcaps. The interior is still in progress, so it was blanked out for the show. Don Audel painted the car bright white in the back of Scollard's cleaners. (Dan Martin.)

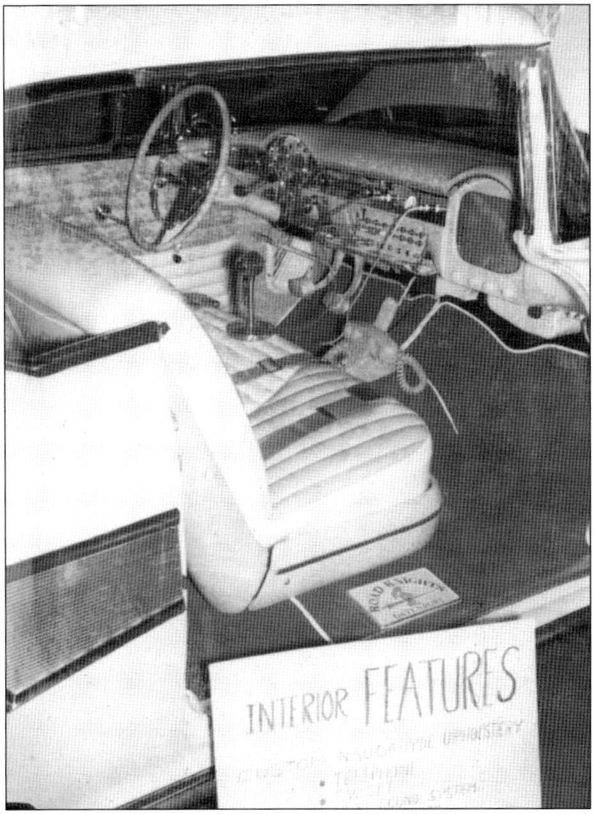

"Miss Elegance" is a 1955 Chevy hardtop built by Road Knights member Paul Savelesky. The interior featured a television, telephone, microphone, and switch for everything in the car. Savelesky's hardtop was powered by a Buick nailhead, with three carbs and a fully upholstered engine compartment. The Chevy was featured in *Rod & Custom* in May 1960 and in numerous other magazines in the early 1960s. (Don Wilbur.)

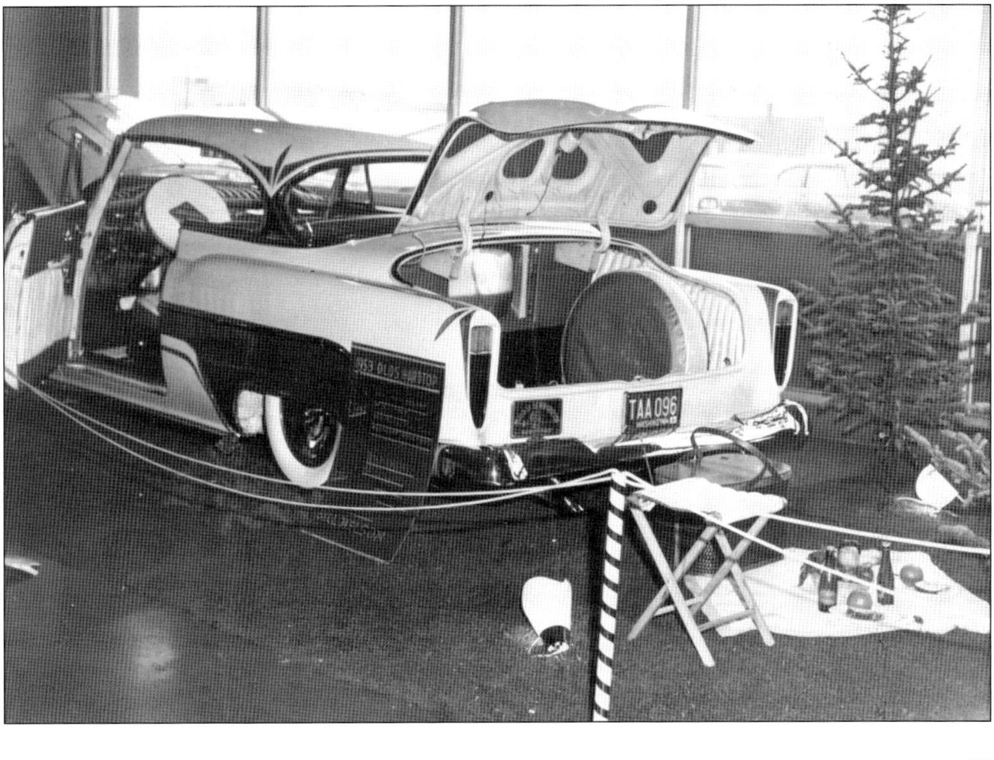

Bill Nelson, another member of the Road Knights, showed his 1953 Oldsmobile hardtop, named the "Picnic," side by side with Paul Savelesky's Chevy. They stayed away from competing with each other by making sure one was in the radical custom class and one was in the full custom class. Lary Phelps painted the car in a gas station on North Monroe Street, and Boots laid out the scallops. (Don Wilbur.)

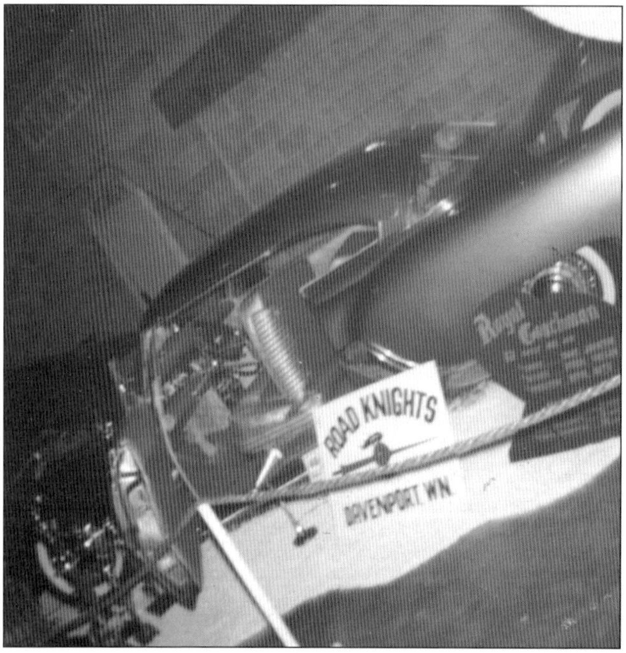

The "Royal Coachman" was Dave Johnson's 1954 Pontiac full custom, built by Virgil Hagger in Reardon, Washington. The car was painted purple, with gold interior done by Royal Upholstery on Sprague Avenue. It was both chopped and channeled, but the quarters were left at the stock height. Canted quad headlights, cad scoops on the roof, and Chrysler wire wheel also made the custom stand out. Dave's Pontiac graced the pages of *Car Craft* and became a show winner throughout the Northwest. (Don Wilbur.)

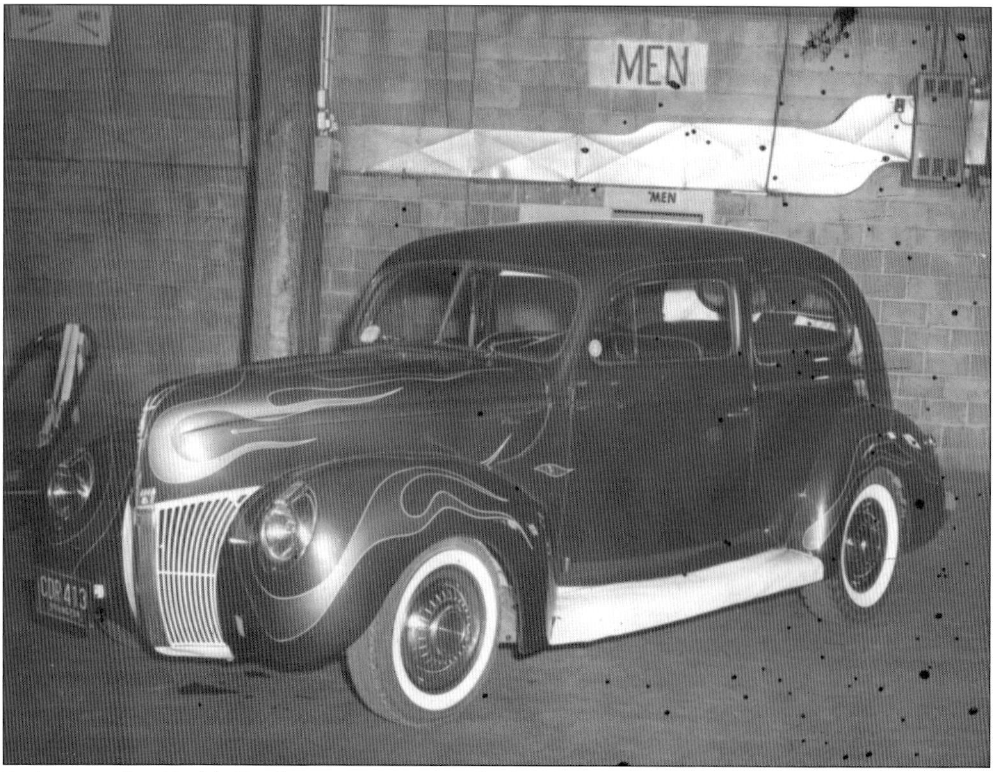

Dukes member Buddy Wickstrom's 1940 standard sedan was painted Plymouth dusty plumb by Art Santa Rosa. The car was powered by an Oldsmobile and backed by an early Ford transmission. The flames were painted a lilac color and striped in white by Don Audel; this was the first of many flame jobs he would do in Spokane. (Don Audel.)

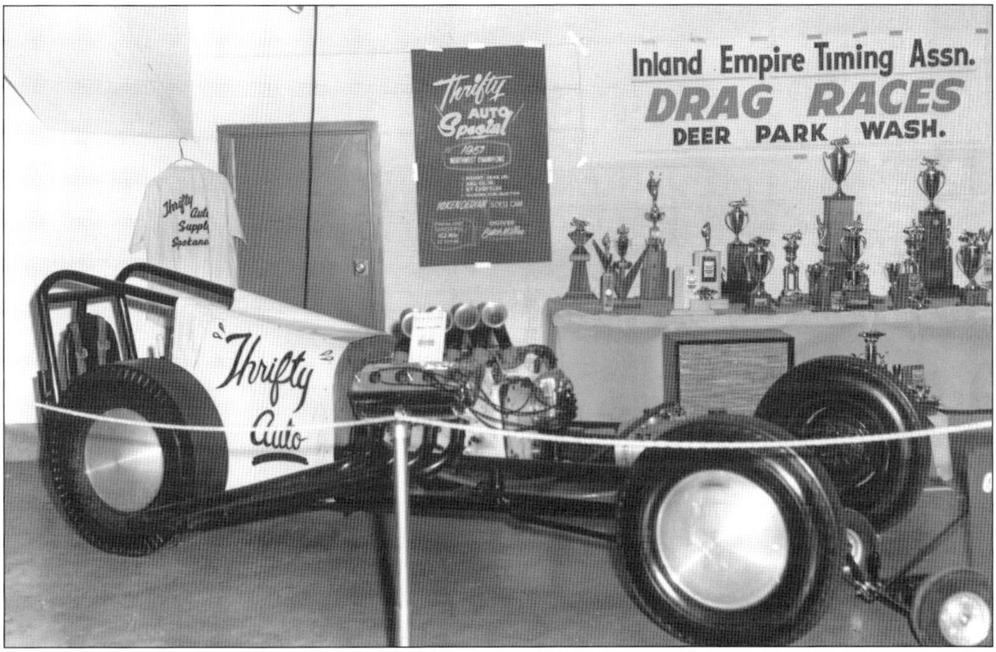

This is the third Thrifty Auto Special. It was the 1957 Northwest champion with Butch Miller driving. The motor was Dick Flynn's 1957 Chrysler 392 with a Harmon and Collins magneto and Howard Cams timing cover. The fuel-injection setup is Hilborn. The car weighed 1,445 pounds and ran at a top speed of 152 miles per hour. Don Audel painted and lettered the body. (Butch Miller.)

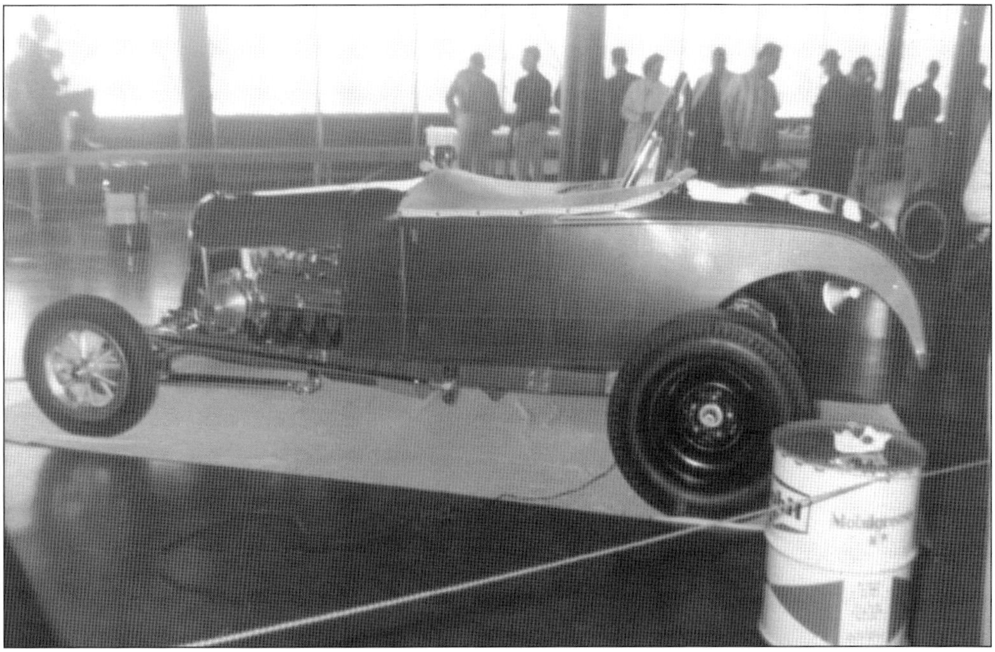

John Langlot's metallic-blue, 1928 Model A altered is seen upstairs in the Spokane Coliseum. Built on a model A frame, the roadster was hemi-powered and had the body pushed way back. It is clear how nice this car was in 1958, and Langlot spared nothing in the detail work. From the chrome grille shell to the overall stance of the car, everything was beautiful. (Frank Moyer.)

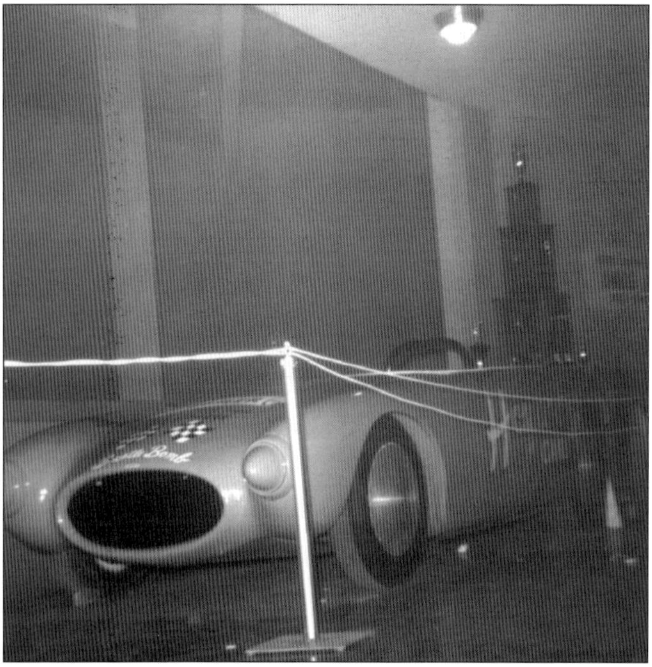

The "Bustle Bomb" is seen here just after Lloyd Scott moved back to Spokane from Long Beach, where the car set multiple records, including the first car to go 150 miles per hour in the quarter mile. It was powered by an Oldsmobile motor in the front and a Cadillac motor in the rear. On the nose is part of the artwork from California, along with the lettering for Scott's new business, Magic Muffler on Sprague Avenue. He would partner with Orville Moe, who supplied the motors when it was raced in the Northwest. (Bob Coutts.)

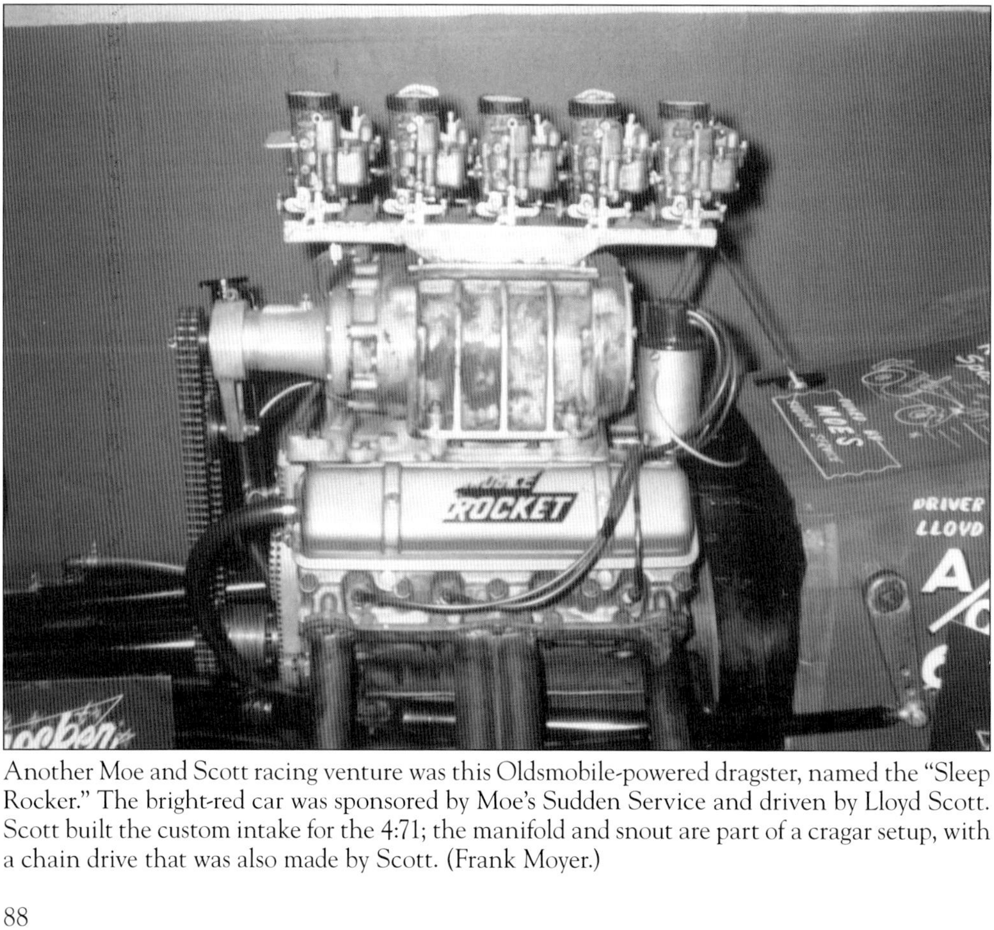

Another Moe and Scott racing venture was this Oldsmobile-powered dragster, named the "Sleep Rocker." The bright-red car was sponsored by Moe's Sudden Service and driven by Lloyd Scott. Scott built the custom intake for the 4:71; the manifold and snout are part of a cragar setup, with a chain drive that was also made by Scott. (Frank Moyer.)

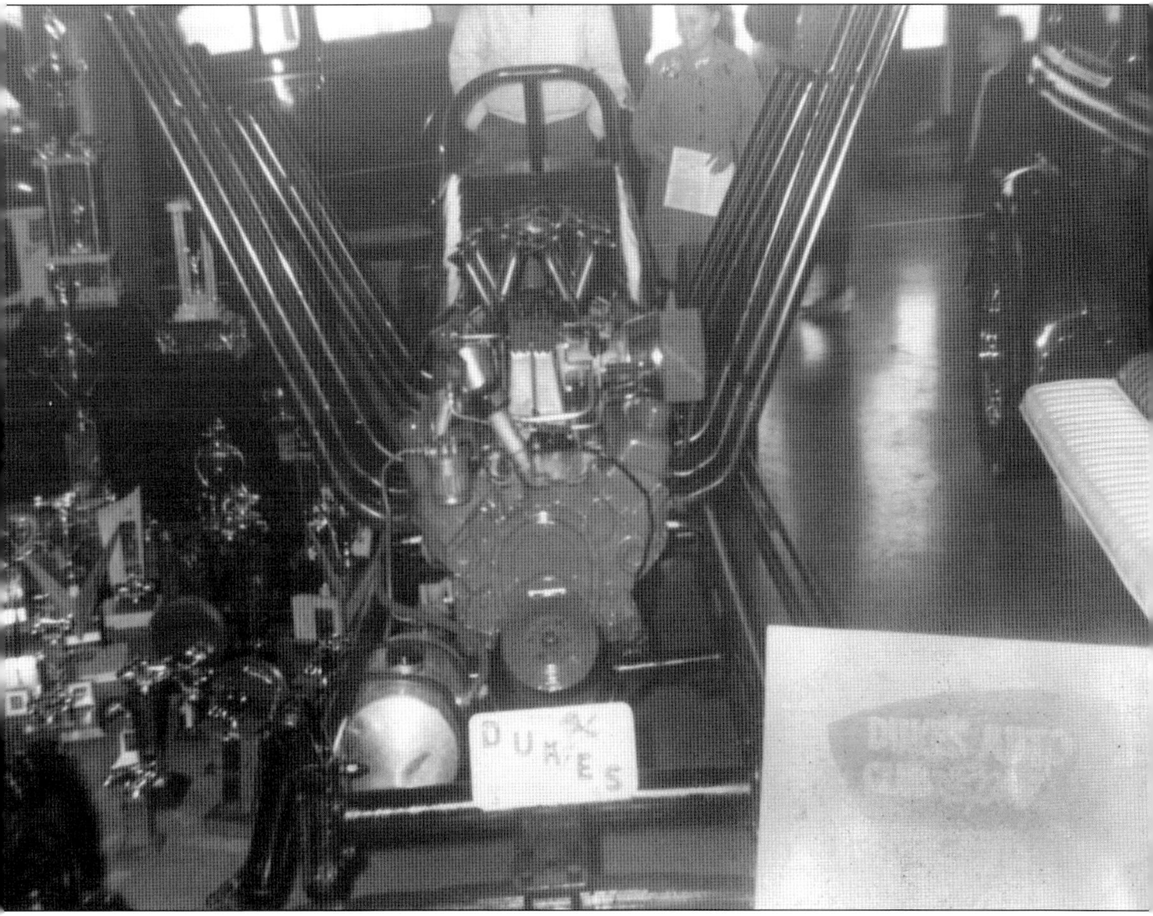

Earl Wham's twin-engine dragster, sponsored by the Dukes Auto Club, at first glance appears to have some of the craziest headers on any dragster. But, considering Wham's background in hydroplane racing and the fact that he used what he had on hand, the headers make sense. He drove the dragster, built in Dick Morphy's garage, along with Kenny Brinkman, Jim Tipkie, and Lee Sherman. The rear engine with the Hilborn fuel injection setup was out of Wham's hydroplane, and the front motor is out of Sherman's everyday driver, a 1957 Chevy convert with factory fuel injection. They would pull the motor out of the Chevy on Friday and install it into the dragster so that they could race all weekend. Then, on Sunday night, they would put the motor back in the Chevy so Lee could drive it to school. (Frank Moyer.)

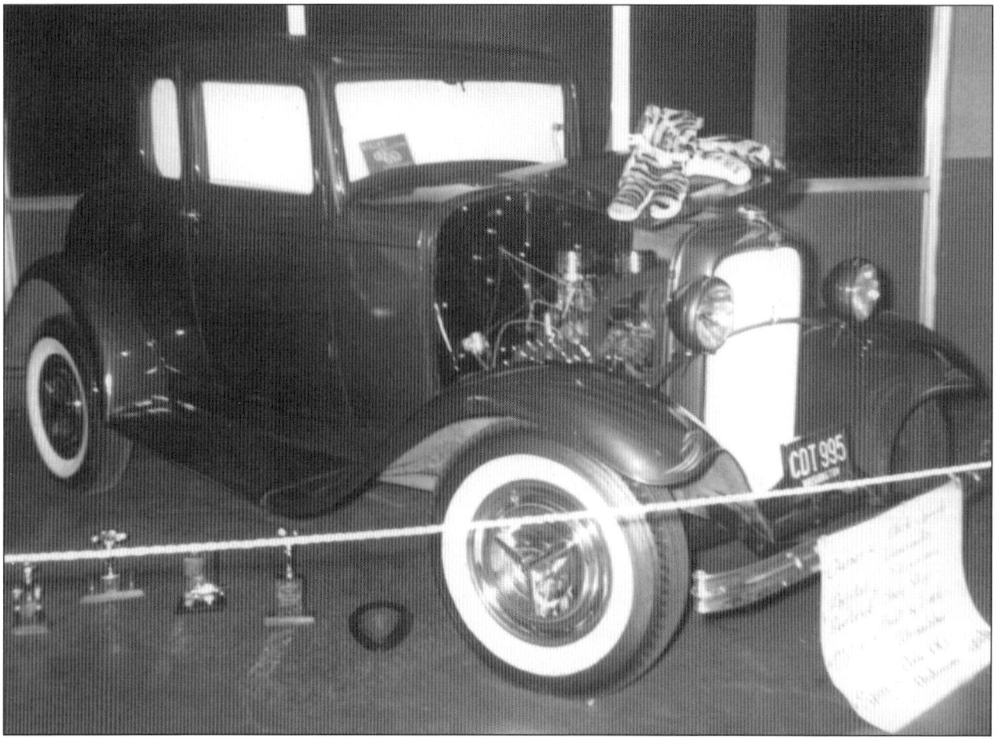

One of the surprises the author experienced while working on this book was this photograph of the 1932 five-window owned by his dad, Richard "Speedy" Gunsaulis. The author had never seen this car before Frank Moyer handed him the photograph. The text on the club plaque on the front windshield is not legible, except for the word "valley;" the show sign is similarly unclear. The interior is obviously not finished, as the windows are blanked out. (Frank Moyer.)

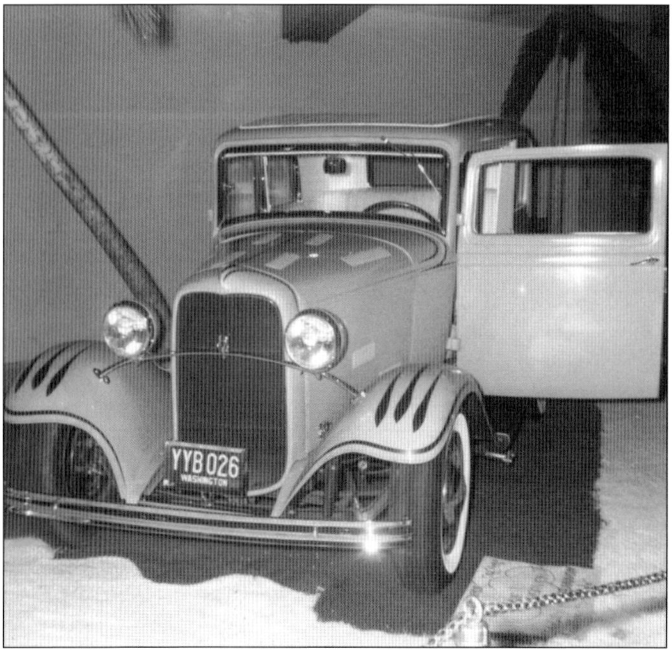

"My Blue Heaven 2" is seen here, when the 1932 Vicky was owned by Bill Bongers, who sold it to Don Wilbur. Buddy Brannon did the upholstery, and the scallops were laid out by Boots. There is a photograph of the Vic in *Hot Rod* magazine in January 1961, when the Road Knights were the club of the month. At that point, it was owned by Don Wilbur, who plated everything on the suspension. Wilbur pulled the car apart to paint it silver and decided to sell it to "Speedy" Gunsaulis, who put it back together and showed it all over the Northwest. (Frank Moyer.)

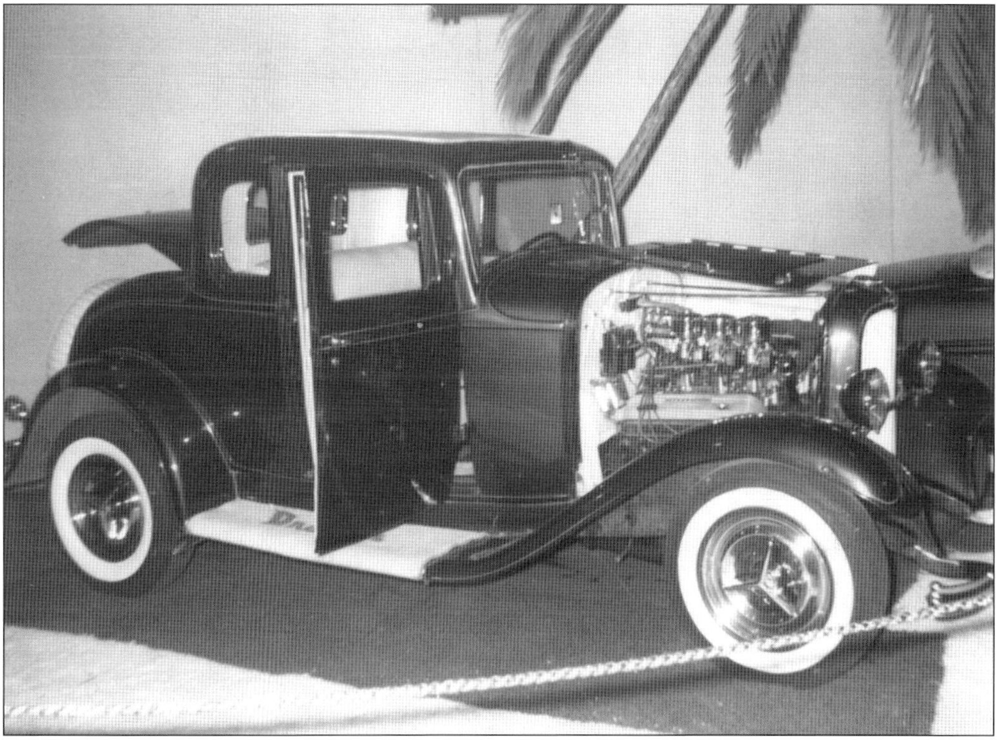

"Lil' Stinker" was featured in *Rod & Custom* in November 1957, when it was owned by Ray Peternell. This photograph was taken in 1958, when the motor was switched from the flathead to an Oldsmobile overhead. Peternell owned the car for over 40 years before it took a path to Canada, then to Jez Hoye in England, who fully restored the car. It then went back to Canada. *Hop Up* magazine did a full feature on the coupe after Hoye restored it. (Frank Moyer.)

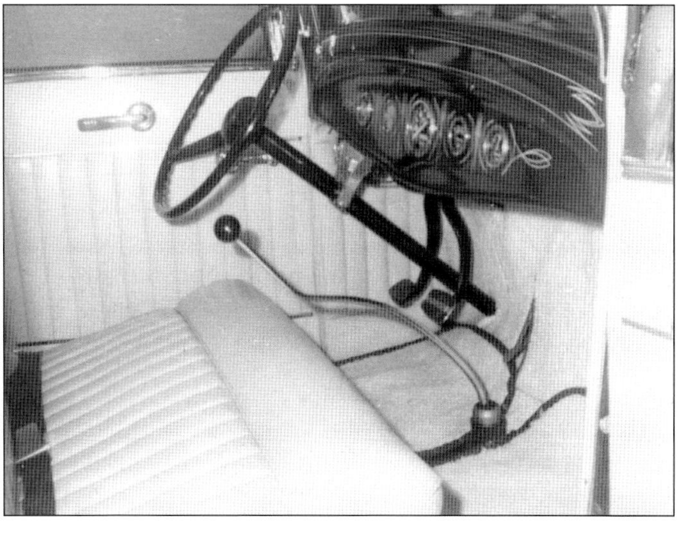

The interior of "Lil' Stinker" is partially the same as it was when it came up from California, with some things added by Buddy Brannon when he was the owner. One detail that was always on the coupe is the chrome trim on the door panels. The door and handles and window cranks are out of a 1949 Mercury. When the motor was changed to an Oldsmobile, a set of hanging pedals was also installed. (Frank Moyer.)

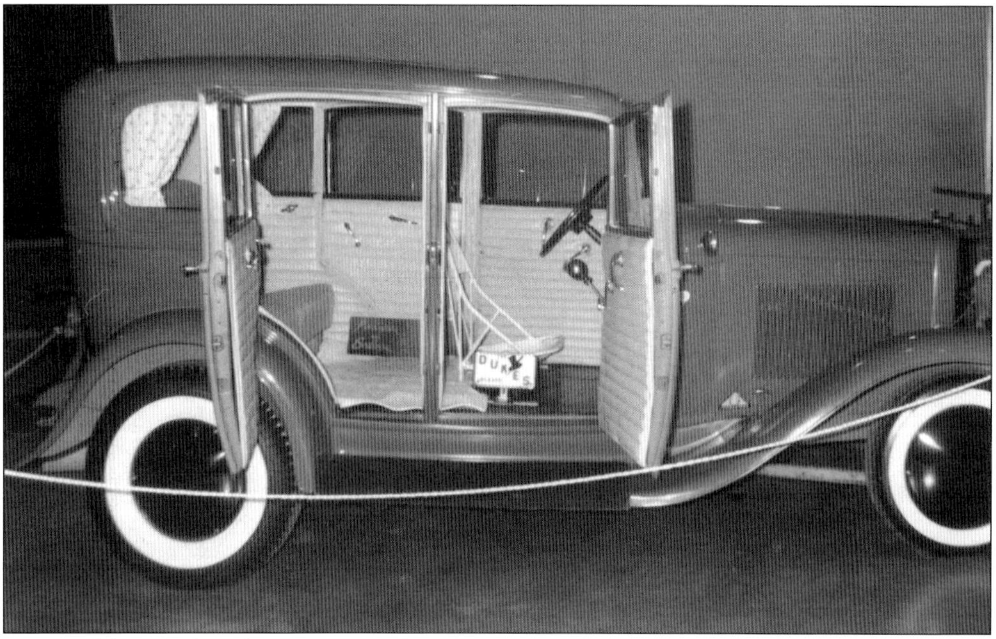

Don Audel's 1932 four-door is seen at the 1958 Spokane Coliseum show. The front seat is out of a helicopter, and Audel detailed it baby blue to match the interior. The exterior was orange with white running gear. The car was powered by a built flathead. Audel had painted a portrait of Mr. Magoo on the cowl, and the shift knob is off a brass bed. (Frank Moyer.)

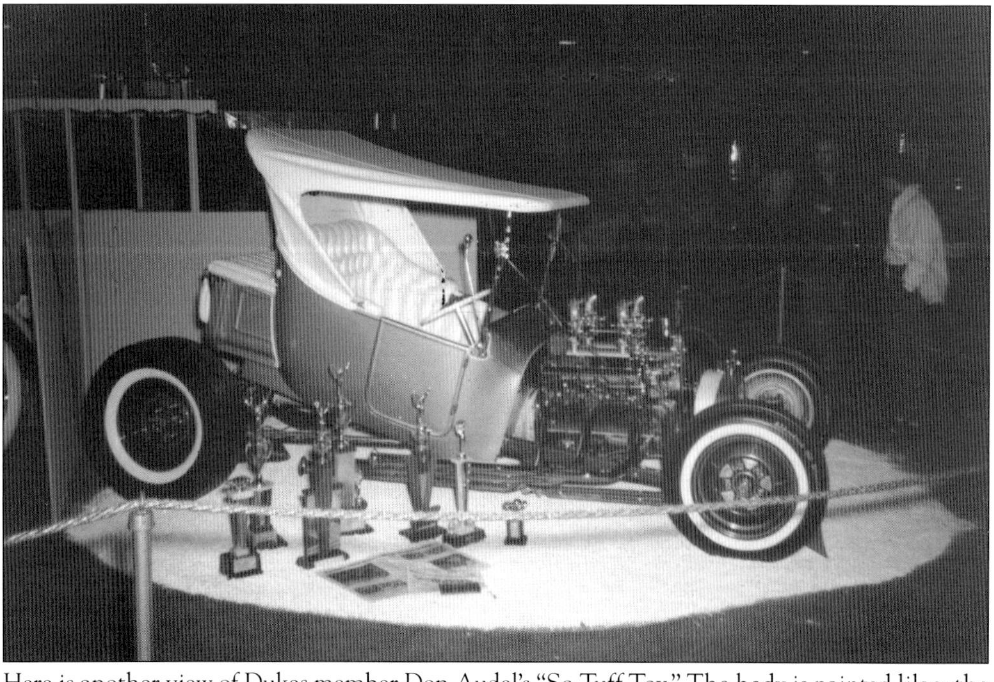

Here is another view of Dukes member Don Audel's "So Tuff Toy." The body is painted lilac; the wheels, motor, and frame are purple. Audel's Model T set a benchmark in Spokane for show cars and was featured in numerous automotive magazines, including *Car Craft* in October 1962 and *Popular Hot Rodding* in March 1964. (Richard "Speedy" Gunsaulis.)

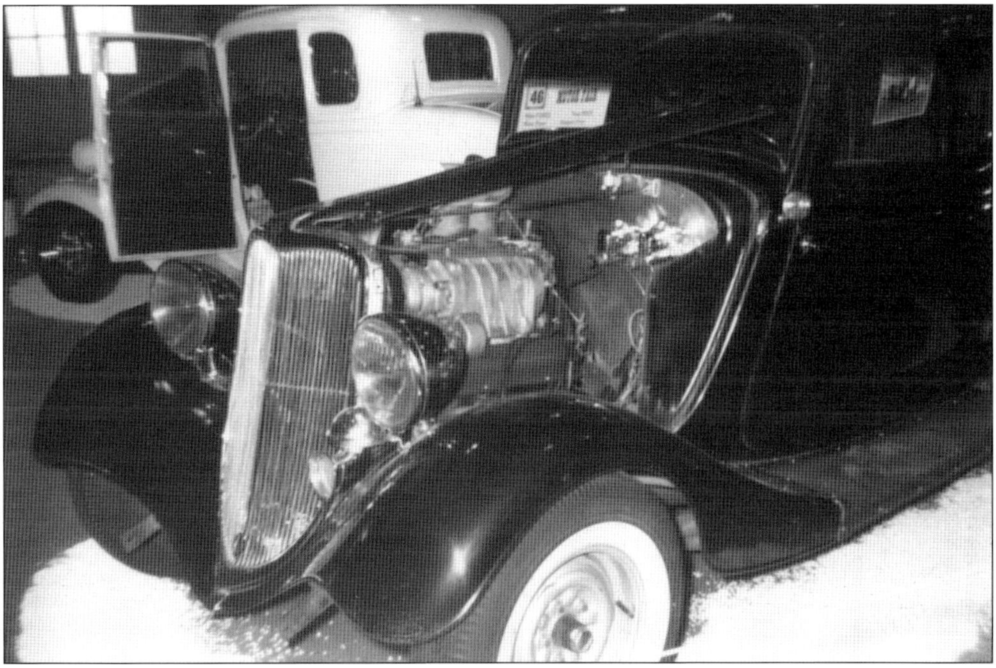

Claude Cuzzetto's 1933 Ford sedan is seen in 1958, after the Studebaker motor was pulled out (it was then put in Don Audel's Model T). The firewall has been set back in this photograph, and the frame is completely hole sawed to lighten it. A roll bar is added to the completely stock mohair interior, with parts of the dash copper plated. The motor is a blown and injected small-block Chevy backed by a four-speed transmission from a '60 Vette. The car has a Chevy rear end. In the background is Richard "Speedy" Gunsaulis's white 1932 Ford, which he sold to Tom Cunningham, who may have owned it at the time of this photograph. (Frank Moyer.)

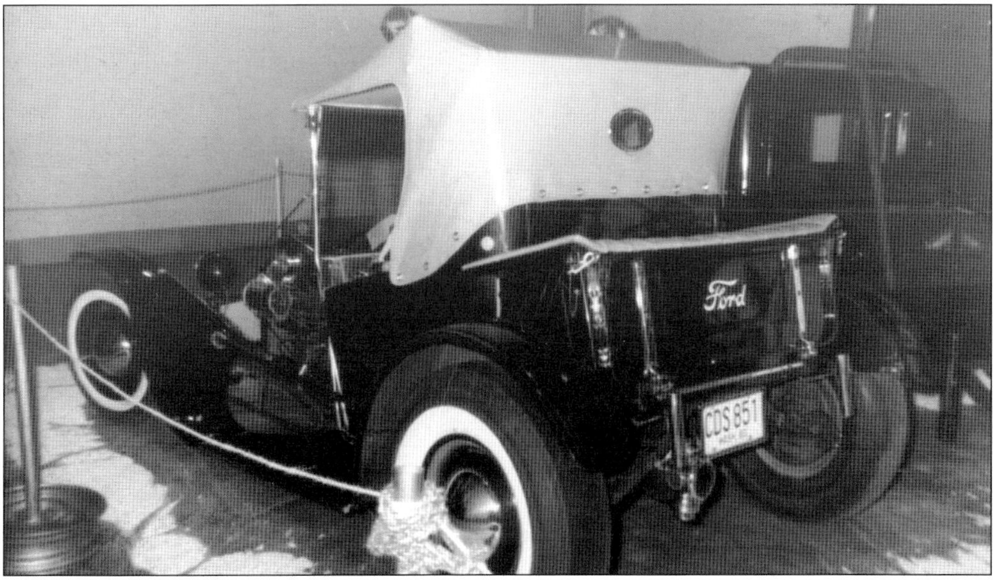

Buddy Wickstrom's Model T is sprung off a '35-'36 rear end with a Model A spring. The top was teal, and the body was blue, heavily raked on a custom tube frame. The area where the hairpin comes through the front fender was later covered with a body-colored upholstery panel. (Frank Moyer.)

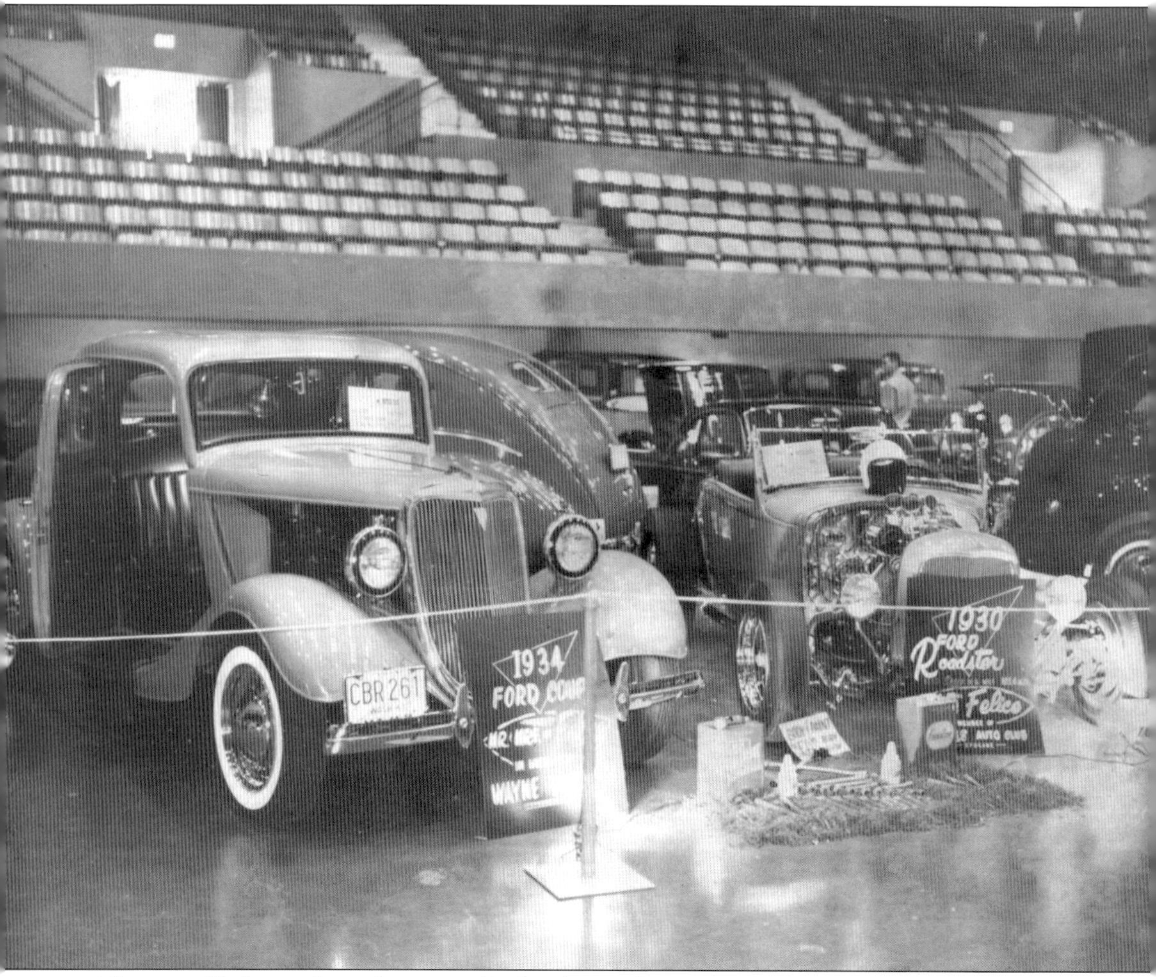

The cars of father-and-son show team Fred and Joe Felice are in the Dukes display in the Spokane Coliseum during the Motor Fair. The red '34 coupe belonged to Fred, and the Model A roadster is Joe's. Fred's car is powered by a flathead, and Joe's is run by an Olds motor, later replaced by a Chevy motor. (Richard "Speedy" Gunsaulis.)

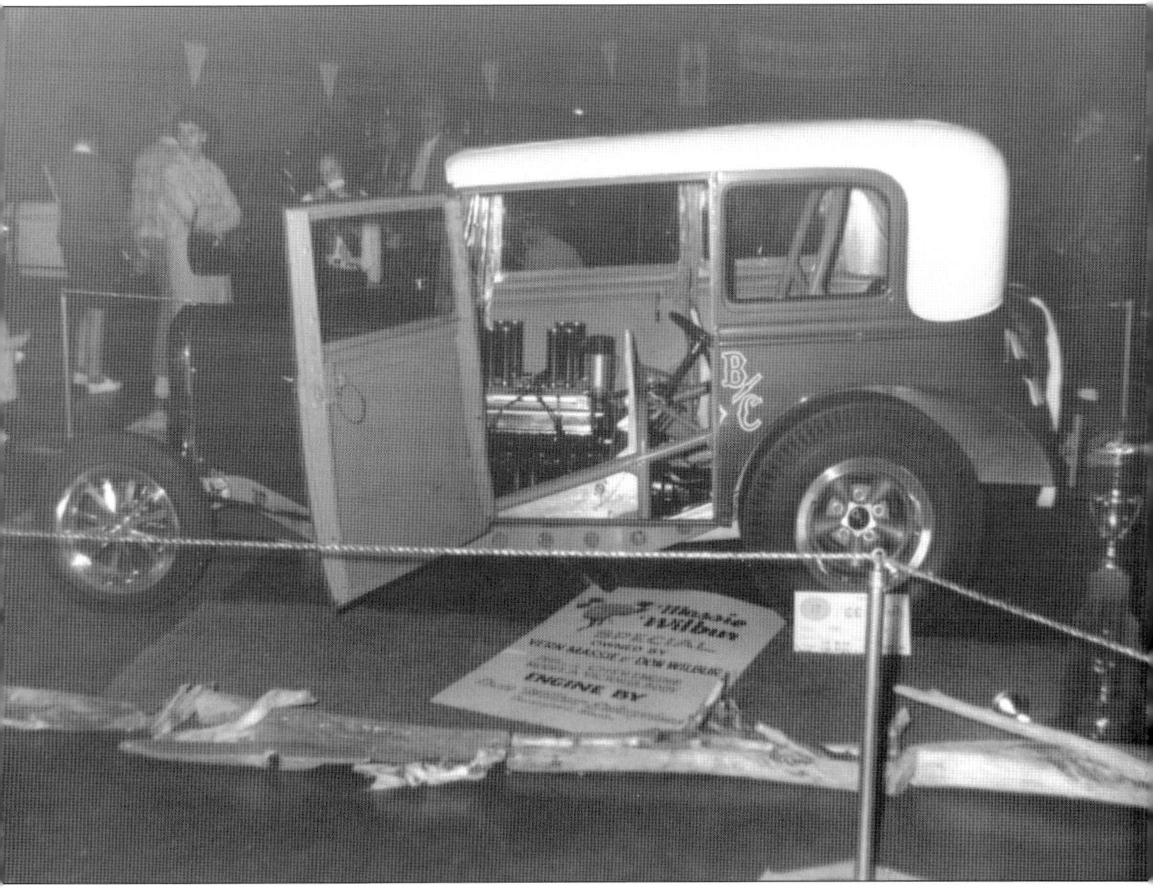

"The 300," Vern Massie and Don Wilbur's '31 Model A Victoria is seen before it evolved into "the Destroyer." The easiest way to tell the difference between the two cars is in the frame. When it was the Destroyer, the A was on a full tube frame that Massie built. In this photograph, it is the same Allstate chassis that Massie used to race with Swede Erickson, so the car is "The 300." When they parted out their car, Erickson took his motor, and Massie took his chassis. Wilbur and Massie then added the Ford body, a fuel-injected small-block Chevy, and campaigned it all over the West Coast. At one of the races on the west side of the state, the front windshield blew out; they pulled the back window out so air could pass through. When they realized the rear window was too small, they pulled it back in the pits and cut the rear window opening out to match the front one. The car was featured as "The 300" in *Popular Hot Rodding* in March 1964. (Frank Moyer.)

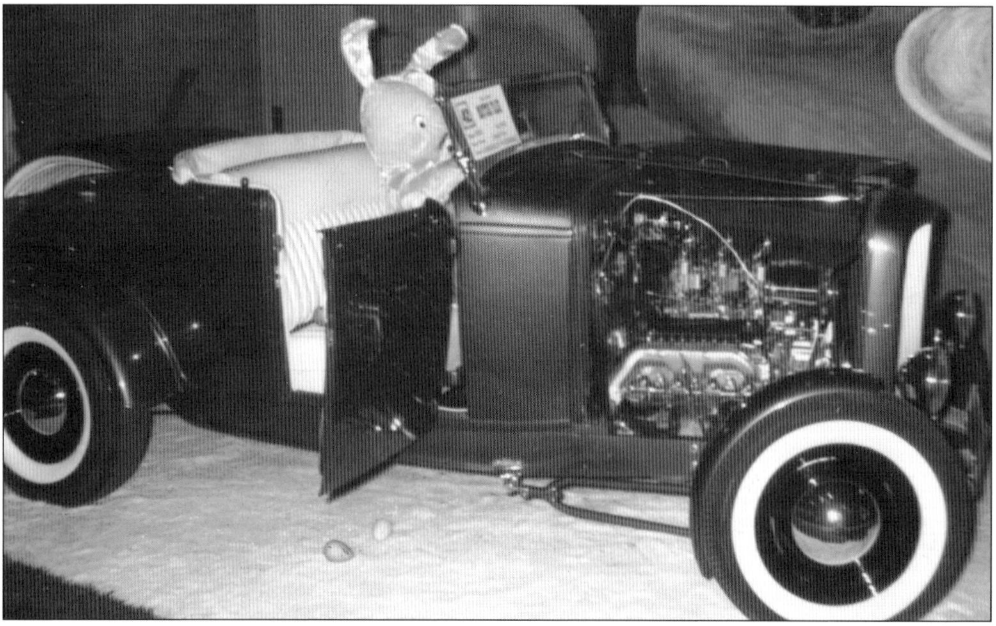

In 1962, the Motor Fair took place on Easter weekend, and Dukes member Richard "Speedy" Gunsaulis planned his show display to match the event. The '32 Ford roadster is emerald green, with a gold Ford Y block, 1939 Mercury steering, and a '33-'34 rear end. The roadster would pop up again in *Rod & Custom*'s 60th-anniversary issue in 2013, with two small pictures in the 1963 section. (Frank Moyer.)

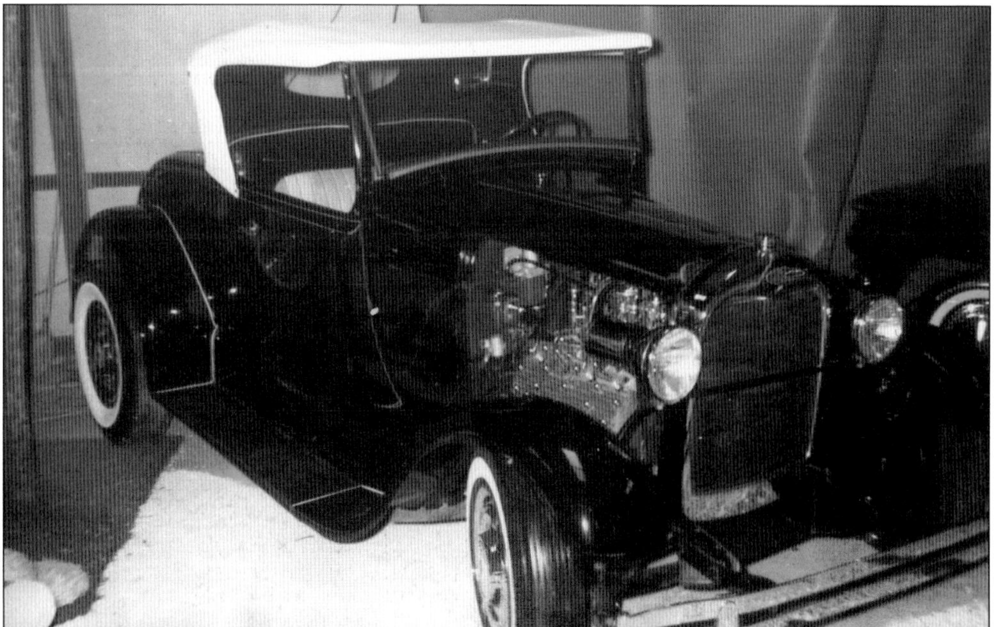

Denny Hoggie's perfect 1929 roadster is shown at the fairgrounds, at Spokane's Auto Boat Speed Show, put on by Don Wilbur and Orville Moe. Danny Martin traded his 1932 roadster for this model A that came up from the Tri-Cities. Hoggie bought the car from Martin and later changed it over to a small-block Chevy. The pinstriping was done by Don Audel. (Frank Moyer.)

Three

STRIP

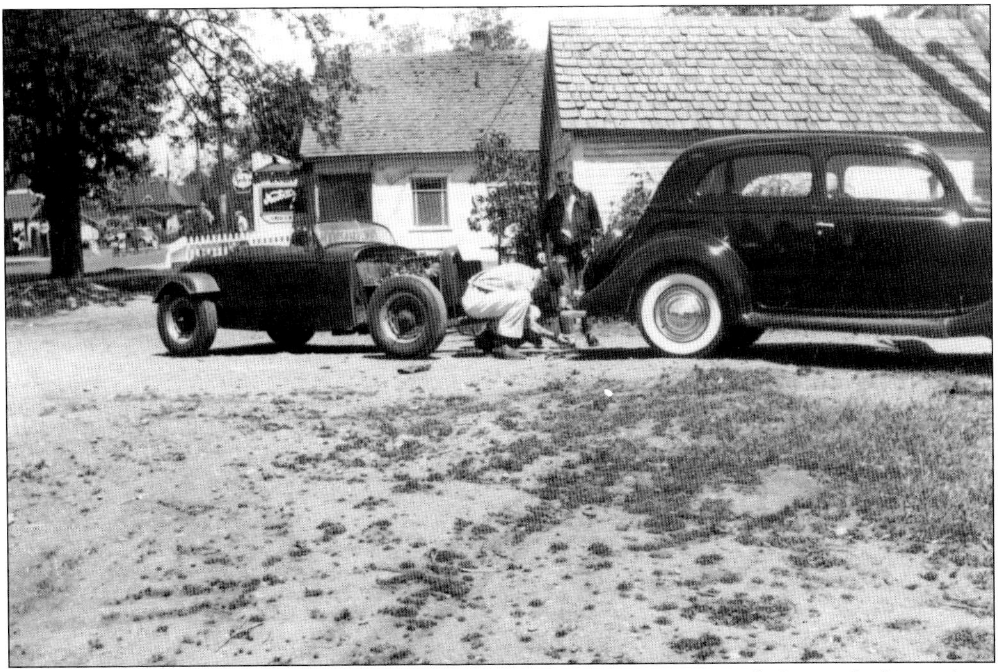

This photograph was taken beside the Hordemannn family store on Ash Street. Jack's roadster is being hitched up to brother Jim's '35 Ford for a day of racing at the Deer Park airport in 1950. This is at the beginning of organized racing in Spokane, with a 20- to 30-member group called the Spokane Roadster Racing Association. Jack's roadster was placed on the chassis of his old four-door after it was totaled. The windshield is made out of parts of a 1937 Ford windshield; a 1940 dash and column were added to the deuce. (Gary Hordemann.)

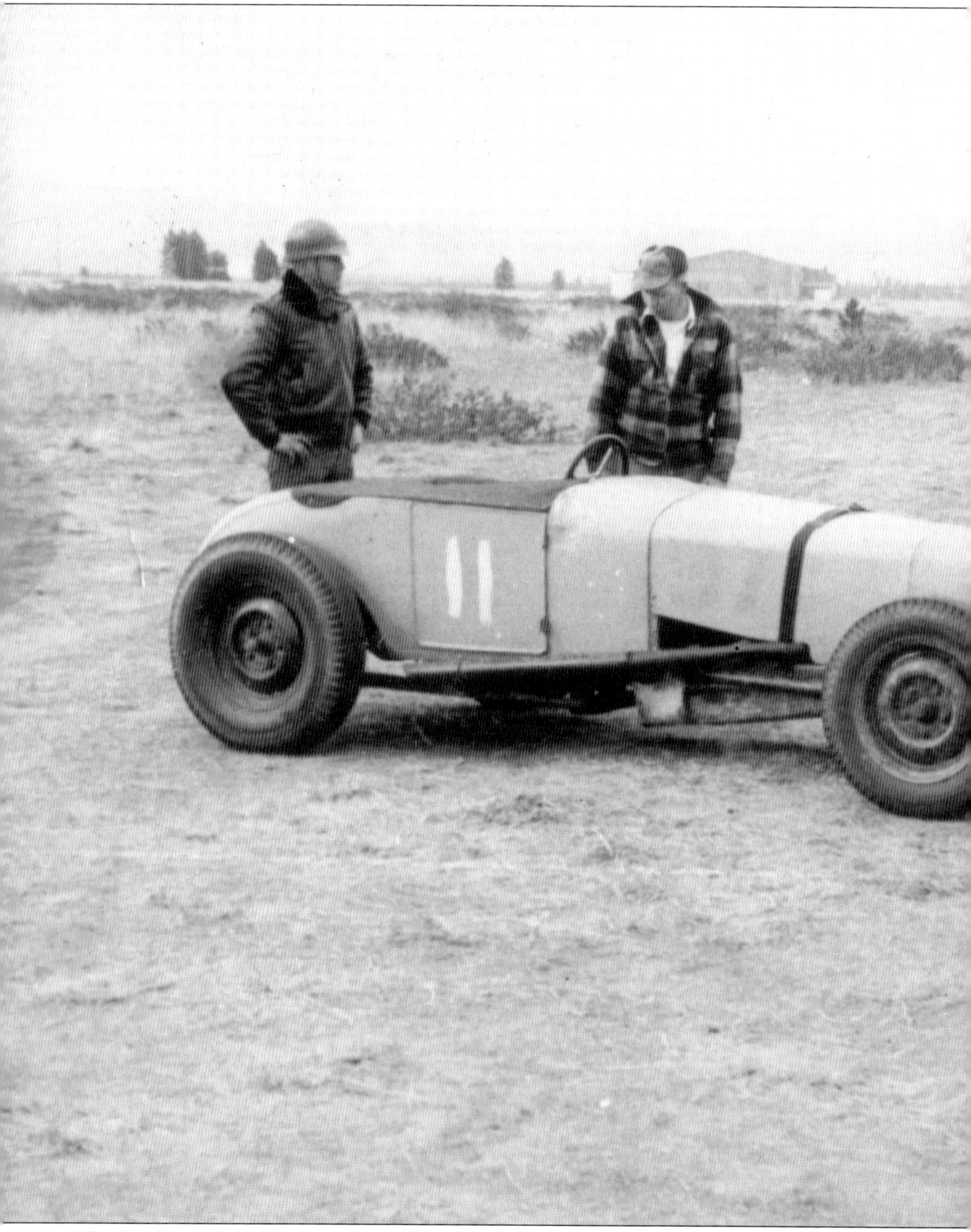

The Smith brothers of Bonner's Fairy, Idaho, raced this altered Model T roadster. This photograph was taken in May 1953. The Smiths found the car in California and brought it up to race at Deer Park. Single-purpose racecars like this were still rare in Spokane at this time, as most hot rods had

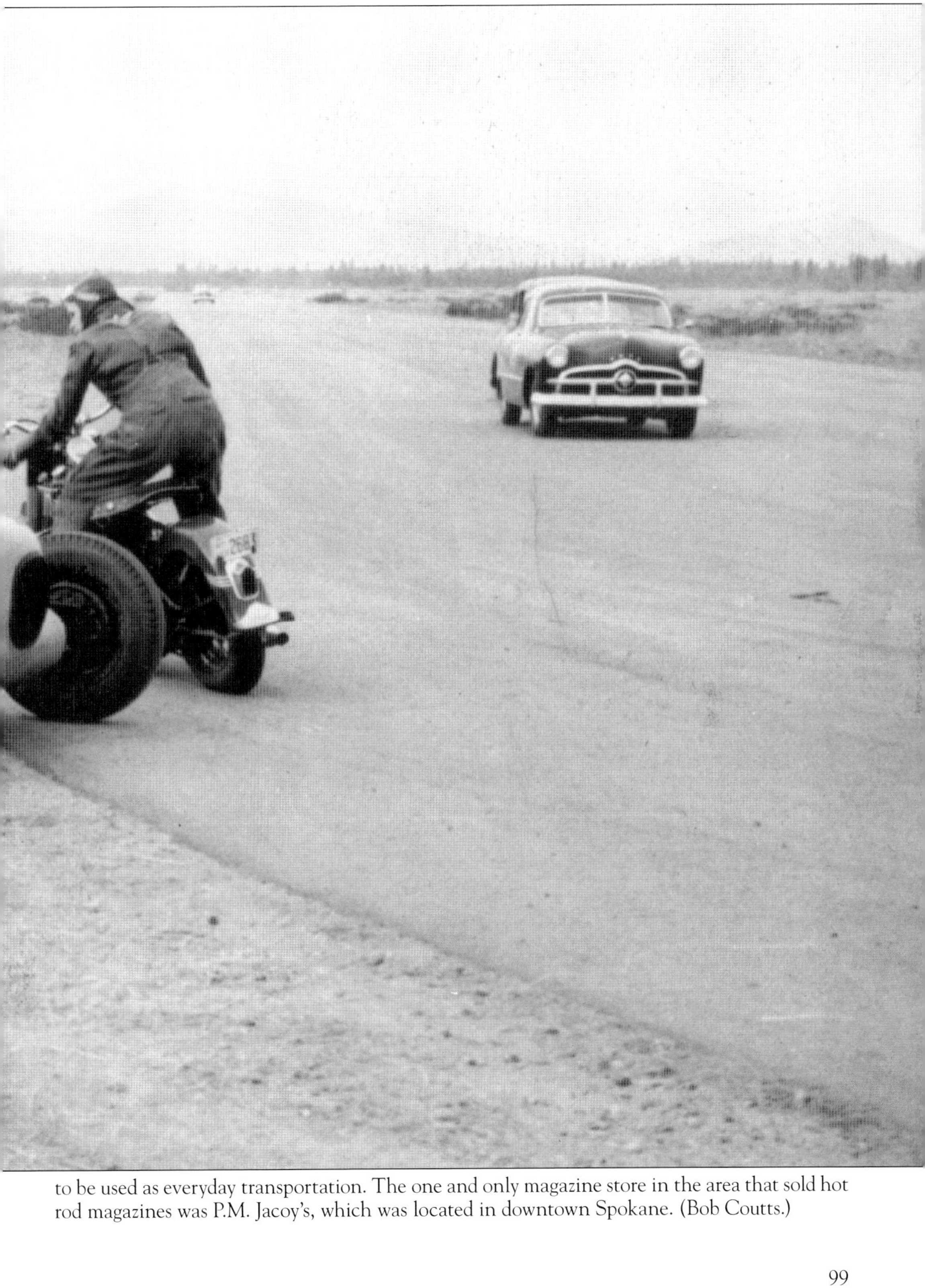

to be used as everyday transportation. The one and only magazine store in the area that sold hot rod magazines was P.M. Jacoy's, which was located in downtown Spokane. (Bob Coutts.)

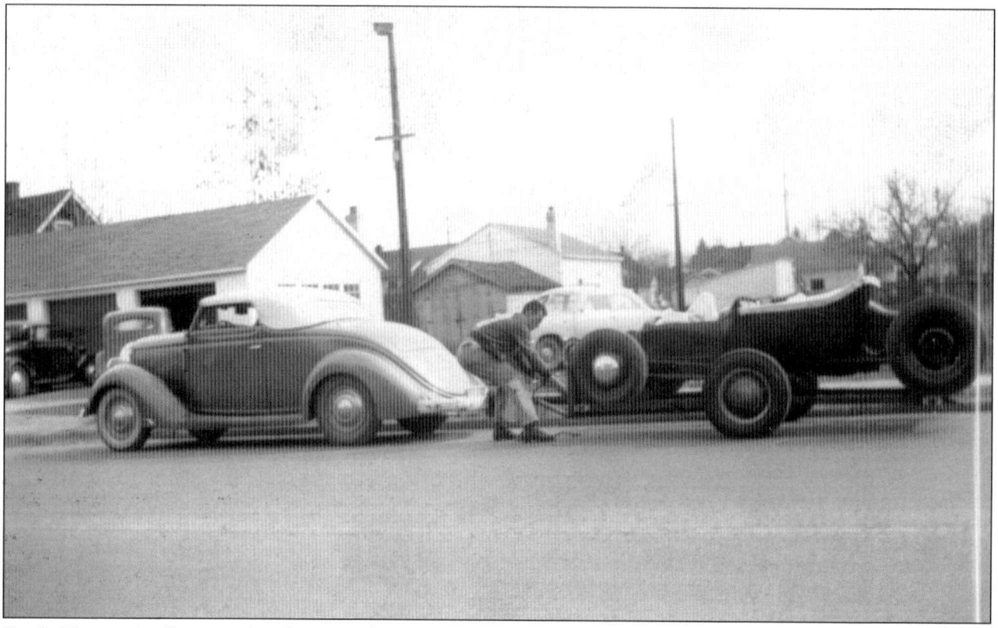

Dick Hogan had quite the show-and-go setup in the early days, although the community trailer belonged to Tim Rochlitzer. This is on Ash Street, in front of the Hordemanns' new three-stall garage, where Corky's Radiator is today. Hogan's 1936 Cabriolet was his daily driver and the tow car for his 1925 Model T racecar. In the background are Jack Hordemann's 1932 three-window (far left) and his brother Jim's '35 (second from left). The T was black primer, flathead powered, and set up on a 1934 Ford frame. (Gary Hordemann.)

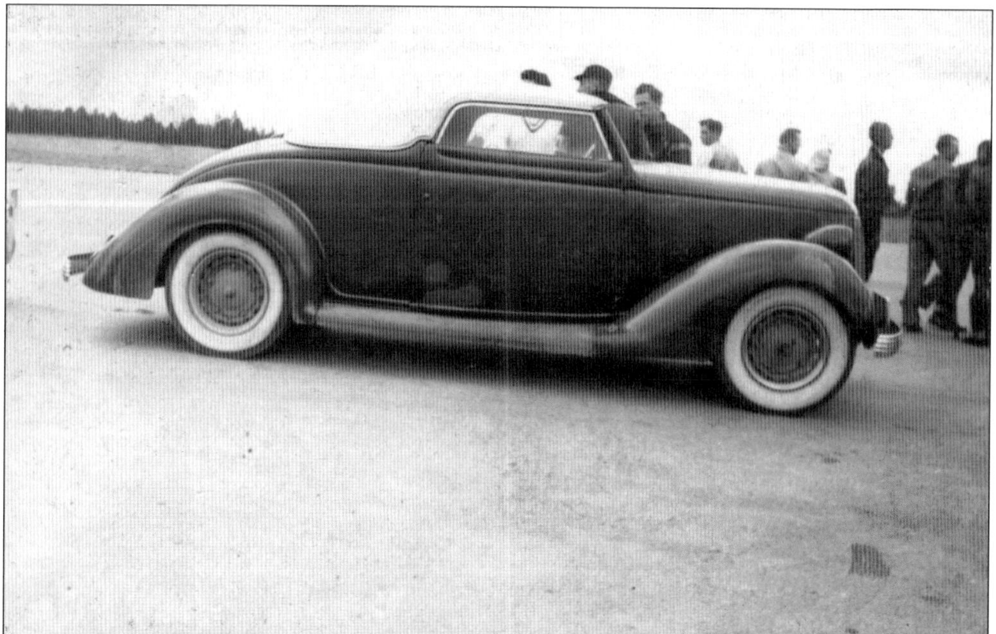

Here is a better photograph of Dick Hogan's 1936 Cabriolet, sitting on the airstrip in Deer Park, hubcaps off and ready to race. The green car had shaved door handles, a Southwind heater, and 1937 Desoto bumpers. Hogan's car was powered by a later-model 59A flathead. (Gary Hordemann.)

Gary Harms sold his roadster to Bob Frankovic and Gary Hordemann, who became the third set of owners. The car came with both V-8 60 motors, the pickup box, and turtle deck. Here, Gary (left) and his brother Jim work in the Hordemanns' shop on the full race motor that came with the T. They are getting ready to head up to Deer Park. Gary and Bob each took a shot at being the driver, but Bob's first run was quicker, and he became the driver from that point on. (Gary Hordemann.)

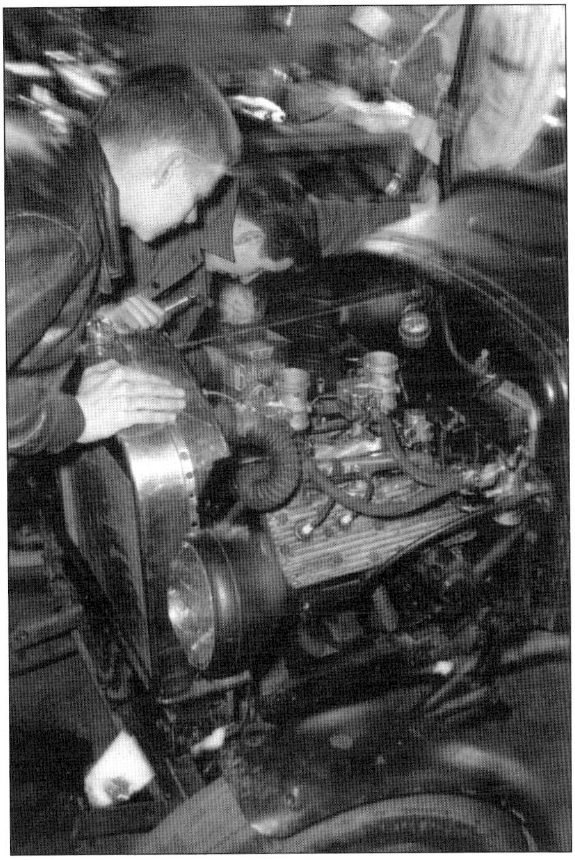

The V-8 60 did not have enough power for the new owners, so they yarded it out and installed the motor out of Jack Hordemann's car. This is at 1620 North Ash Street, in front of the Hordemanns' shop, which became a hangout for early Spokane hot-rodders. Jack Hordemannn (left) and Bob Frankovic look over the roadster. Larry Johnston is in the background. (Gary Hordemann.)

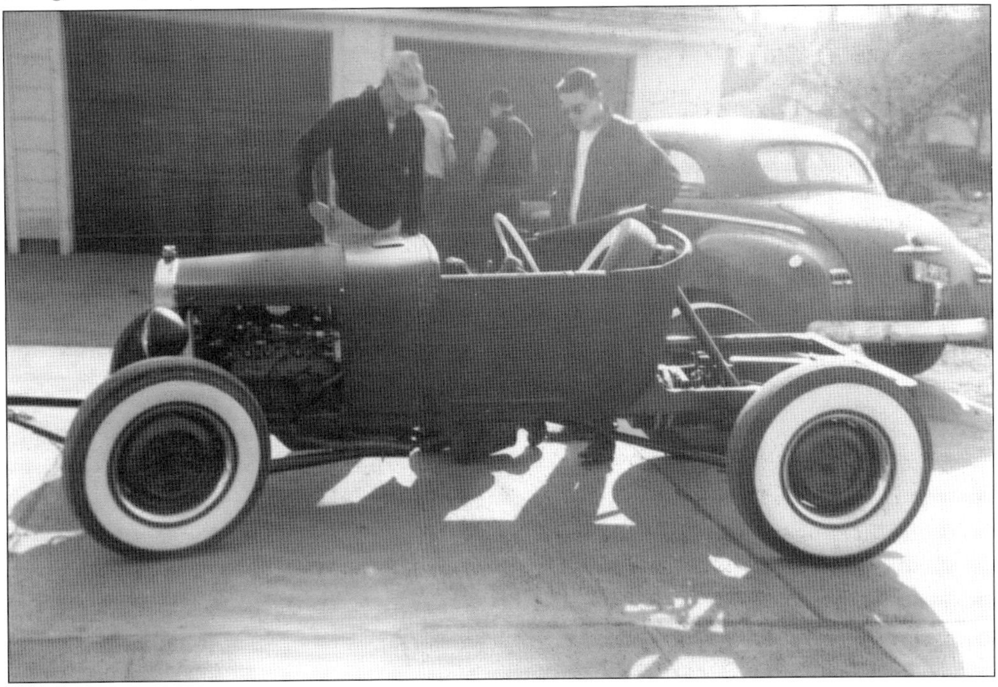

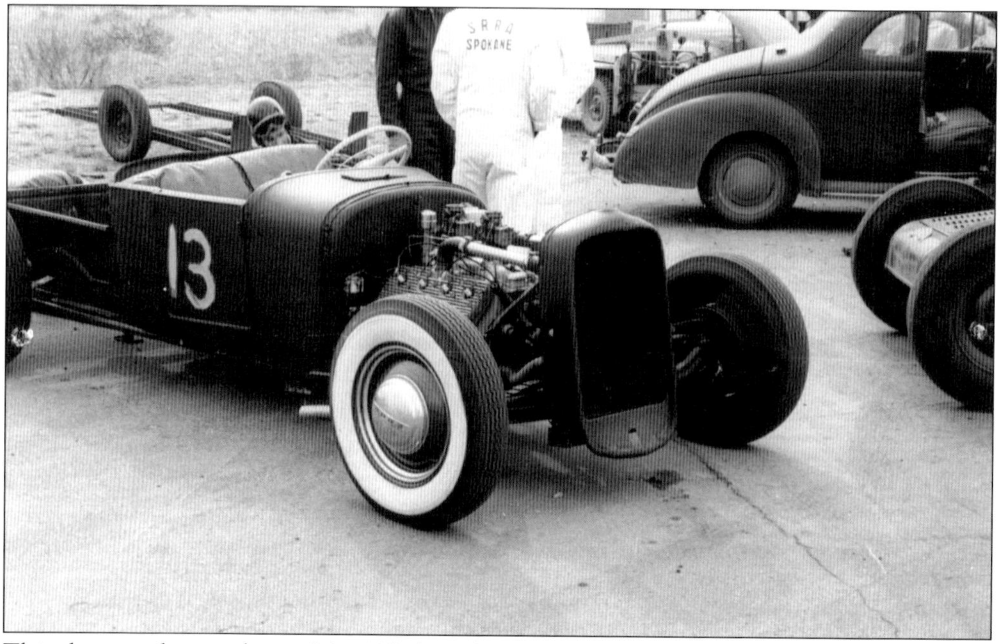

This photograph was taken in May 1953 by Bob Coutts. In the background is a racing participant wearing his SRRA overalls. For a small group, SRRA was very active in promoting racing. Besides the overalls, the short-lived group made license-plate toppers, plaques, and dress shirts. (Bob Coutts.)

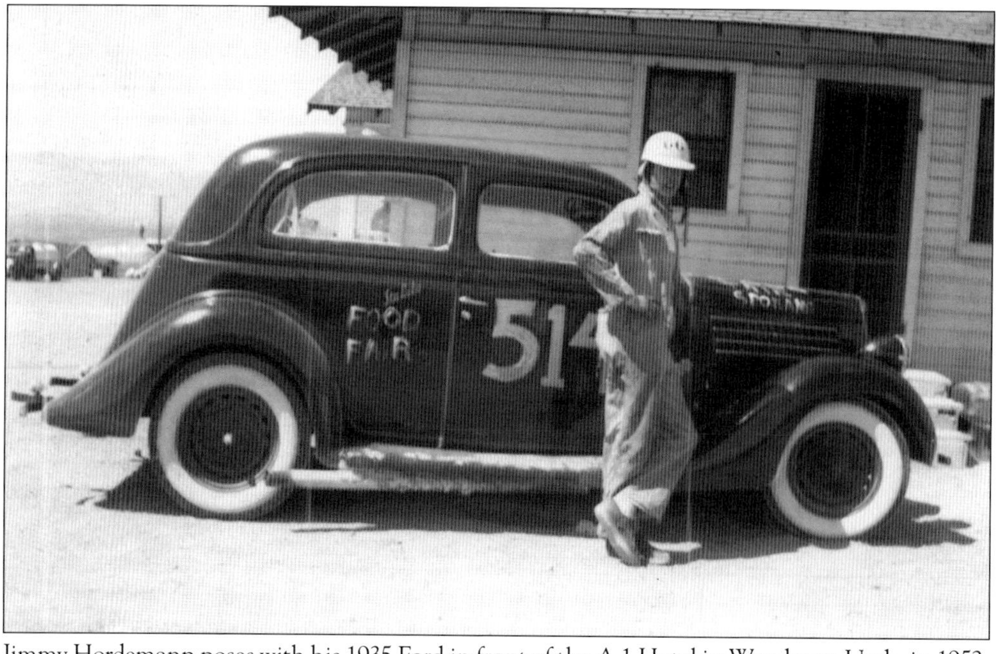

Jimmy Hordemann poses with his 1935 Ford in front of the A-1 Hotel in Wendover, Utah, in 1952. He drove the '35 down from Spokane to race it on the salt flats. Tim Rochlitzer also raced his V-8 60 powered T in 1952. It was the same roadster that Hordemann's brother would later own. Rochlitzer went down with Art Santa Rosa and George Petterson, trailing the roadster behind Patterson's '40 Ford sedan. They ran the No. 582. (Garry Hordemann.)

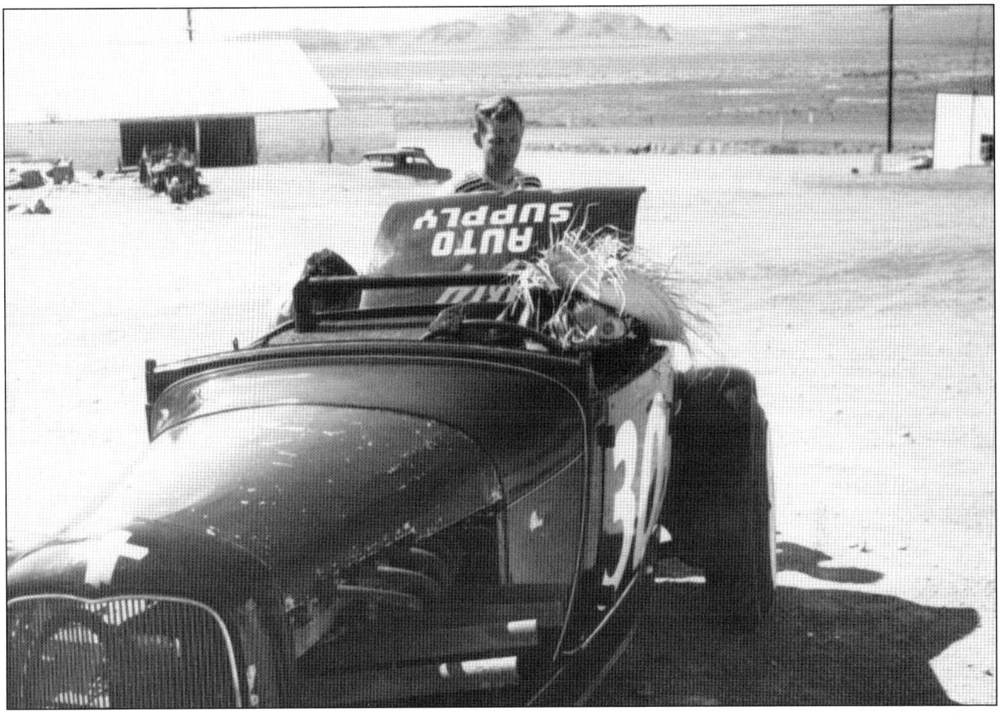

In 1953, Bruce Robinson and Doug Smith drove the 730 miles to race their 1929 Ford roadster at the Bonneville Salt Flats. Here they are in front of the A-1 Hotel in Wendover, just 10 miles from the track. The car is decked out with No. 306 and is sponsored by Thrifty Auto Supply. It was powered by Smith's GMC and backed by a Ford three-speed. The motor featured a Vertex Magneto, Spaulding cam, and a Howard Johanson log manifold. The roadster, originally rodded by Gary Rupert in Spokane, was powered at that time by a Ford flathead. (Bob Coutts.)

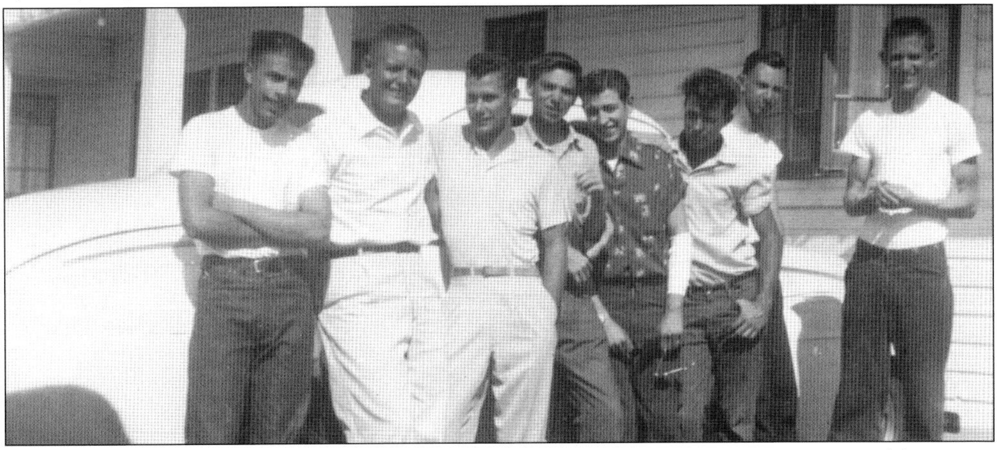

Posing in front of the A-1 Hotel are, from left to right, Art Santa Rosa, Tim Rochlitzer, an unidentified friend who traveled out with Rochlitzer, Gary Harms, Jim Hordemann (with his arm bandaged up from a wreck on the way to Bonneville), Tom Bellmore, Bob "Bones" Markley, and Charlie Markley. The 1941 Ford coupe belonged to the Markley brothers and was powered by a flathead (later exchanged for a Desoto motor). It had a dropped axle and big and littles to finish off the stance. At this time, Rochlitzer was stationed in Kentucky after finishing up at Gonzaga, where he was in the ROTC. (Gary Harms.)

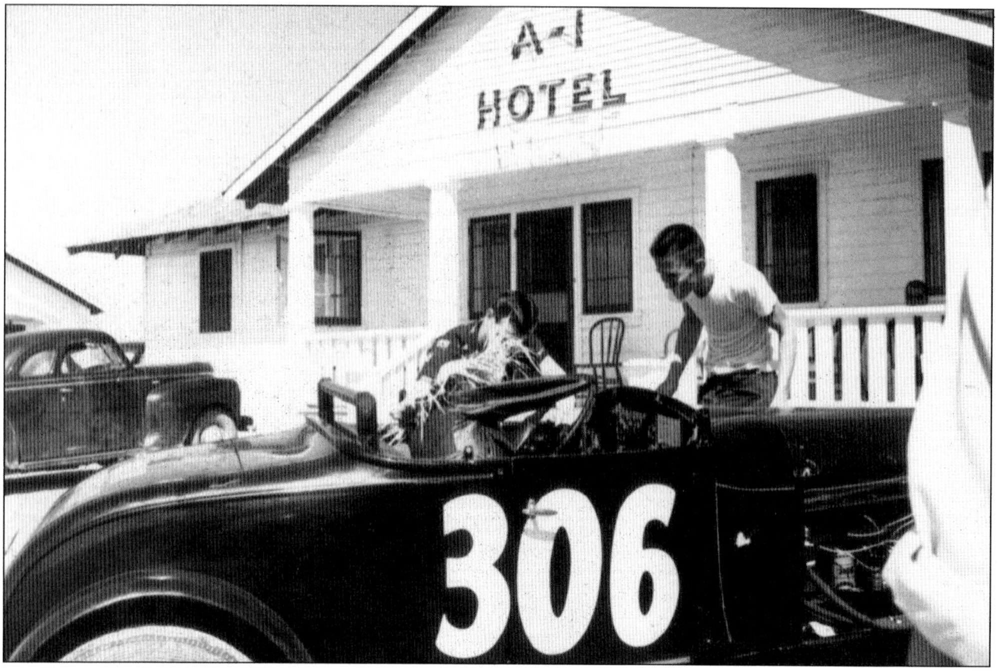

Jim Hordemann (left) and Charlie Markley are seen in front of the A-1 Hotel. Charlie, 21, was stationed at Fairchild Air Force Base (less than 20 miles west of Spokane) in Airway Heights, Washington, from 1952 to 1955. His brother later joined him at Fairchild and was stationed there from 1954 to 1955. They were both from San Carlos, California, and rented a small room from Art Santa Rosa's parents in Spokane. Doug Smith, who was part owner of the No. 306 car, also rented a room at the Santa Rosa house. Originally from Connecticut, he was stationed at Fairchild. (Bob Coutts.)

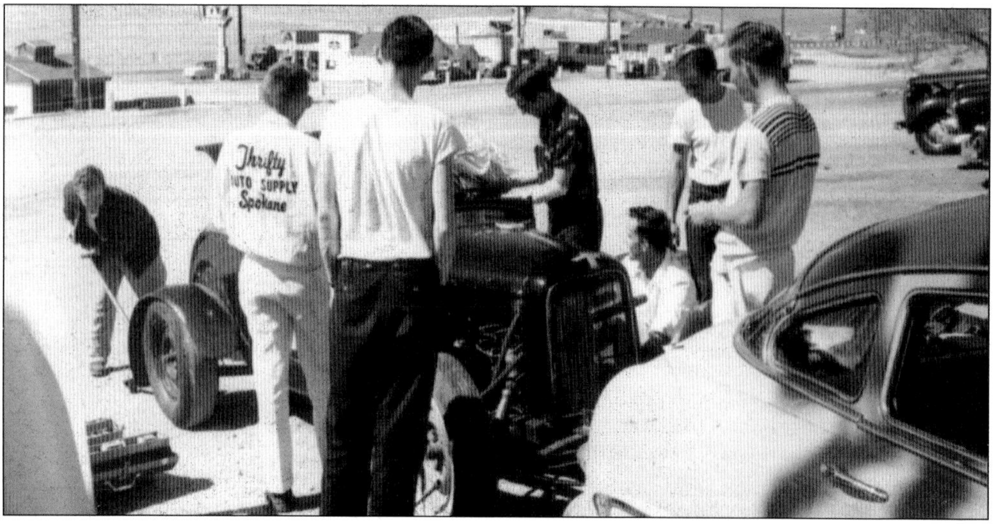

In front of the A-1 Hotel in Wendover, the crew from Spokane starts to get the car ready to race. Step one was to lose the fenders. Shown here are Bruce Robinson (wearing the Thrifty shirt), Bob "Bones" Markley (hands in pockets), Jim Hordemann (dark shirt), Doug Smith (kneeling by front wheel), and Art Santa Rosa (second from right). In front of the roadster is the Hudson that towed the car down to Bonneville. (Bob Coutts.)

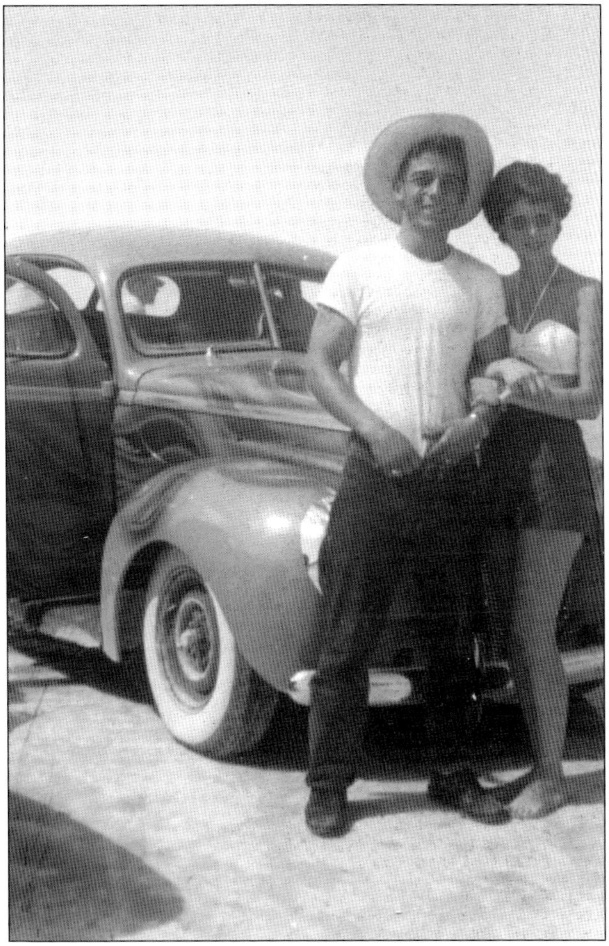

Steve Pick snapped this photograph of his wife, Connie Pick, and Stu Young when they just happened to run into each other on the salt flats. Steve and Connie were on their way back to Spokane after he had been stationed in Illinois. Young came up to Bonneville with some friends from San Diego, where he was stationed with the Navy. (Gary Harms.)

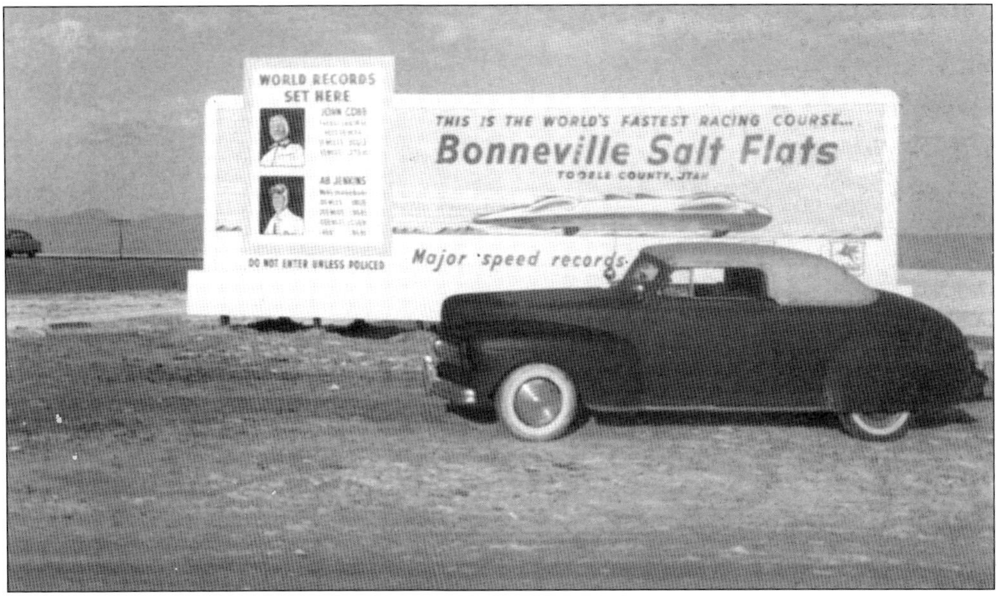

Car No. 594 belonged to Vampires C.C. member Dusty Rhodes, who took his custom Merc convertible down to race in August 1953. The car was powered by a 59A Merc motor with Edelbrock heads and an Offenhouser manifold, and the rear end was a Columbia two-speed. Rhodes's custom ran four passes, the slowest being 99.55 miles per hour. He attained a top speed of 106.38 miles per hour on his fourth run. (Dusty Rhodes.)

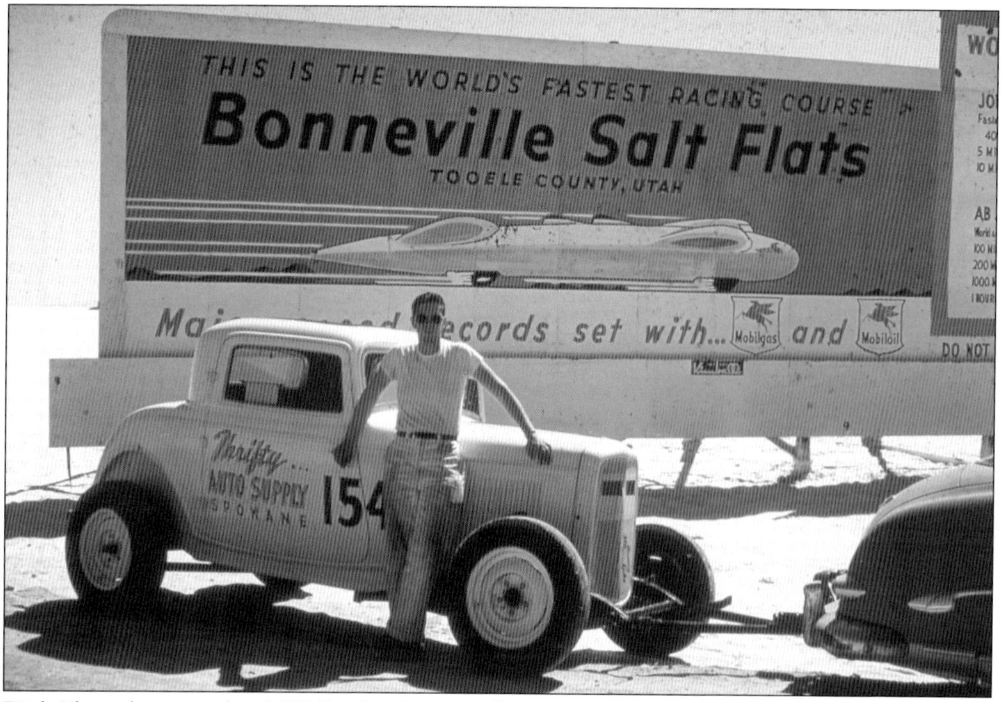

Dick Flynn leans on his 1932 Ford at Bonneville in 1955. Flynn and Ron Hammel towed the car down from Spokane behind Hammel's Hudson. This is the same three window that Jack Hordemann had owned and raced. Flynn added his Desoto, and Thrifty Auto started sponsorship. Art Santa Rosa painted it white. Flynn spun out on the first run and decided to hand the wheel over to Steve Pick so that he could focus on the engine. Pick and Flynn ended up with a top speed of just over 157 miles per hour in the coupe. (Dick Flynn.)

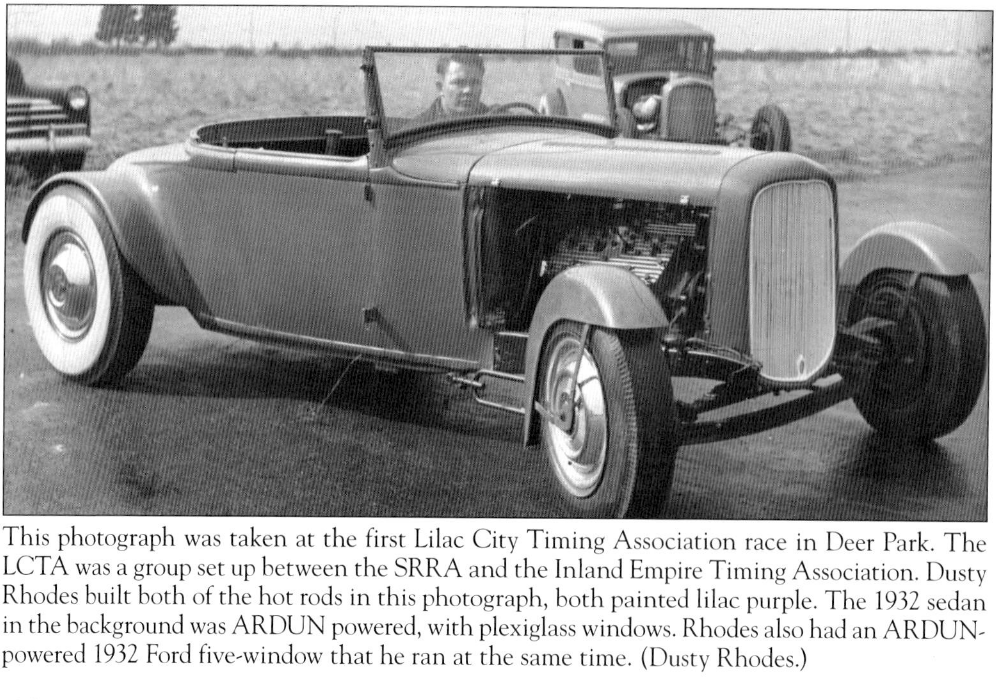

This photograph was taken at the first Lilac City Timing Association race in Deer Park. The LCTA was a group set up between the SRRA and the Inland Empire Timing Association. Dusty Rhodes built both of the hot rods in this photograph, both painted lilac purple. The 1932 sedan in the background was ARDUN powered, with plexiglass windows. Rhodes also had an ARDUN-powered 1932 Ford five-window that he ran at the same time. (Dusty Rhodes.)

Bob Coutts is seen with the 1925 T that he bought from Dick Hogan for $450 in the summer of 1954. This photograph was taken in a garage he rented from his neighbor at Morton Street and Indiana Avenue. The roadster ran a 276 flathead with three carbs on a Weiand intake and Weiand heads. In 1956, Steve Pick's flathead was installed in it, and the car won the Seafair championship in Seattle. Finally, they stuffed Dick Flynn's Desoto motor in the T and ran it for a season, with Butch Miller driving it. (Bob Coutts.)

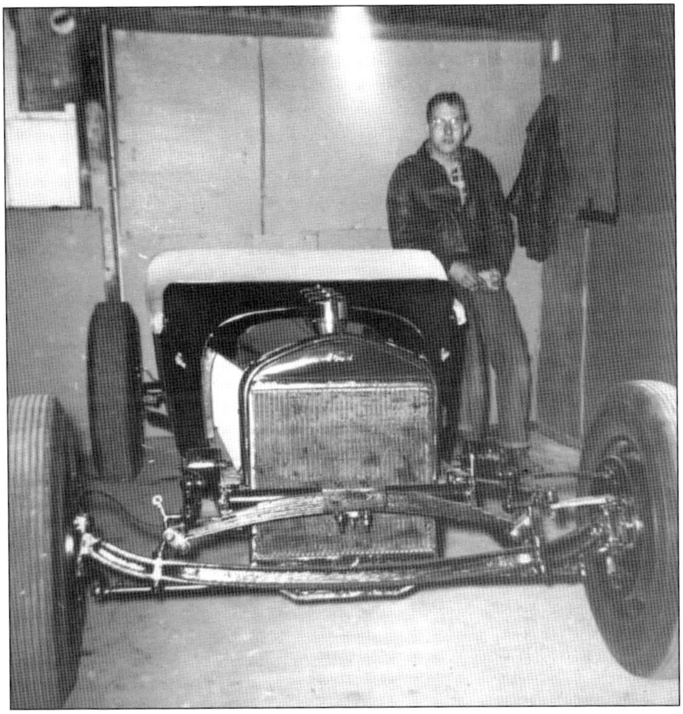

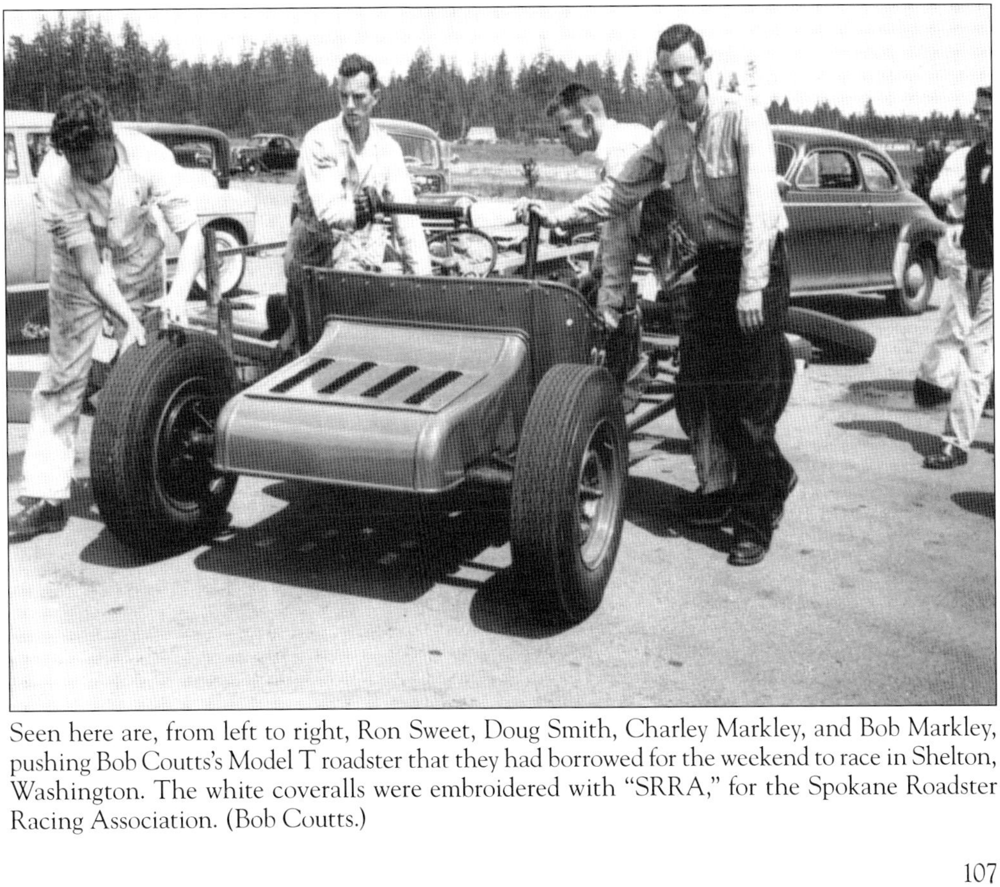

Seen here are, from left to right, Ron Sweet, Doug Smith, Charley Markley, and Bob Markley, pushing Bob Coutts's Model T roadster that they had borrowed for the weekend to race in Shelton, Washington. The white coveralls were embroidered with "SRRA," for the Spokane Roadster Racing Association. (Bob Coutts.)

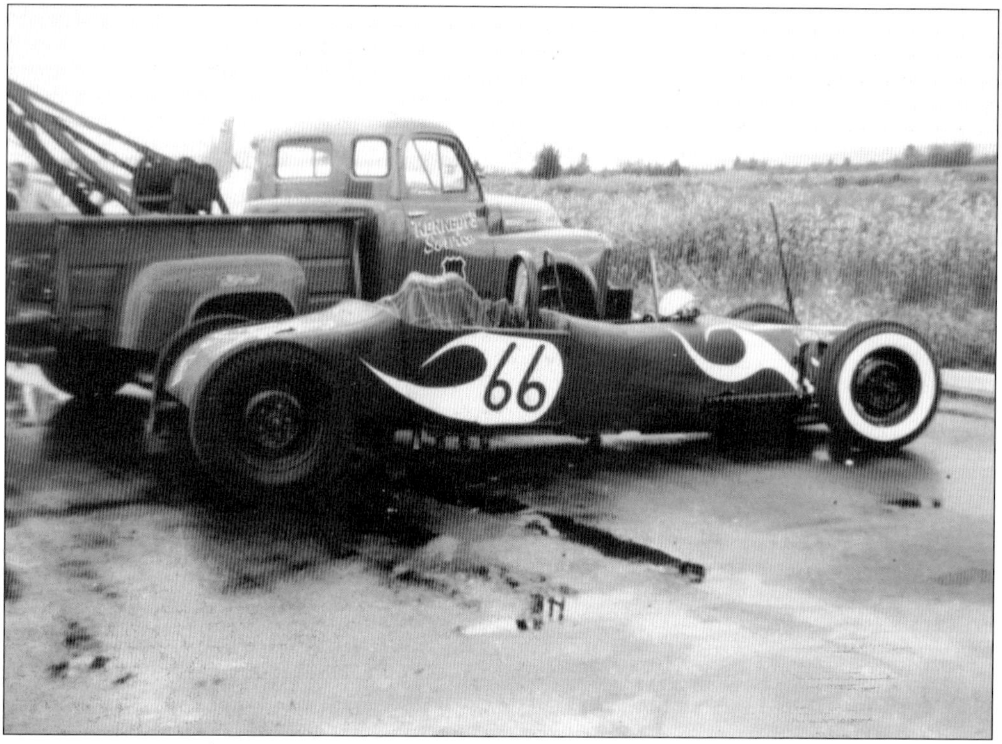

Larry Armitage worked at Lucas Auto Parts on Indiana Avenue and Monroe Street. He and his friends Clarence Bennett and Art Santa Rosa built this crude-looking but very quick rear engine Model T roadster. The car was powered by a 292 Desoto motor and ran 133 miles per hour on nitro methane. Jim Kennedy's Philips 66 station on Northwest Boulevard sponsored the car and is the reason for the No. 66. (Bob Frankovic.)

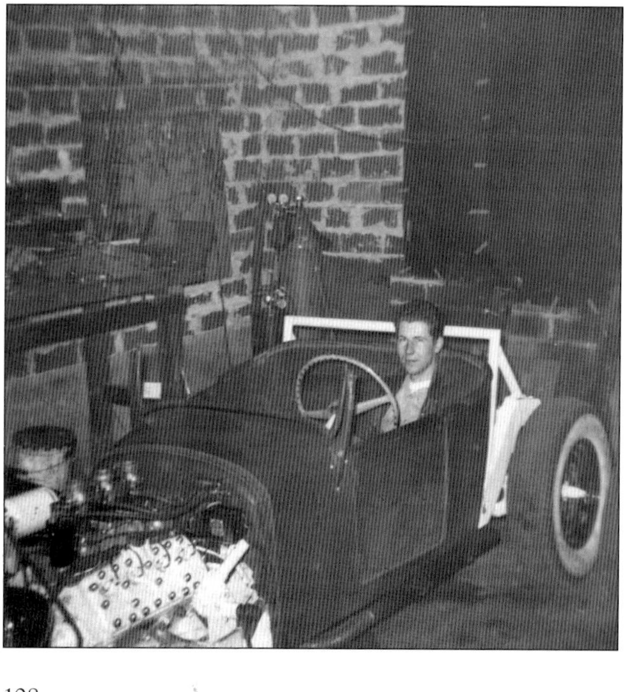

Walt Holderman's T made it into *Hot Rod* magazine in September 1955 in an article on the NHRA Safety Safari coming to the drag races in Deer Park. Bob Coutts took this photograph of Holderman sitting in his T in his garage on North Perry Street. Holderman bought the flathead from a friend in Seattle and ran a three-carb manifold with stock heads. (Bob Coutts.)

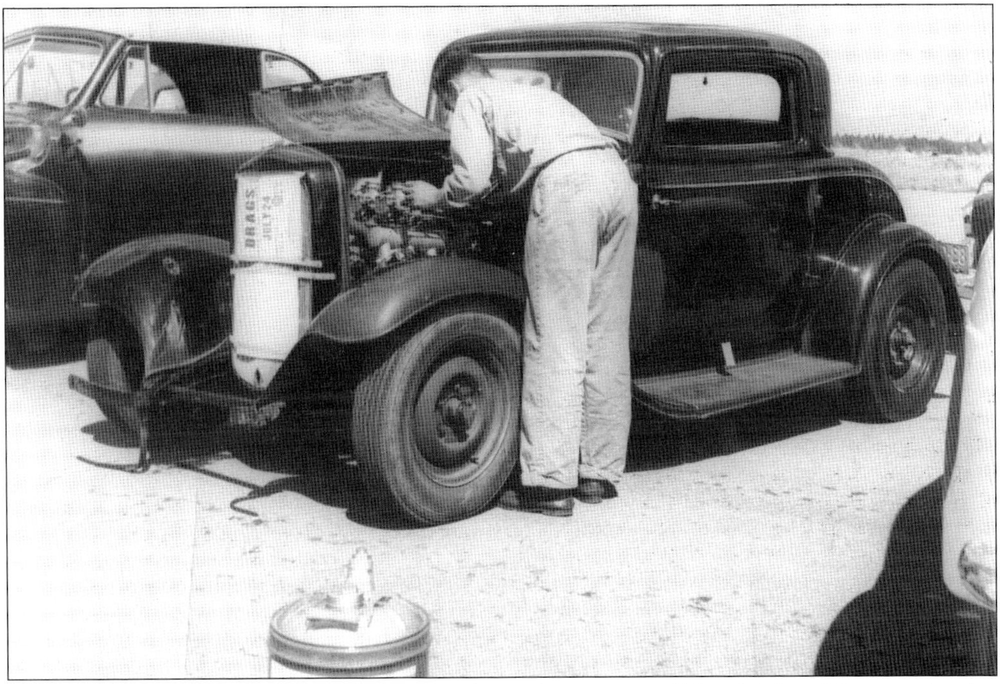

Dick Flynn's 1932 Ford three-window is seen here when it was still black. Here, Flynn readies his Desoto at the Deer Park strip in 1955. By the end of this meet, he had pulled the fenders off to lighten the body. Butch Miller drove the car in the "B" altered class, and the coupe was running just over 105 miles per hour. (Bob Coutts.)

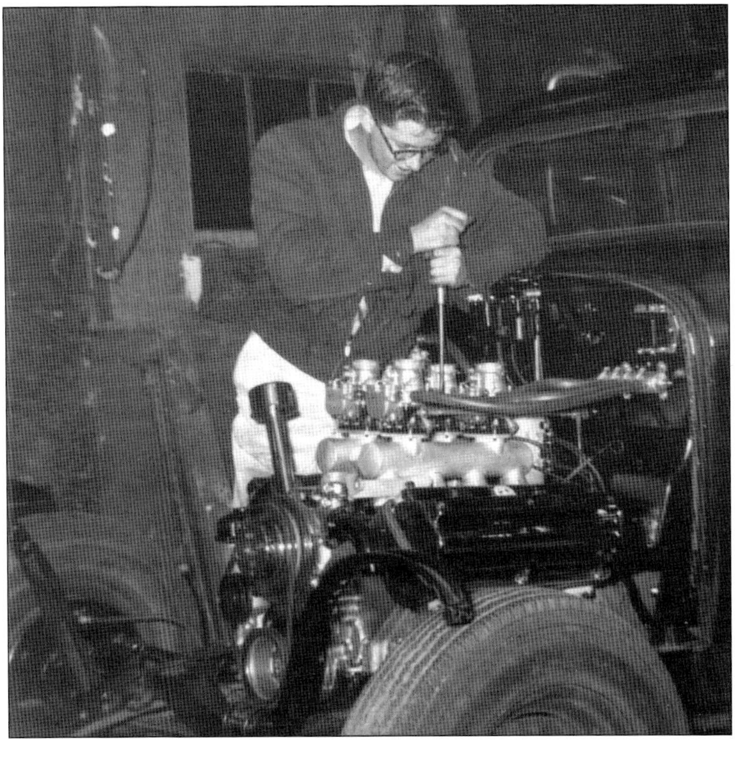

Dick Flynn works in his garage on Baldwin Avenue and Lidgerwood Street, just east of Thrifty. The Desoto ran six Stromberg 97s on a U-Fab log intake. The rest of the coupe was basically untouched at this point and included a bone stock interior that was so nice that the rear curtain still worked. Flynn sold the coupe so he could focus on dragsters and faster speeds. (Bob Coutts.)

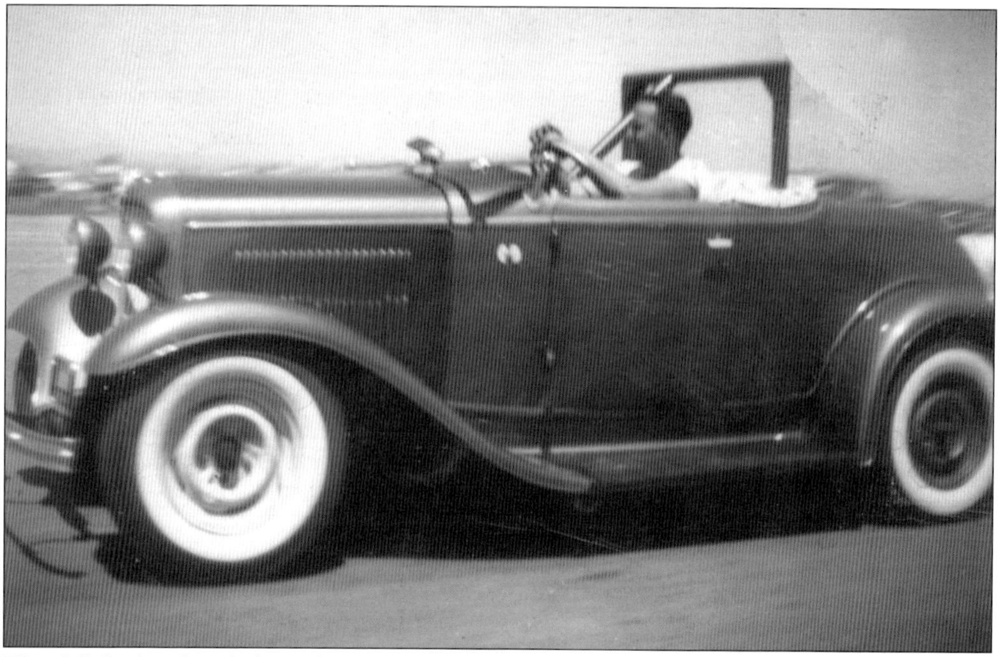

This full-fendered '32 belonged to Jack Henderson, a member of the Dragins Auto Club. It was powered by a small-block Chevy. Later, the '32 was owned by Danny Martin while he was working at the Rainbow station at 4200 North Division Street. A guy from Kennewick pulled in driving a beautiful Model A roadster and offered to trade Martin $500 plus the model A for the deuce. Bill Payne would end up bringing the '32 back to Spokane, where it is still owned by Bill's son and is now powered by a Desoto hemi. (Billy Payne.)

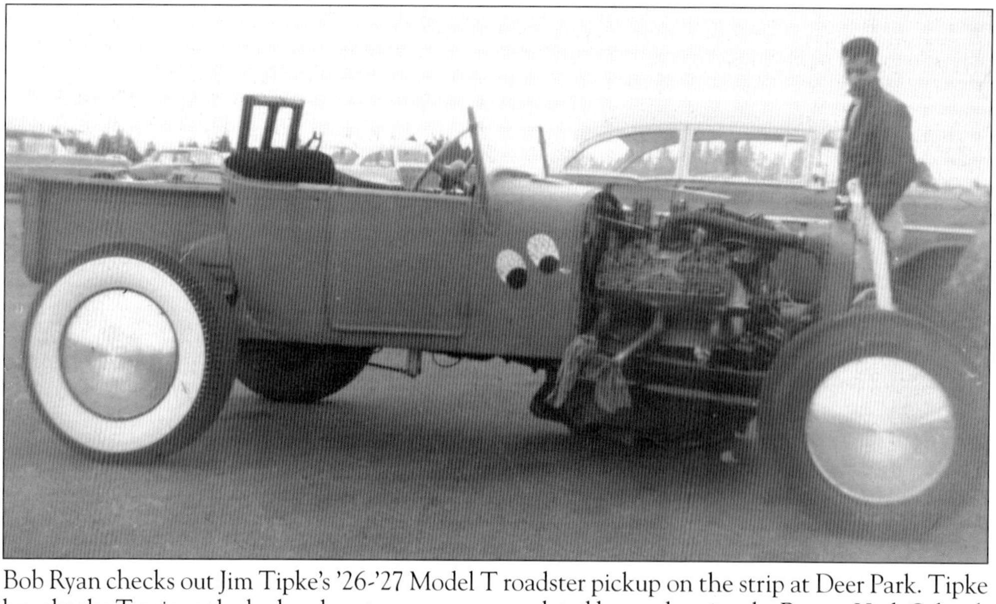

Bob Ryan checks out Jim Tipke's '26-'27 Model T roadster pickup on the strip at Deer Park. Tipke bought the T, minus the bed and motor, as an uncompleted hot-rod project by Rogers High School. He pulled the motor out of his convertible and added a pickup box to the back. Tipke would go on to build some of the best racecars that came out of the Northwest, including cars that would end up racing at the Indy 500. (Frank Moyer.)

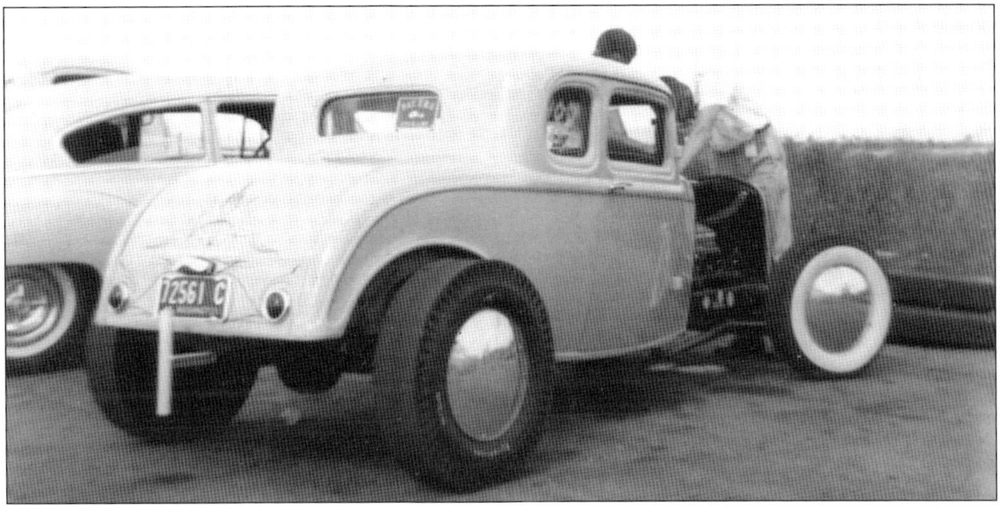

Jack Henderson's 1932 coupe was previously owned by Dusty Rhodes. The coupe was bright yellow. The writing below the pinstriping and above the Hollywood light reads, "Harvey shaken from cross breeding." It was a nod to Von Dutch that pinstriper Joe Burnett added to the car. In the background is Larry Taylor's '49 Chevy, which ran the stock six with two carburetors on it. (Larry Taylor.)

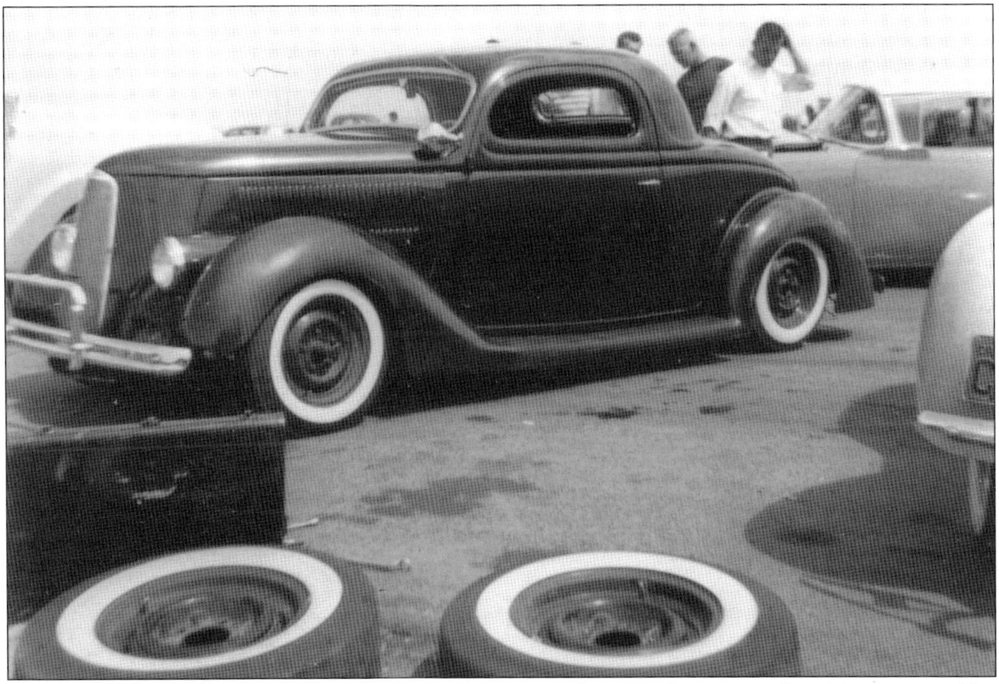

The Calori coupe looks just as mean on the strip as it does on the street. The '36 was owned by Bill Bongers at the time of this photograph at Deer Park. The car is probably running a small-block Chevy after the flathead was pulled out and put in Bob Adams's Custom 42 Ford. It is hard to tell what could be powering the coupe in Spokane photographs, since it had a long history of motor swaps when it was located here. When the car came to Spokane, it was flathead powered. Next, it went to a small-block Chevy. From that point, it went back to a flathead, then Buick, Pontiac, and one more flathead motor before it went back to California. (Larry Taylor.)

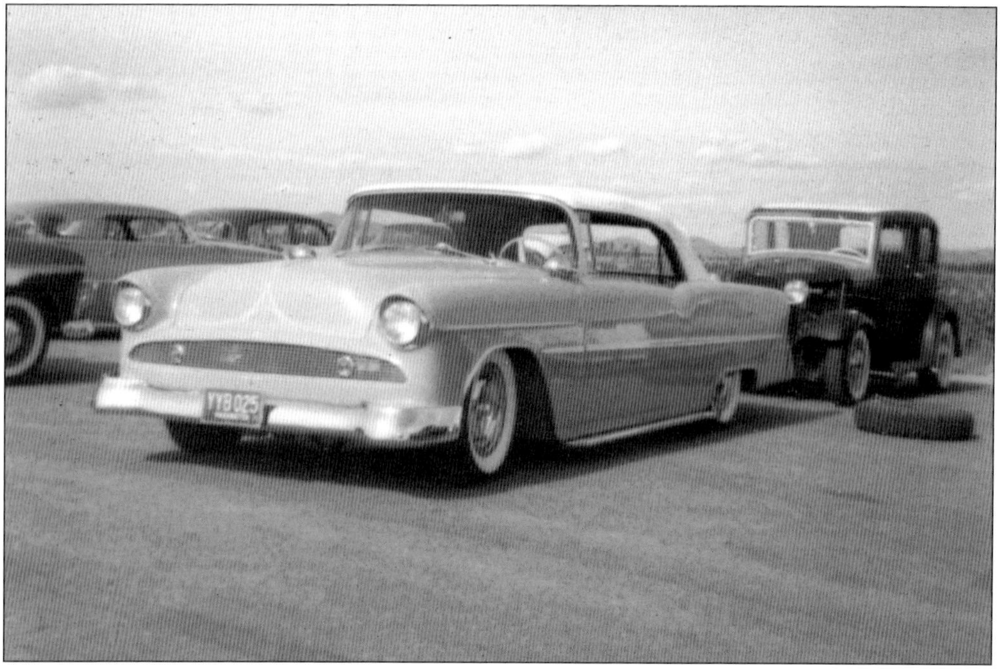

Hot Rod magazine called Bill Bongers's '55 Chevy convertible "Fast and Fancy" in November 1957. The grille had a T-bird style, but it was made from Desoto mesh with GM parking lights. The lake pipes were added after the *Hot Rod* feature. The small-block Chevy had dual fours and was out of a '56 Corvette. The hubcaps are Olds Fiesta. The rims are painted red—that thin lip of red is the perfect accent to the sky-blue body. In the background is Bongers's 1932 Vicky, previously owned by John Mehl. (Larry Taylor.)

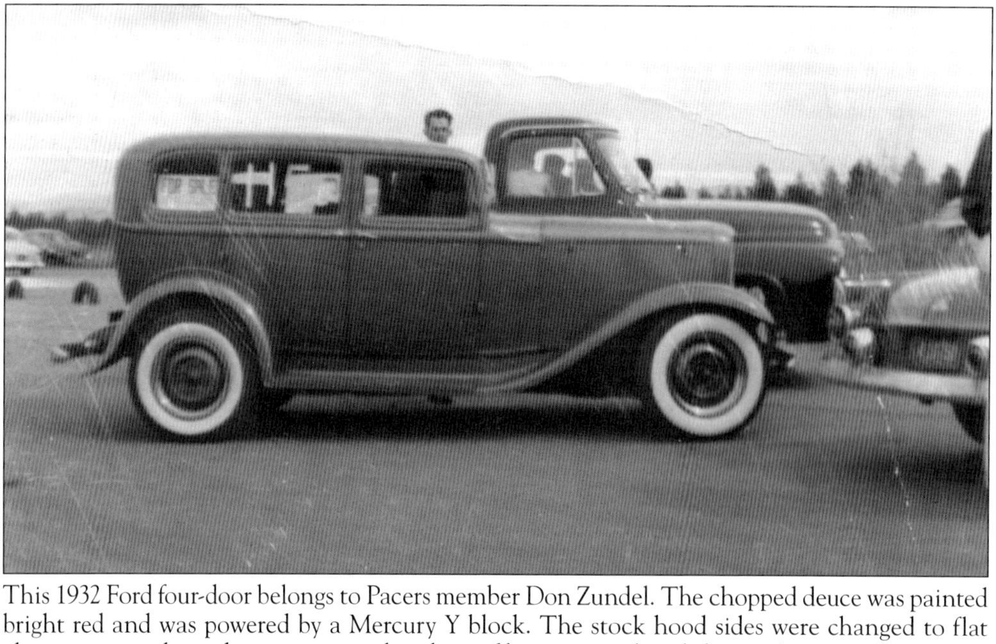

This 1932 Ford four-door belongs to Pacers member Don Zundel. The chopped deuce was painted bright red and was powered by a Mercury Y block. The stock hood sides were changed to flat aluminum panels, and a more streamlined set of bumpers replaced the stock set. Just visible are the tops of small headlights popping up in front of the grille. (Glen Harbison.)

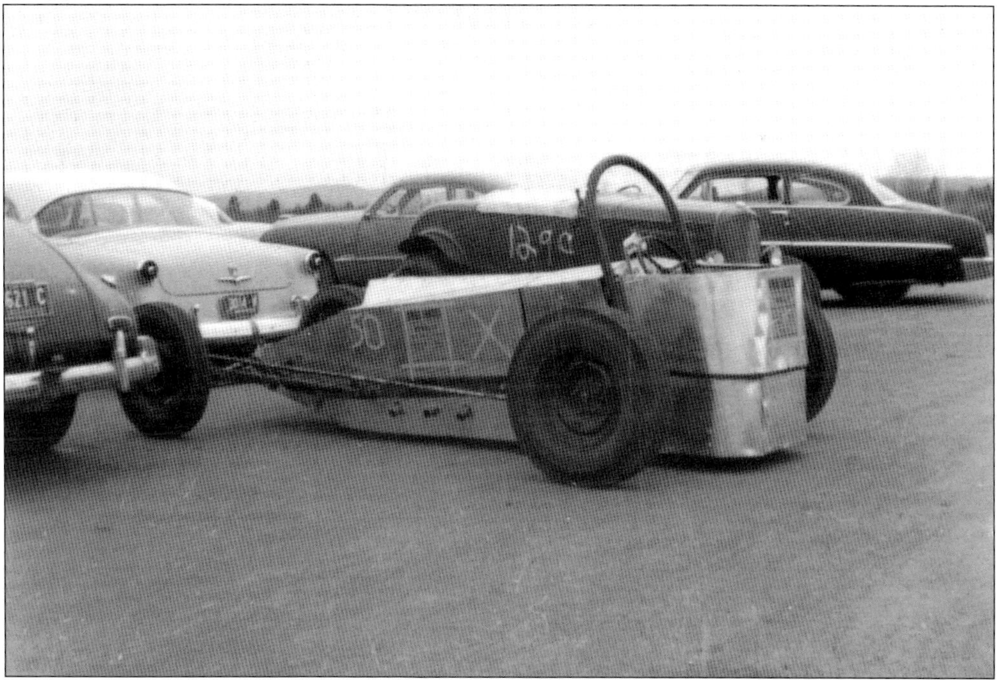

Gary Rupert and Doug Smith's early dragster was powered by a flathead when the body was on, and a GMC when the body was removed. In the 1955 Safety Safari meet at Deer Park, the dragster ran a top speed of just over 109 miles per hour with the GMC motor. In the background is Bud Prufer's 1932 roadster. (Glen Harbison.)

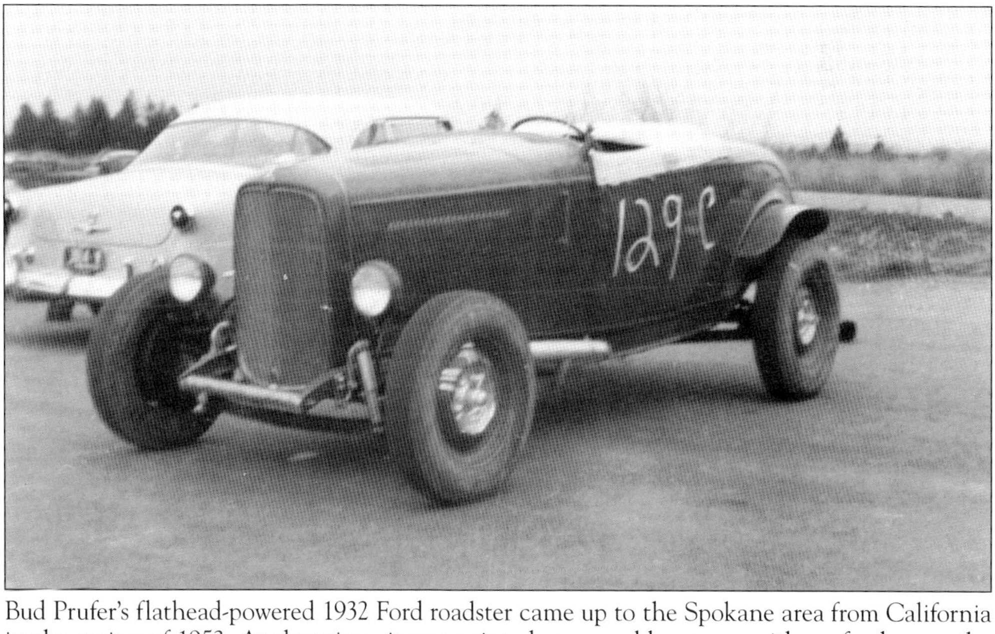

Bud Prufer's flathead-powered 1932 Ford roadster came up to the Spokane area from California in the spring of 1953. At that time, it was painted an aqua blue green with no fenders on the rear. Bud added the bobbed fenders and painted it dark blue, with a white tonneau cover and a louvered hood top. Note the way Prufer flat-towed the car with a custom bar, made to replace the stock front spreader bar. (Glen Harbison.)

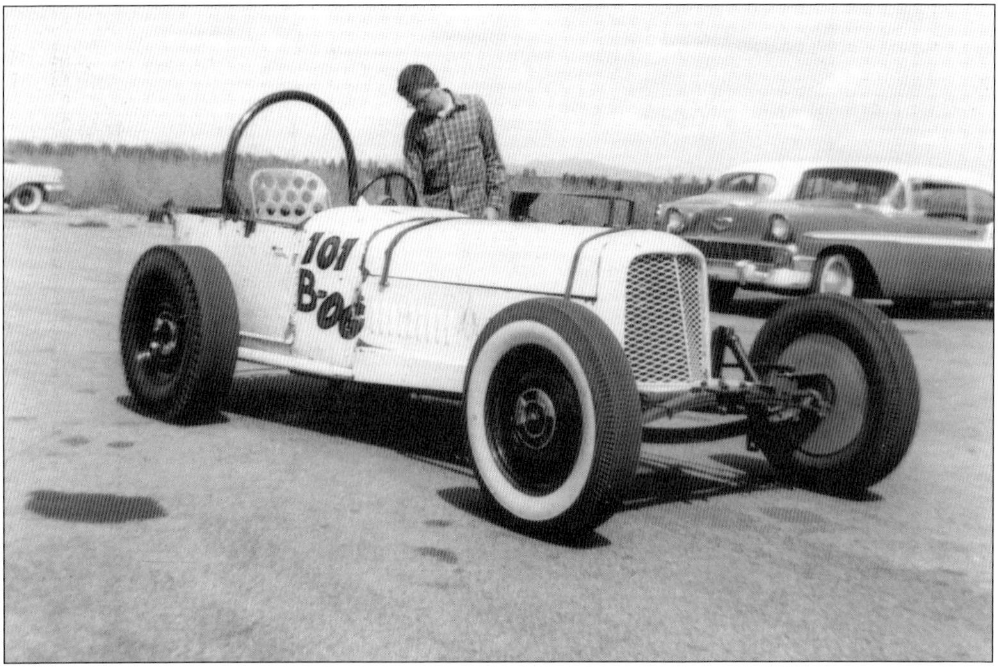

One of the nicest guys in Spokane hot rodding was Dick Morphy. This is his first dragster, a GMC-powered car built out of a '26-'27 Model T. Morphy was a member of the Dukes Auto Club. His T was white with black suspension. He would go on to race a dragster named the "Mickey Mouse Special" powered by a small-block Chevy. (Larry Taylor.)

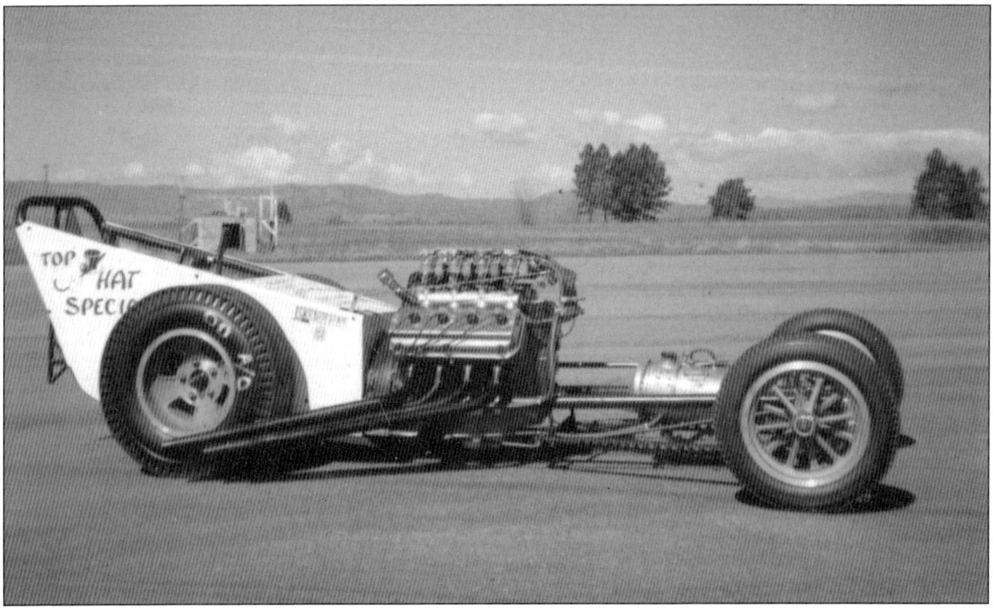

The "Top Hat Special" was painted white for the 1959 season. The dragster was built at Jack Hordemann's house, 922 West Cascade Way, on the north side of Spokane. The front end and rear are out of the same T they raced earlier, and the motor is a 442 Chrysler 292. Jim Hordemann was the driver and main fabricator on the rail, but the team members included Ed Vicara, Larry Johnston, Bud Brown, Larry Wandler, Pete Norrie, Larry Taylor, and Ron Niedriger. (Larry Taylor.)

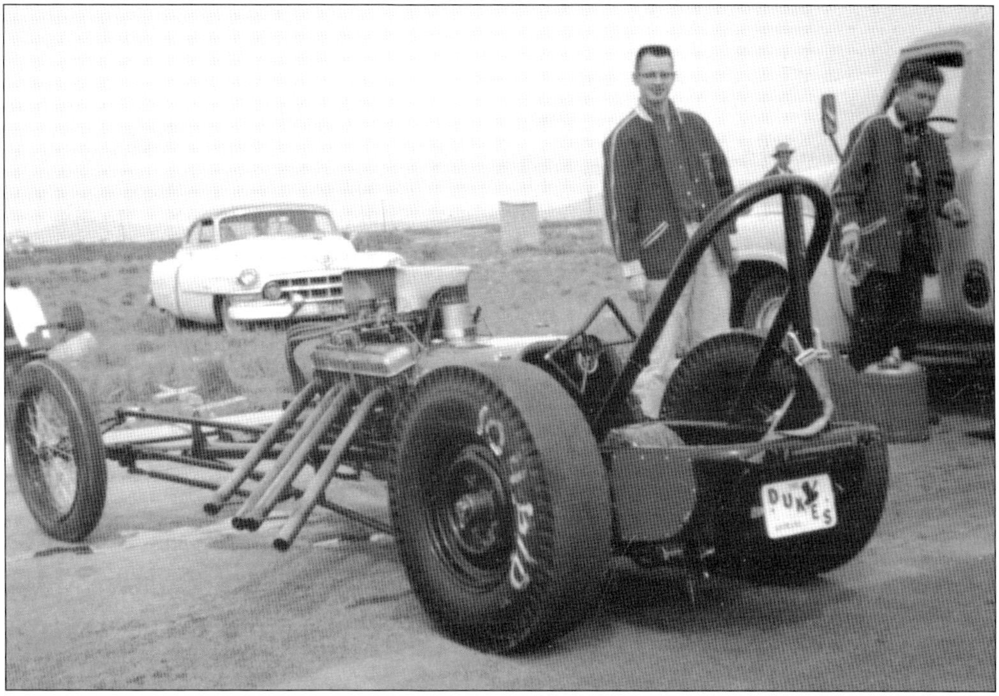

Dick Morphy's second dragster, the "Mickey Mouse Special," was a big step forward from his GMC-powered T. Morphy proudly displays his Dukes club plaque, and fellow club members Kenny Brinkman (left) and Buddy Wickstrom (right) are helping out with the rail. The 265 small-block Chevy is topped with four Stromberg 97s, but it later ran a Hillborn setup. John Meads's Cadillac is on the grass in front of the dragster, and to the right is Morphy's '55 Ford push truck. (Larry Taylor.)

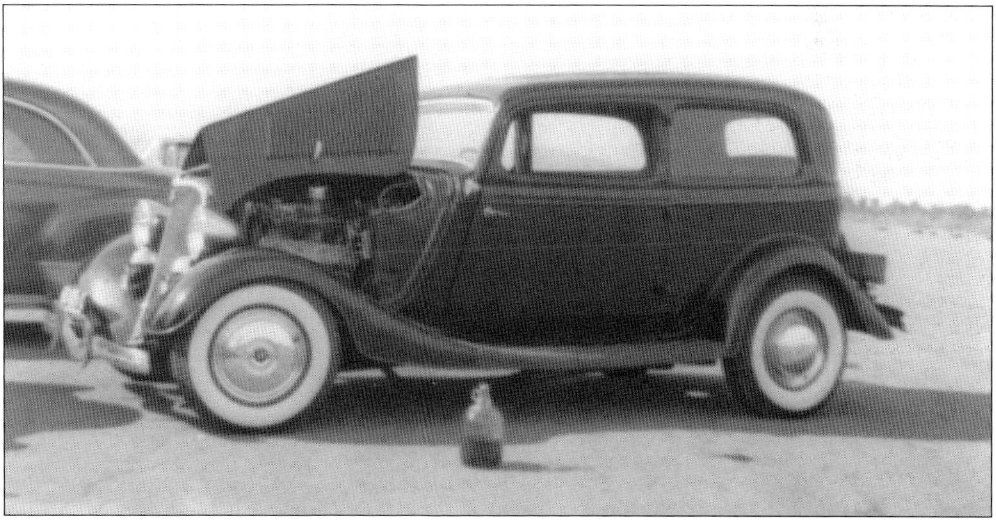

Claude Cuzzetto's 1933 Ford sedan has become a fixture of Spokane hot rodding. Claude bought the car from Mike Kantz with the Studebaker motor already installed in it in 1958. In this photograph at Deer Park, the firewall is still stock, as is the running gear. Claude became a member of the Dukes with his 33 and raced it all over the northwest and as far south as Bakersfield, California. The Stude motor was pulled out for a small-block Chevy, and became the power plant for Don Audel's "So Tuff Toy." (Larry Taylor.)

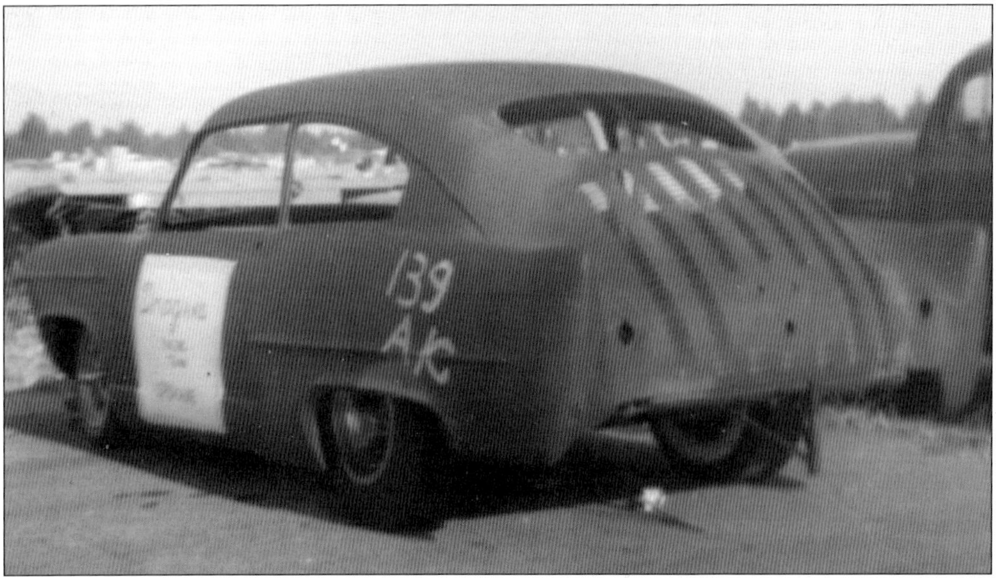

This car is the combination between the Sears Allstate that was Vern Massie's everyday driver, and the Desoto motor out of Swede Erickson's 1932 three-window show car, named the "Party Doll." The brown-primered car was only raced in 1960. It was part of the Dragins racing team. The Allstate body was removed from the frame, and Massie partnered with Don Wilbur. They started running a Model A Vicky body on the chassis. (Bob Coutts.)

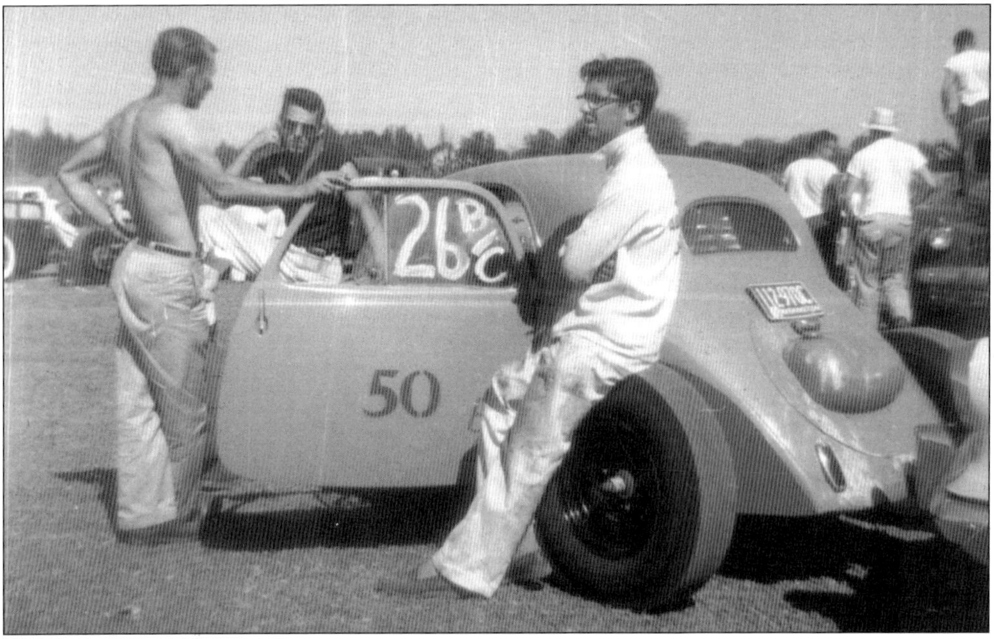

Dick Flynn, wearing his Thrifty Auto coveralls, sits on the tire of Gary Rupert's Fiat Topolino. Randy Scissor is facing the camera at the front of the car. The Fiat was powered with a 296 flathead that ran on nitro. Rupert built the frame to a scale drawing he made on the floor of his garage, and the suspension used a mixture of early Ford parts. The license plate and taillights are deceiving, as Rupert did not use this as a street car; the lights were set up for flat-towing it to races. (Butch Miller.)

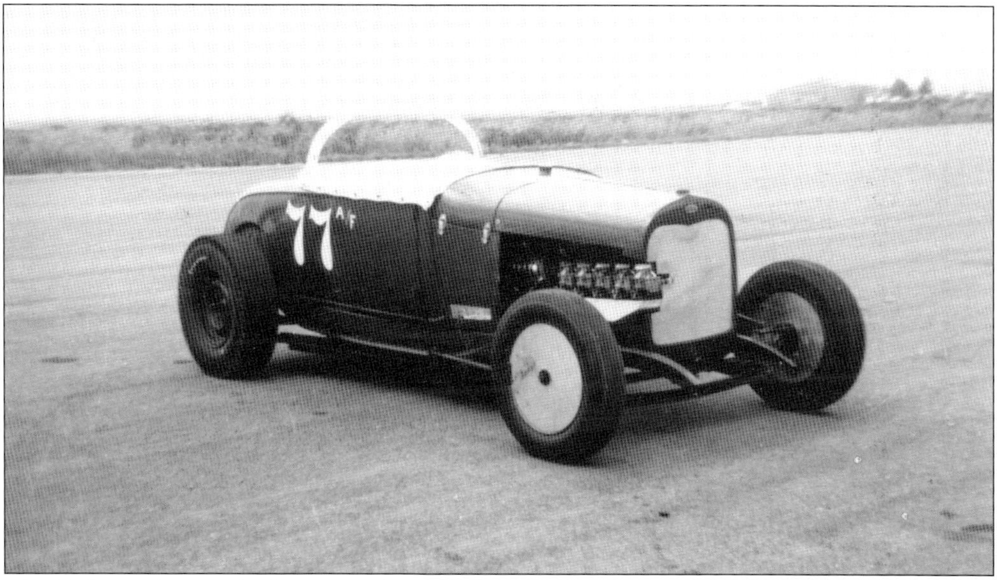

The Kelly roadster with the crank-driven blower setup on an Oldsmobile motor was made by Keith Miller, who later became an engineer for Oldsmobile. The roadster is running a Model A grille shell with this setup, so they did not have to cut the '32 shell that was usually on the car. The Kellys were a big part of running the IETA, from being officers in the organization to Jim's mother, Edith, taking care of the newsletters and running the clocks. Jim's father, Ned Kelly, ran a small repair and speed shop in Hillyard, at the corner of Francis Avenue and Market Street. He was also very active in the IETA. (Bob Frankovic.)

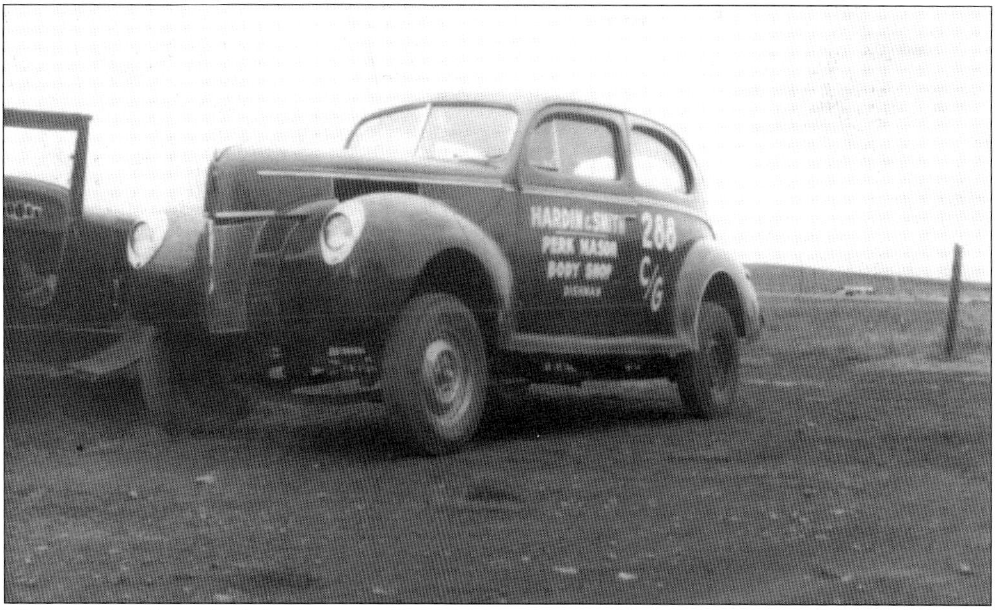

This 1940 Ford was built by Gene Kitcha in 1958 and became the Hodge & Kitcha racing team's car. They ran a 265 with mechanical Hillborn injection, backed by a '37 LaSalle transmission and Oldsmobile rear end. The car was running mid-10s to 11s when they sold it to Hardin & Smith, minus the motor. That 265 went into a '37 Chevy and became the Ron's Drive-In car. (Tim Hein.)

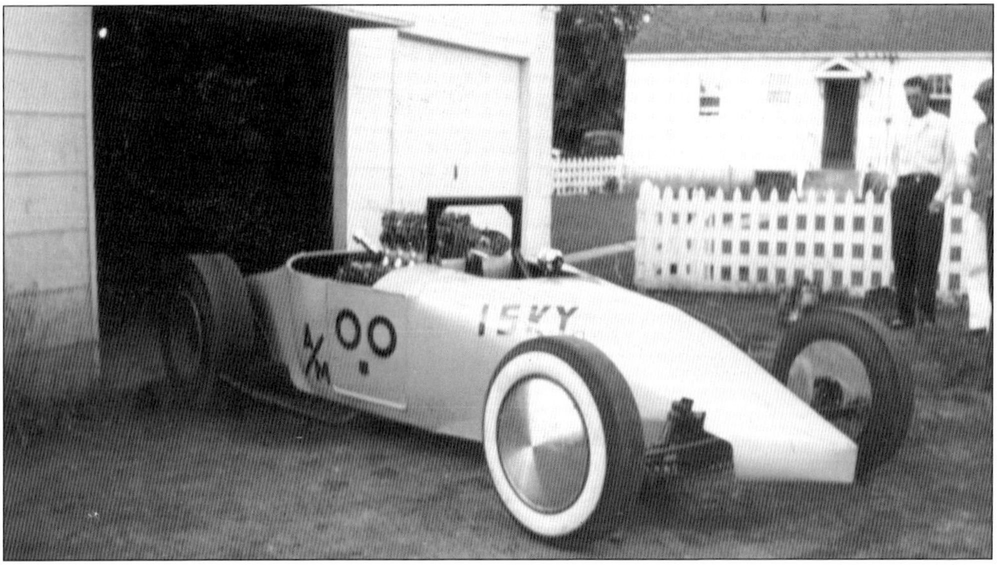

This is the same Model T roadster that Tim Rochlitzer and Gary Harms owned, powered by a V-8 60. The Hordemann brothers made it into a bright-yellow, rear-engine drag car with a 292 Chrysler that was bored and stroked. The frame was built in the basement of Jack Hordemann's house at 4808 North Adams Street. He also made the aluminum nose and changed the shape of the cowl for this version. Buddy Brown (second from left) and Ron Niederiger look at the T after it was rolled out of Jack's garage. (Gary Hordemann.)

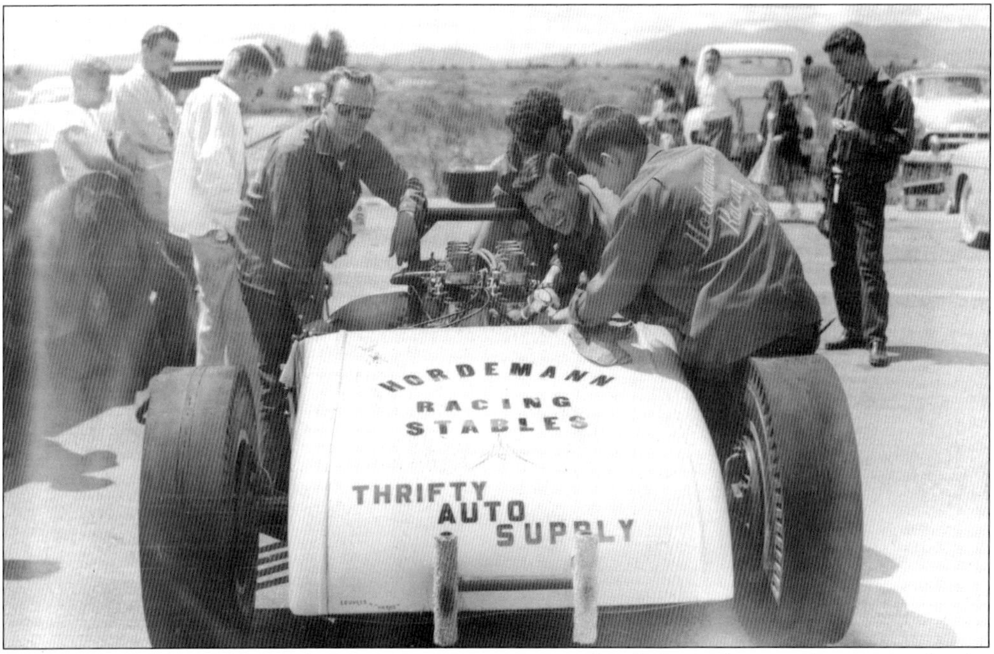

In this photograph of the Hordemanns' T are Byron Brownlee (left, in white coat), Larry Taylor (in sunglasses, looking at the camera), Jim Hordemann (working on the motor), and Larry Johnston (at right, sitting on wheel). Johnston is wearing the Hordemann Racing Stables shirt. Thrifty Auto is now sponsoring the roadster, and this is how it looked when it was in *Hot Rod* magazine in 1956. The lettering on the lower left of the turtle deck reads "Louvers by 'Harms.' " (Butch Miller.)

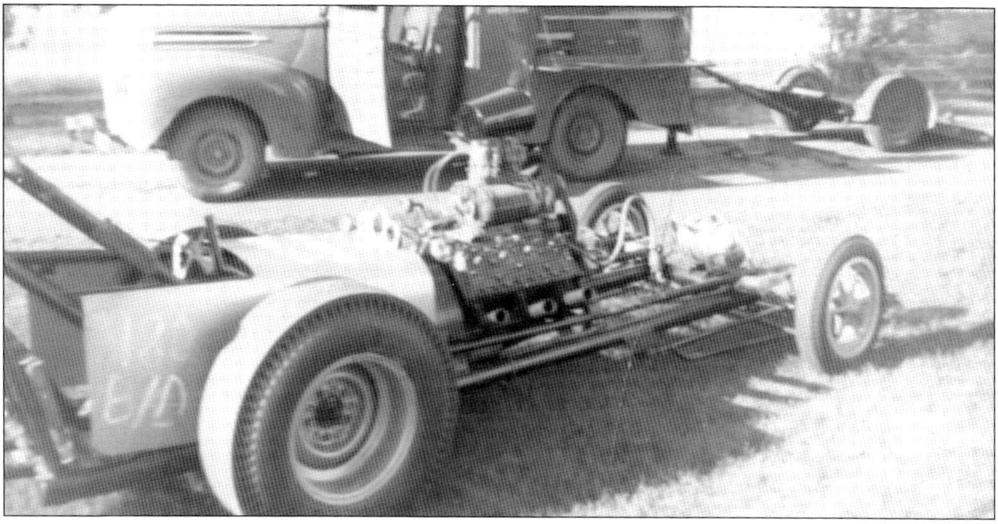

This is Greg Nelson's flathead in the Dragins Racing Club dragster. The club had purchased a Chassis Research frame and had it shipped up to Spokane for $247 plus freight. At one of the club meetings, the members realized that nobody was using it, so Greg Fury and Dave Nelson decided to run it. Within a week, they had dropped Nelson's motor in the rail, and it was ready to go. With a wastebucket scoop on a Scot blown flathead, the car ran 112 miles per hour with an 11.98 ET in 1961. (Greg Fury.)

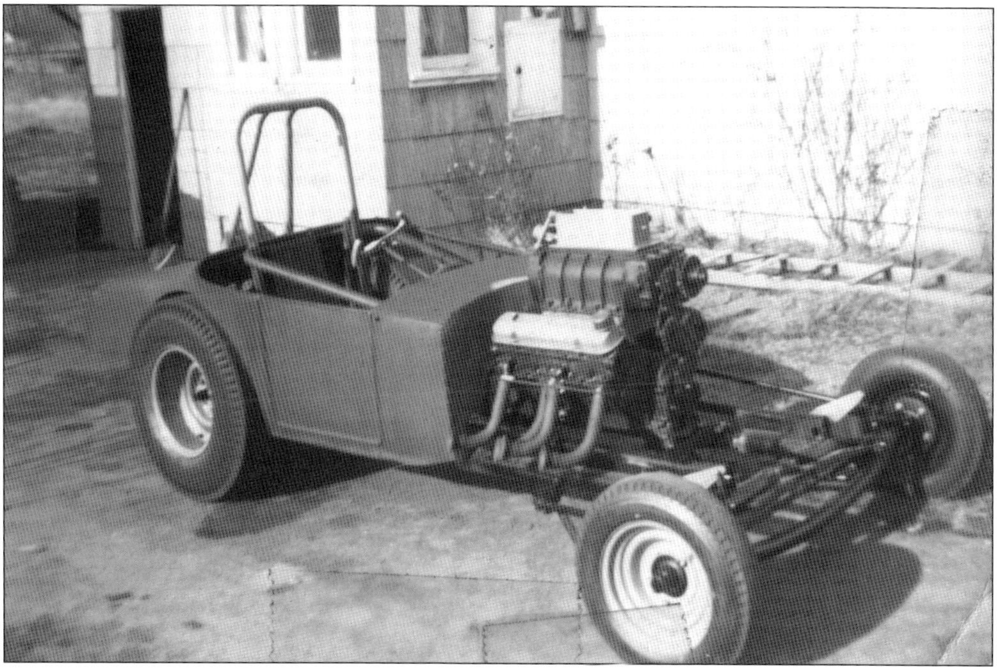

The last Spokane guy to build a car out of the T roadster body was Greg Fury in 1961. As seen here, the top of the cowl is still altered from the rear engine car. Fury's car was running a Pontiac with a chain-drive setup he made when he worked at Thrifty Auto on Division Street. Fury was a member of the Dragins race team. The car was running 120 miles per hour with the Pontiac. He later changed it to a blown Chevy. With Joe Blaylock driving it, the car topped out at 178 miles per hour. (Greg Fury.)

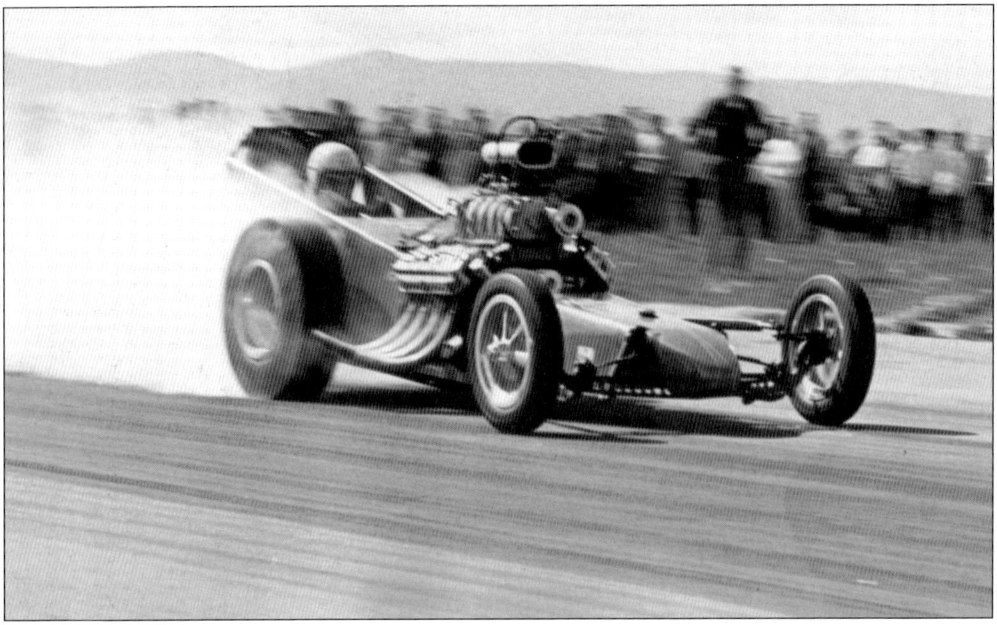

This is the same chassis as the "Top Hat" car, now painted orange and sponsored by Kelly Automotive. Jack Hordemann made the chassis, the body was built by Al's Body and Fender, and the car is running a Blown 392 Chrysler. The important detail in this photograph is the tube running into the injector scoop. That tube is part of a home-built nitrous setup that Hordemann made. During this time, Spokane racers like Jack Hordemann and Dick Flynn started experimenting with spray nitrous oxide systems. (Larry Taylor.)

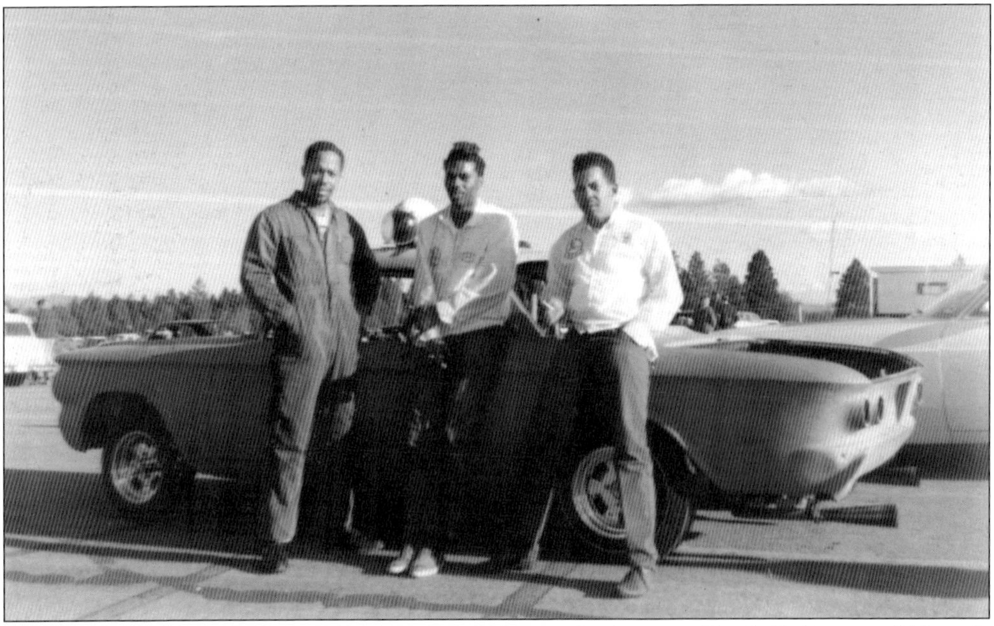

Willie Ritchie and his dad ran a Corvair repair shop in Spokane on Foothills Drive and Nevada Street. They also were competitive with a Corvair race team that ran at Deer Park. Willie was known in Spokane for his skills as a motor builder, and developed parts and methods to fix Corvair issues. (Pat Riggins.)

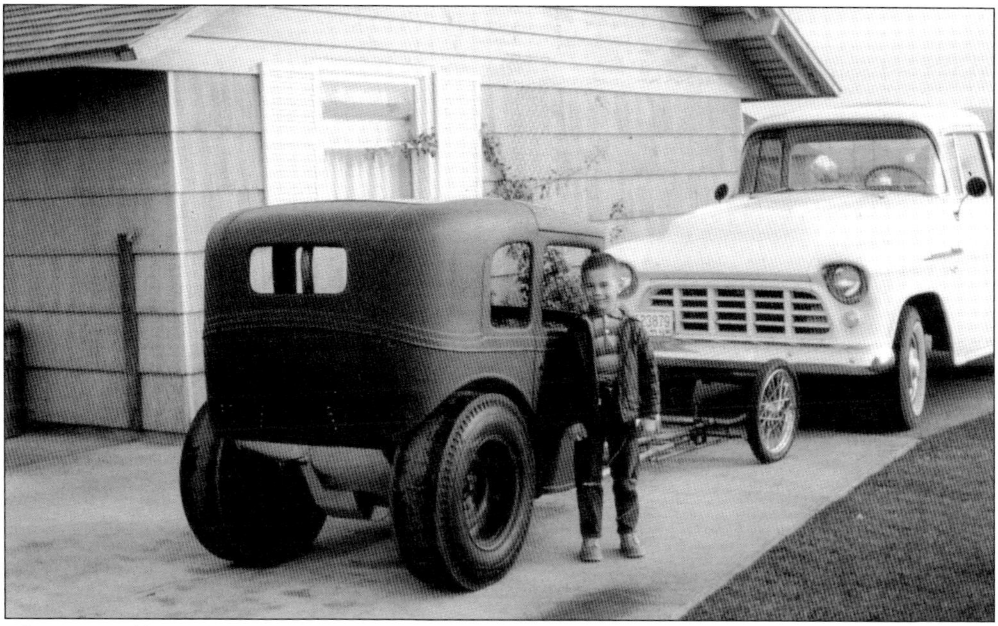

Chris Cornell stands next to the Bantam belonging to his dad, Duke, at their house on Desmet Avenue in the Spokane Valley. Vern Massie and Duke set up the chassis on the Bantam, powered by a 283 Chevy bored out to 301. Terry Frost did the machine work on the banjo rear end. The total weight of the car was 1,100 pounds, and it had a top speed of 137 miles per hour. Years after the Bantam left Spokane, it was tracked down by Chris Cornell, who restored it to its 1960s glory. (Duke Cornell.)

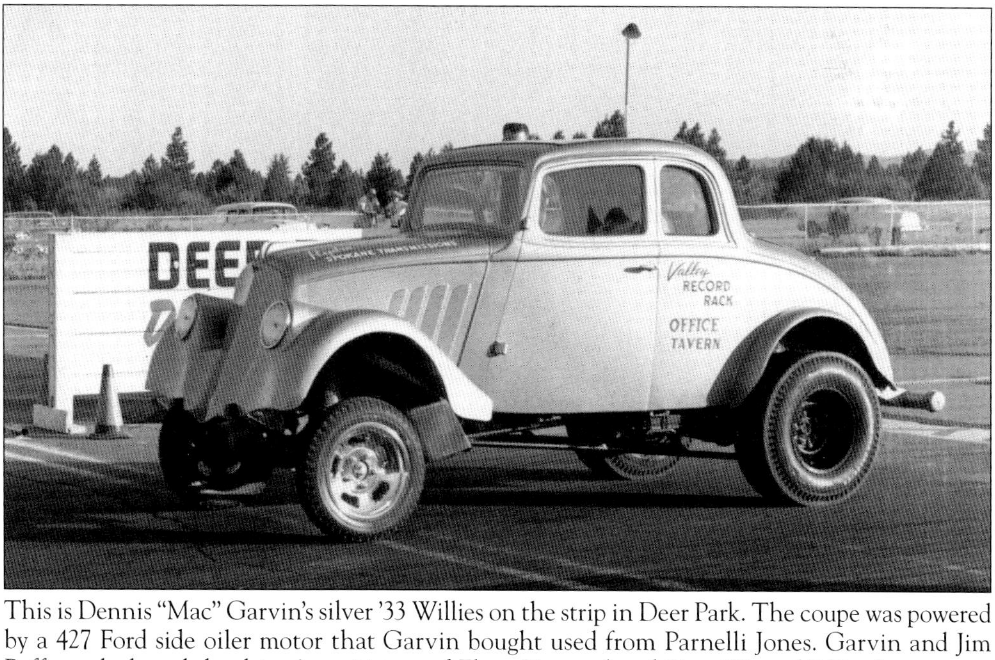

This is Dennis "Mac" Garvin's silver '33 Willies on the strip in Deer Park. The coupe was powered by a 427 Ford side oiler motor that Garvin bought used from Parnelli Jones. Garvin and Jim Poffenroth shared the driver's position, and Elton Hammel and Gary "Stretch" Groskreutz were team members. The car was sold to the Weaver brothers, who replaced the body with a real '33 Willies sedan delivery body after a fire destroyed the coupe. (Greg Fury.)

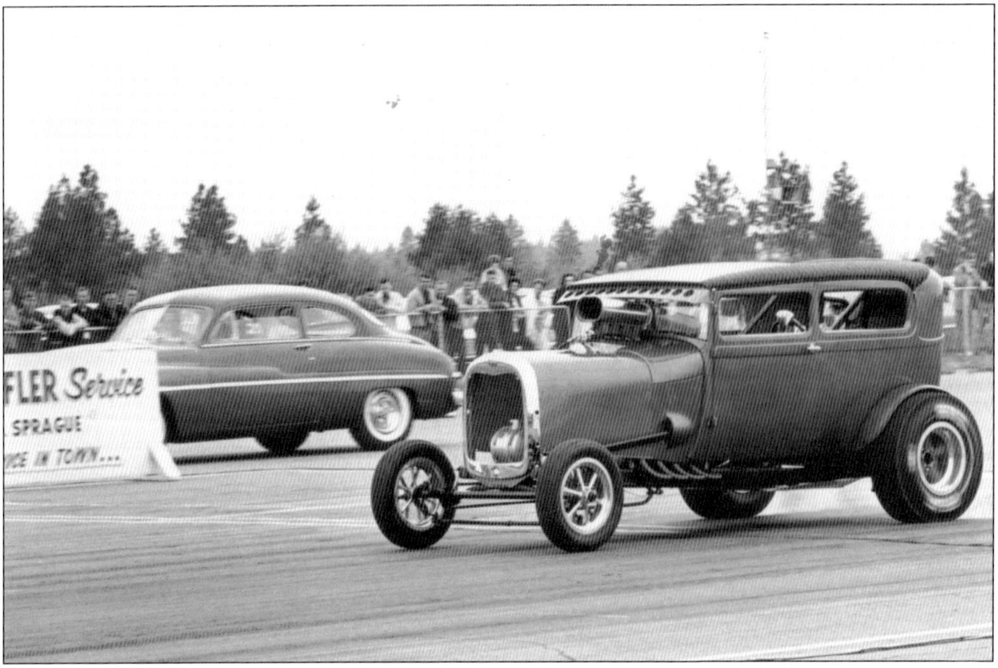

Originally from Walla Walla, Terry Frost moved to Spokane with this amazing Model A sedan. The car was painted '55 Buick Tahitian red and ran a 354 Chrysler, built by Ned Kelly and backed by a '38 Cad tranny. The motor is topped off by Clarence Bennett's Hillborn setup. The way the body was stepped off the frame allowed the exhaust to run between the cowl and the frame, creating a beautiful detail. (Greg Fury.)

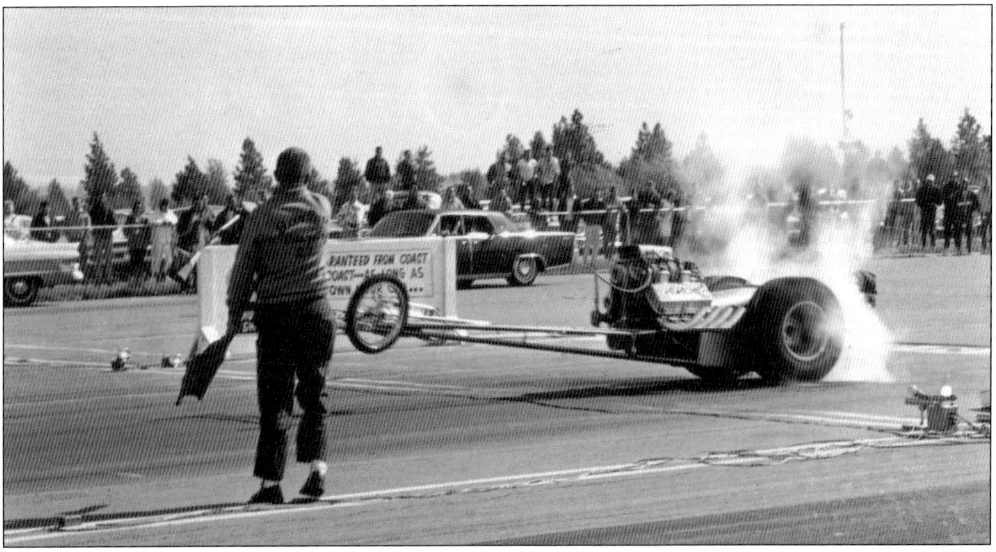

Dukes member Darryl Cambell flags Frank Rupert in the purple "Eagle Electric" dragster off the line. Jim Hordemann originally drove the dragster before turning it over to Rupert. The frame for the "Eagle" was built by Woody Gilmore of Race Car Engineering. It was powered by a 392 hemi. The car ran 202 miles per hour. The crew chief was John Mead. Team members were Ken Brinkman, Rod Cosgrif, Jack Forney, Pete Galina, Alvin "Red" Haugan, Russ Livengood, John Meade, Dick Morphy, Bill Payne, Frank Rupert, Ed Vacura, and Bill VanDouris. (Greg Fury.)

Four

CLUBS

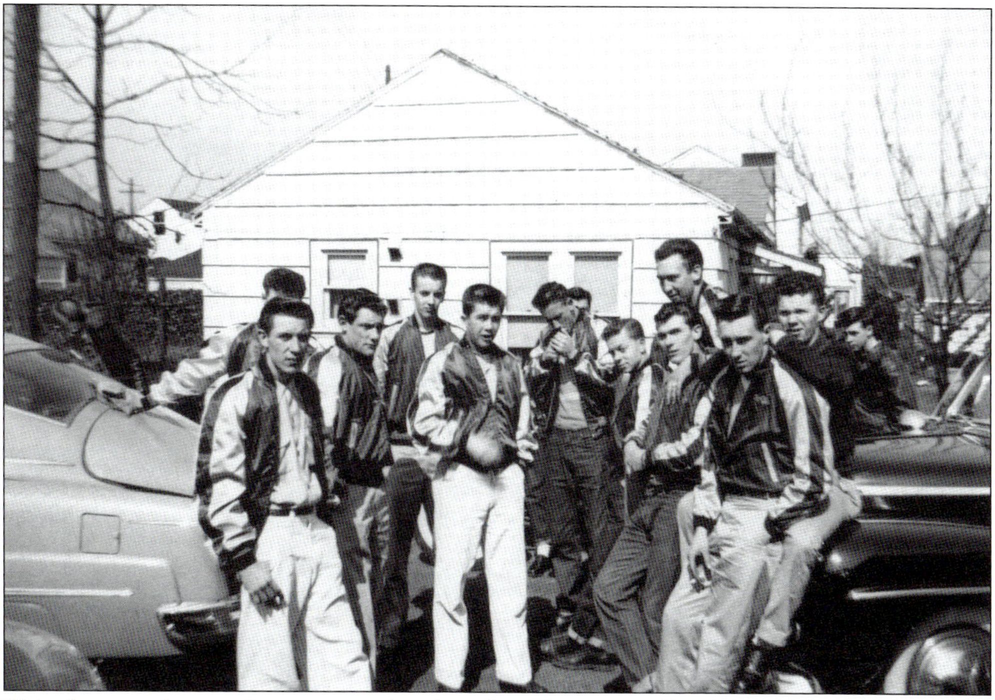

This photograph was taken in a motel parking lot. The cars are Duane Wolf's 1932 five-window, Butch Miller's 1948 convertible (left), and Jack Currie's Oldsmobile (right). This is a great photograph of the Dukes' early satin jackets. They were replaced in the mid-1950s by wool clicker-style coats. (Butch Miller.)

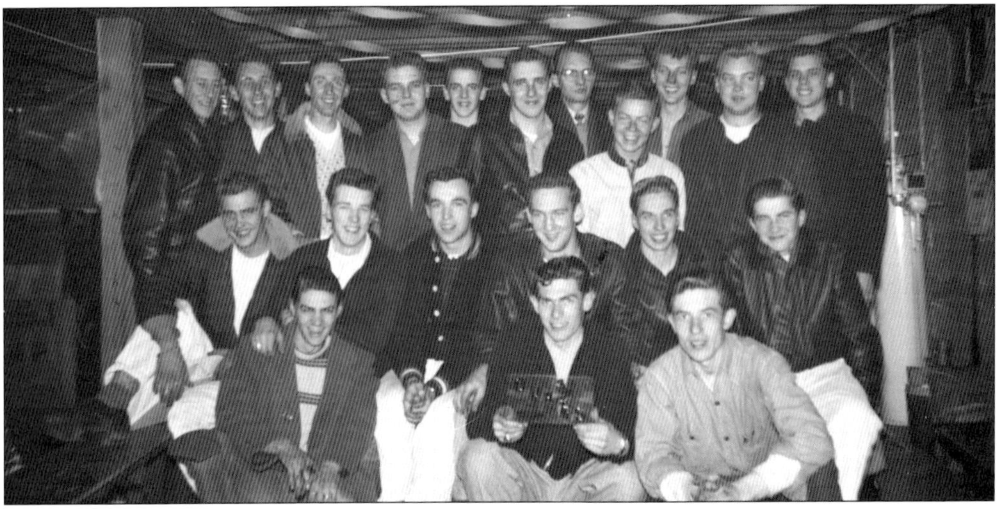

This is an early Dukes meeting in Jerry Hoover's basement. Jerry Hoover (first row, center) holds one of the early, clear-plastic Dukes plaques. Among those pictured here are Bill Wymann, Don Noack, Bob Brown, Duke Rogers, Larry Hovick, Don Miner, Dusty Rhodes, and Chubby Barton. (Harry Prouty.)

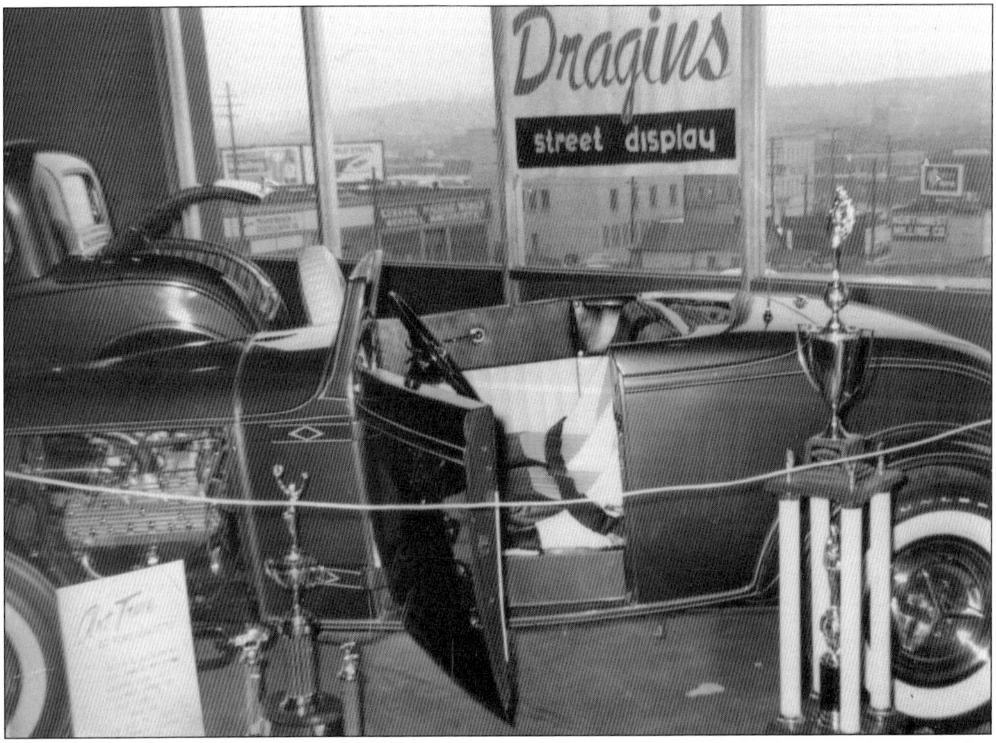

Art True's 1932 Ford Cabriolet is seen in the Dragins display at the Spokane Coliseum. The Dragins Auto Club was formed in 1954 by four guys in the Spokane Valley: Bob Adams, Denny Mahoney, Bill Vandouris, and Swede Erickson. Later members include Bud Branam, Buddy Vought, Ray Peternell, Don Stockman, Bill Bongers, Speedy Gunsaulis, and others. By 1960, the club had transformed into a racing team, with Bob Adams, Vern Massie, Greg Fury, Ron Dixon, Walt Johnson, Bill Rowe, Terry Frost, Joe Blaylock, Larry Carey, and others. (Bob Adams.)

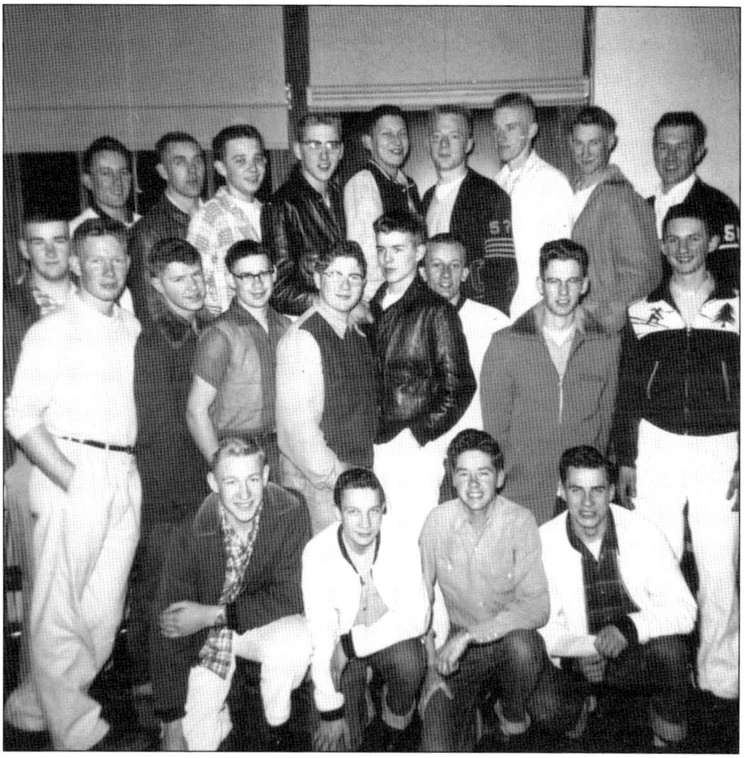

The Road Knights of Davenport, Washington, 35 miles from Spokane, became major participants in the area. Don Wilbur (back row, third from left) not only built some of the best show cars and racecars, but also ran the Auto Boat Speed Show with Orville Moe for nearly 50 years. (Don Wilbur.)

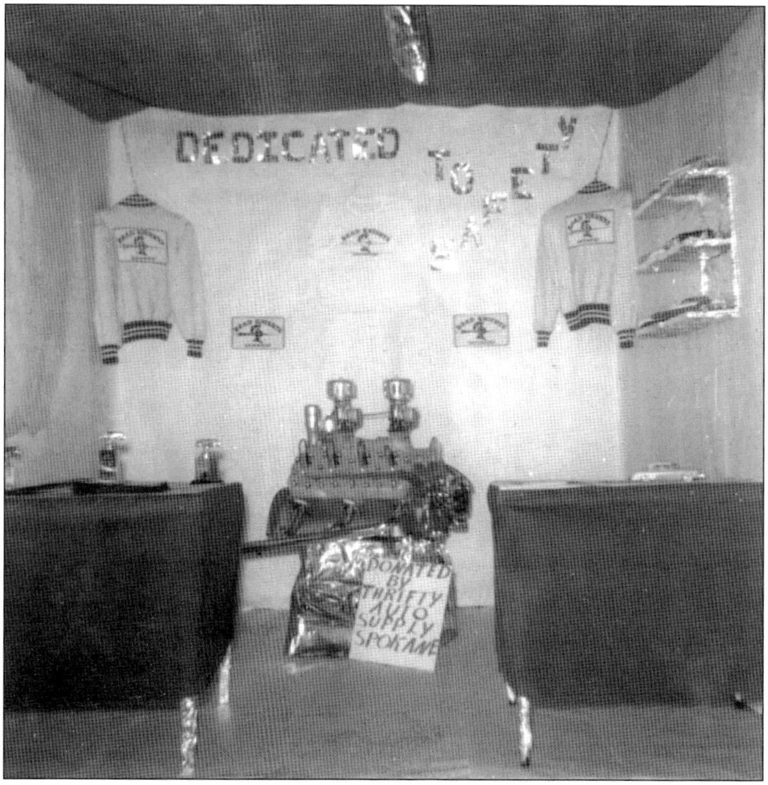

The Road Knights' fair display includes a flathead donated by Thrifty Auto Supply. When the club formed in 1955, there were 25 members. The original officers were Frank Kruger (president), Frank Heriza (vice president), John Sawyer (treasurer), Don Wilbur (reporter), and inspectors Tom Griffin, Daryl Ziemer, Gary Moats, and Melvin Janke. (Don Wilbur.)

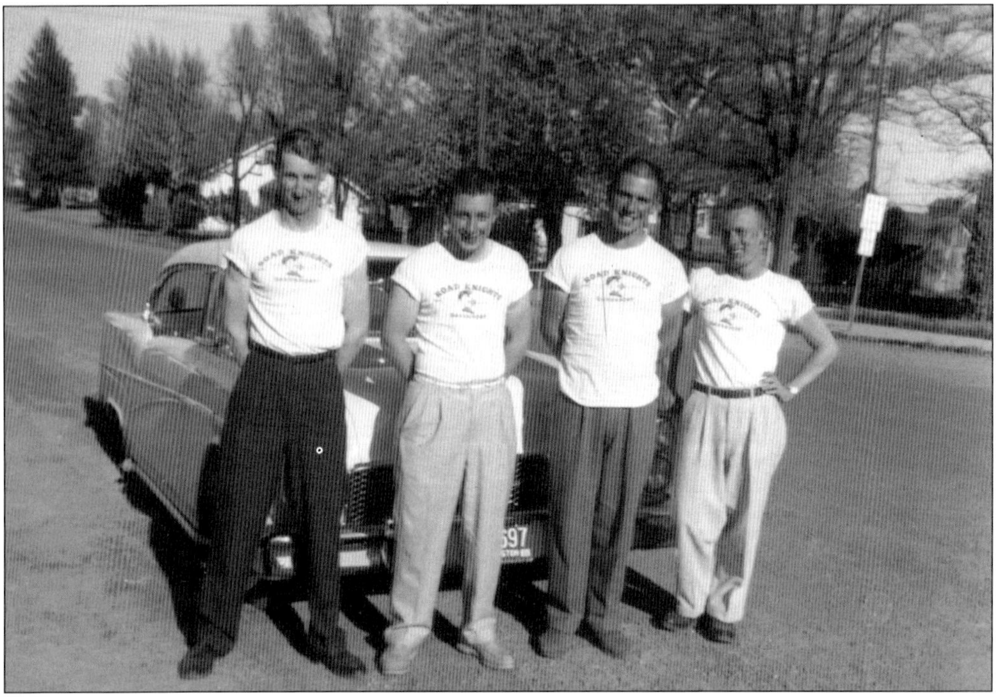

Members of the Road Knights of Davenport stand in front of Paul Savelesky's 1955 Chevy, "Miss Elegance." Savelesky is on the far right, and Bob Nelson is second from left. Nelson also showed a custom 1953 Oldsmobile, the "Picnic." (Richard "Speedy" Gunsaulis.)

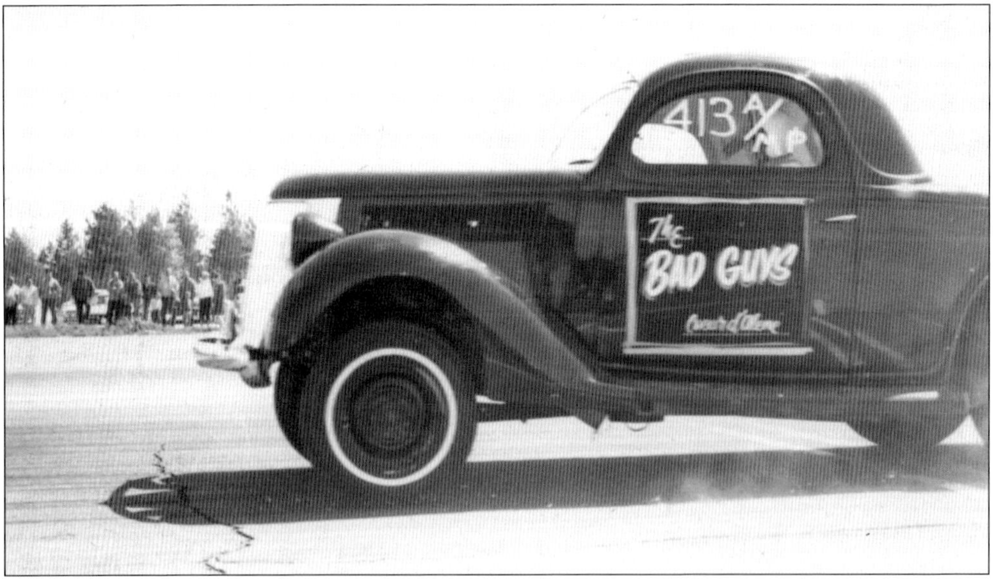

Harold Shockley was a member of the Bad Guys Car Club from Coeur d'Alene, Idaho, 30 miles east of Spokane. The Coachmen and the Lakemen were also from Coeur d'Alene. Other Spokane clubs include the King Pins, the Gents, the Eliminators, the Street Tin, the Wanderers, the Camelots, the Centurions, the Pacers, the Vampires, the Road Angels, the Downshifters, the Knights, the Majestics, Malibu Car Club, the Saints, the Rakers, the Road Rods, the Mystics, and the Mariners. (Tamatha Shockley.)

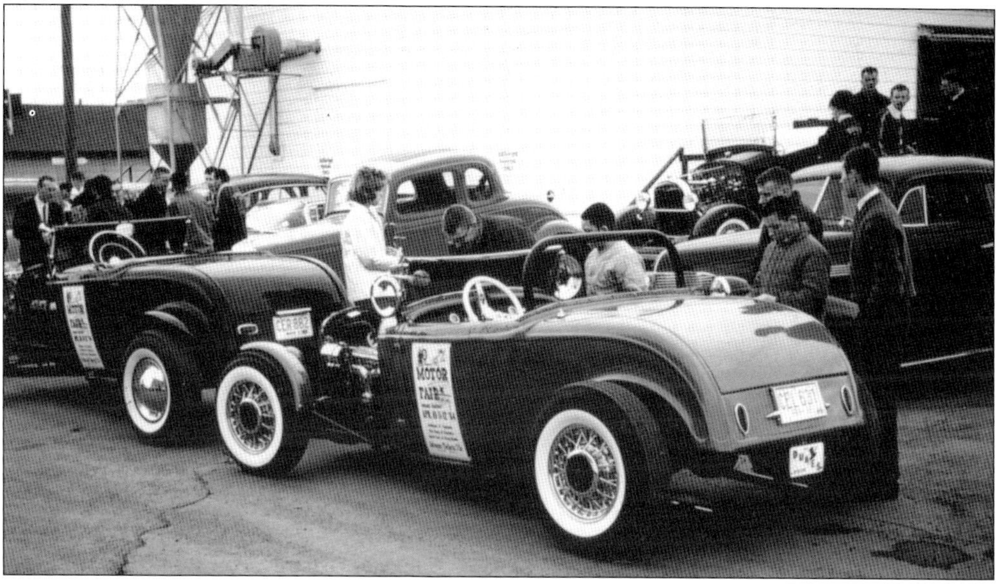

A local radio station asked the Dukes to help promote the Beach Boys when they came to town. Members of the club picked the band up at the airport and drove them through downtown Spokane. Ron Corkum's Stude-powered '32 roadster is seen here in front of Frank Moyer's '32. In the back row is Fred Felice's five-window coupe and Denny Hoagie's Model A roadster. In the crowd are Al Davis, Frank Moyer, Cathy Moyer, Don Audel, Darrel Larson, and Don Gorman (in the tie). (Frank Moyer.)

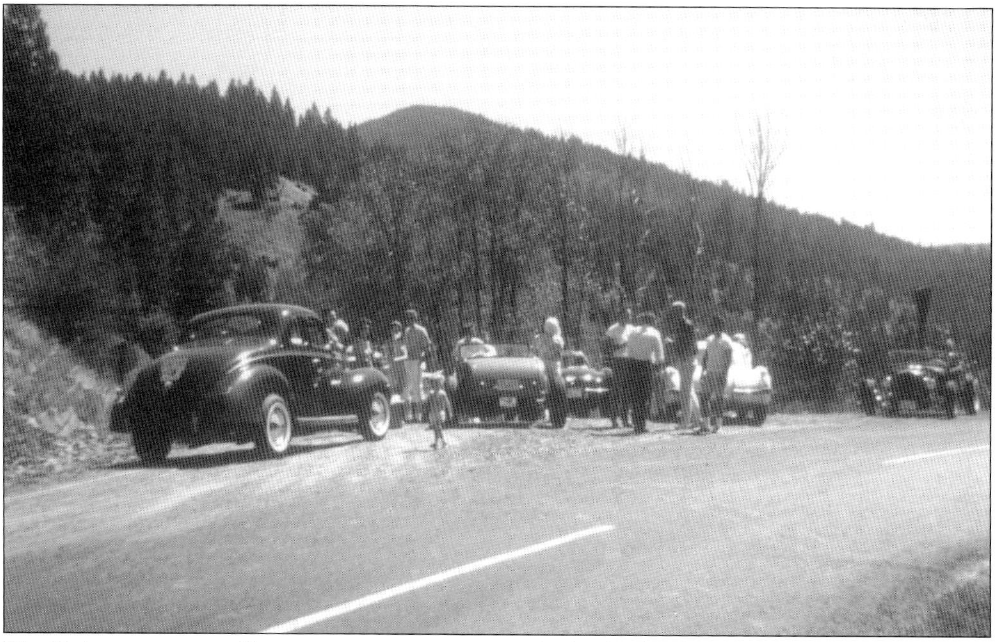

The Dukes are pictured here on a run to a resort on the backside of Coeur d'Alene Lake. The cars are, from left to right, Don Gorman's '40 coupe, Frank Moyer's '32 roadster, Buddy Wickstrom's black Vette, Danny Martin's white Vette, and Joe Felice's 1930 Model A roadster. On the street are Don Audel, Joe Felice, Bruce Crow, Al Davis, and Barbara and "Speedy" Gunsaulis in front of Moyer's car. (Frank Moyer.)